JACKPOT

High Times, High Seas,
and the Sting That Launched the War on Drugs

JASON RYAN

LYONS PRESS
Guilford, Connecticut
An imprint of Globe Pequot Press

*To Elizabeth, who provided love
and encouragement from the start.*

Lyons Press is an imprint of Globe Pequot Press.

Text design by Sheryl Kober

Library of Congress Cataloging-in-Publication Data
Ryan, Jason.
 Jackpot : high times, high seas, and the sting that launched the war on drugs /
Jason Ryan.
    p. cm.
 Includes bibliographical references and index.
 ISBN 978-1-59921-976-9
 1. Drug traffic—United States. 2. Marijuana—United States. 3. Drug control—United States. I. Title.
 HV5825.R93 2011
 363.450973—dc22

                    2010054487

Printed in the United States of America

10 9 8 7 6 5 4 3 2 1

Contents

Prologue

Charleston, South Carolina
August 2008

The wind whipping through downtown Charleston mattered little to the young girl throwing Pop-Its firecrackers on the sidewalk of Meeting Street, her arm flinging the paper-wrapped explosives to the bluestone. They snapped despite swift gusts that feathered their fall. Farther along, the wind tossed the hair of the family posing for a picture in front of a mansion, and gusted past the women selling sweetgrass baskets a block away on the steps of the city's main post office, next to the Charleston Federal Courthouse. The craftswomen struggled to control the flapping blankets placed beneath their woven wares, and one wondered if they feared seeing their larger, and most expensive, baskets blown halfway across town—$400 tumbleweeds skipping down cobblestone streets and racing past the creaking wooden wheels of tourist-filled horse-drawn carriages.

The blustery weather was a welcome reprieve from South Carolina's crippling August heat—a gift from Tropical Storm Fay, which zigzagged across Florida. Perhaps especially grateful were the South Carolina lawyers spared from sweating in their suits that week, including the pair heading to the federal courthouse for a sentencing hearing in the case of *United States of America v. Ashley Brunson*.

The federal courthouse and its annex stood with the post office on the southwest corner of Charleston's storied Four Corners of Law. Sharing the intersection were City Hall, the Charleston County Courthouse, and St. Michael's Episcopal Church. Inside the old buildings of granite, marble, stucco, and brick, one could conveniently seek resolution in matters within municipal, local, federal, and spiritual jurisdictions, should one have that many problems. Ashley Brunson, for his part, had just one problem, though it was a serious one: his guilty plea two months earlier to a federal felony charge of conspiring to import tons of marijuana and hashish into the United States. More remarkable than the substance of his crime was that it had occurred three decades earlier. Brunson had dodged the long arm of the law for more than twenty-five years, spending much of that time sailing across the world. He now sat in Courtroom 2, handcuffed, awaiting his punishment.

Courtroom 2 was small, no bigger than a classroom, and its pews held only a few spectators the morning of August 21, 2008. Considering Brunson had spent a lifetime on the run, the tiny crowd and absence of news crews wasn't surprising. The man had been forgotten.

He had been arrested a year earlier at the southern border of the United States, trying to enter California from Mexico with a passport bearing the name of a deceased man from Chicago. For decades he had used the alias without a problem, obtaining the false identification in 1985 and renewing the passport without incident in Seattle in 1995 and in Hong Kong in 2005. For some reason his passport raised a red flag on his entry to the United States in June 2007, and his fingerprints rang a match with the National Crime Information Center, revealing him as a wanted man. The computer database didn't forget that Robert Ashley Brunson had been wanted since 1983, a fugitive from the largest drug investigation in South Carolina history—Operation Jackpot. Brunson had outlasted more than a hundred other men and a handful of women who went to jail for smuggling-related crimes. He was the last of South Carolina's gentlemen smugglers.

The only other remaining fugitive was his wife, Kathy, who hunkered down at their home in Mexico. In exchange for her freedom, Brunson pleaded guilty to helping smuggle sixty thousand pounds of marijuana and hashish into the United States. He had been tempted to fight the charges, to force the government to prove beyond a reasonable doubt his involvement in smuggling ventures that occurred nearly three decades ago. Brunson and his lawyer knew the government's roster of witnesses had been depleted in recent years, with key smugglers and kingpins passing away. Other potential witnesses refused to talk, just as they had during related trials held decades earlier. But Brunson chose to spare his wife the chance of incarceration, pleading guilty so long as the government agreed to leave her alone and drop the charges against her.

During a plea hearing two months earlier, Assistant U.S. Attorney Robert Jendron, a veteran federal prosecutor in South Carolina, outlined Brunson's offenses, which included driving a car loaded with hashish on June 9, 1980. Working by faint moonlight that night,

Brunson helped transfer thirty thousand pounds of hashish off the seventy-one-foot ketch *Second Life*, which had just arrived at an abandoned dock near Hilton Head Island, South Carolina, after sailing for more than two months from war-torn Beirut, Lebanon.

"As it turned out, they were short of drivers," Brunson told Chief U.S. District Judge David C. Norton at his plea hearing. "And I mistakenly volunteered."

"No good deed goes unpunished," the judge responded, wryly.

Jendron continued detailing the smuggling that occurred that evening. The prosecutor had devoted much of his career to Operation Jackpot, including four busy years in the 1980s when the bulk of Brunson's coconspirators were brought to justice, many hauled into courtrooms after dramatic captures across the country and world. Jendron was the only federal prosecutor remaining in the U.S. attorney's office from the Jackpot years, his colleagues from that era all using the investigation's success as a springboard to other prominent positions.

Jendron noted Brunson's position as a crewman on the *Love Affair*, a forty-one-foot sailboat stopped by the Coast Guard off the Bahamas in November 1978, its cabin stuffed with nearly eight thousand pounds of Colombian pot. The Coast Guard had decided to perform a safety check of the sailboat after spying it one evening forty miles west of the island Great Inagua, its running lights suspiciously turned off., The check for proper safety equipment would oftentimes result in the discovery of more serious infractions, as it did this time, when the Coast Guard boarding party couldn't help but notice the abundance of pot packed below deck.

"It was another time they needed an extra crew member, and I volunteered," Brunson said to Norton.

Now, at the sentencing hearing, with the wind blowing outside, the sixty-year-old Brunson was again before Norton, calmly seated and wearing a striped prison jumpsuit and glasses, his gray hair neatly combed. Brunson's lawyer, Diedreich von Lehe III, asked the judge to consider America's changed attitudes and laws toward drugs since Brunson committed his crimes.

"It's a case that took place in a different world," von Lehe said. "It was a time before there was any such thing as President Reagan's War on Drugs. It was a time when cocaine had not yet entered the scene, not to mention crack and the other scourges that we face today . . . There was no violence associated with drugs, people didn't carry guns when they brought this stuff in, and they didn't have shootouts."

Von Lehe argued that Brunson had been punished enough by being imprisoned for the last fourteen months on false passport charges, and, more painfully, by having isolated himself from his family for a quarter of a century. In 1983 Brunson was sitting in the cockpit of his sailboat in Antigua when he spied a man coming to the edge of a nearby dock. Peering through a pair of binoculars, Brunson saw it was his wife's brother. In his hand was an indictment. Among the forty names on the indictment, Brunson soon read, were his own and his wife's. In response, he pulled up the anchor and set sail, not to be seen by friends, family, or the authorities for twenty-five years. Among those left behind, too, was a young daughter, Brooke, whom he had conceived with another woman a few years prior. She was six when he last laid eyes on her on the island of Bequia.

During his time abroad Brunson delivered yachts for wealthy clients, living in the Philippines, Hong Kong, Vancouver, and Mexico. It was after a sixty-day sailing trip from Mexico to the Philippines in 1987 that he and his wife found out they'd soon be parents to twin boys. They stayed in the Philippines to start their family, then discovered Hong Kong, where real money could be made moving corporate pleasure junks between the British colony and Borneo, Malaysia, and Singapore. Once Hong Kong was returned to China in 1997, many boats in the region were sold, and Brunson found work sailing them to Okinawa for their new Japanese owners. In time Brunson moved his young family to Mexico. Such adventure sounds romantic, von Lehe conceded to the court, but Brunson lived uneasily.

"He wondered when there would be a knock at the door, so to speak, and the feds would be there to take him away," said von Lehe. "It hasn't been carefree for him."

Throughout the years Brunson would send home the occasional Mother's Day or Christmas card. His older sister remembers seeing a picture of the boys when they were about four years old. The sporadic correspondence hardly made up for her brother's absence. In a letter to the judge, she spoke of his flight and the hardship it caused.

"He could not share the birth of his sons with his family. We do not know his wife. Ashley's mother and father grew old and died. He was not there for them," she wrote. "Two of his brothers died, and he did not know about it. I sent him a picture of myself, so he could recognize me as I am now seventy-seven years old. He doesn't know his nieces and nephews. Ashley cut himself off from all his family, the love and companionship of all of us. I think family is important for Ashley, and this was a great sacrifice."

Brunson's recent arrest and forced homecoming caused more turmoil in the lives of his loved ones. At home in Mexico, von Lehe said, the twins were devastated by their father's apprehension. They knew their father by his alias, Lyle, and never questioned why they were an American family living abroad.

"I can't imagine any greater price that this gentleman has had to endure already and pay than having to tell his sons, 'Boys, your father is not who you think he is,'" said von Lehe. "There can be no overriding purpose for this gentleman to get any punishment other than time that he has already served on this offense."

Norton listened to von Lehe's arguments, wondering aloud how he could justify a sentence considerably lighter than ones received by Brunson's coconspirators.

"Because he didn't do what he's supposed to do, you want me to give him less, a time served sentence, plus his wife gets a walk," said Norton. "So how do I justify that in the light of the ten or fifteen or twenty other people who got sixty months? One got three hundred months, some of them are on lifetime, you know, special probation . . . Tell me how to get around that, besides the fact of mercy."

Von Lehe said they would take mercy, if that's how the judge wanted to characterize it. Norton seemed irked by this response.

"Oh, I understand, nobody wants justice, okay? Nobody whoever walks into that door wants justice," said the judge. "Everybody wants mercy."

As to the men who earned stiffer sentences in Operation Jackpot, von Lehe argued they were more senior members of the drug smuggling conspiracy. Brunson was a minnow among marlins.

In fact, Brunson's sister said in her letter, it was these men—a group of deviants "more sophisticated" than her brother—who led him down the wrong path.

"He went away to the University of South Carolina with Dockers pants, cashmere sweaters, and a London Fog jacket," she wrote, "and he came home with sandals, long hair, and a mustache."

Her words had merit. The kingpins who controlled much of the East Coast marijuana trade in the 1970s were not unaware of their corrupting influence, and even cautioned their potential associates about joining their informal smuggling fraternity. Indeed the kingpins seemed to have crystal balls in the pockets of their designer clothing, and could see that their decisions, no matter how carefully considered, would one day guarantee their presence in a courtroom. But when life is fast and fun, it's one thing to read the writing on the wall and another to actually heed it.

Decades earlier, upon paying Brunson for the first time for his participation in a smuggling run, Bob "The Boss" Byers remarked to his fellow kingpin, Barry "Flash" Foy, about the significance of the payout.

"Barry, here he goes," said Byers. "Another good man bites the dust."

PART I:
THE GENTLEMEN SMUGGLERS

Chapter One

On any given day, the view from the top floor of the Coconut Grove Hotel was spectacular. One looked over an enchanting scene of colors rarely seen in everyday life. The water of Biscayne Bay was not blue, but turquoise. The Miami sunset was not gray and yellow, but instead a mesmerizing mélange of cream, ivory, gold, ochre, and magenta. Between the bay and burning sun was the Atlantic Ocean, stretching out toward Africa and Europe, its vastness interrupted by the assorted bits of unseen land that made up the Bahamas. From one of these Bahamian islands, Orange Cay, came something even more fabulous than the exotic water and sky. Its hue was comparatively unremarkable, nothing more than a dull white. Its size was minimal, just a speck in the distance, though it loomed larger as the day and evening wore on. But to the men gathered in the twenty-two-story hotel penthouse, the small and drab object was gorgeous, if only because it would make them very, very rich. Doing their best to speak soberly, they radioed to their friends on the horizon, advising them that the coast was clear, so hurry up and come on home.

Barry Foy and Les Riley, two men united by a hometown bond and a love of marijuana, received these transmissions. While their friends waited nervously ashore that afternoon in the fall of 1974, Foy and Riley cruised fifty miles from the westernmost Bahamas to Miami, destined for the canal-side community of Gables by the Sea, just past Key Biscayne. There, behind a vacant home, Foy had rented use of a dock. It was a straight shot, and their only concern was the Coast Guard, for whom they kept an alert watch, as did the men in the penthouse. They'd had enough hassles on this trip already. The deceivingly straightforward logistics of the smuggling operation—send a boat to Jamaica and bring it back loaded—had become exceedingly complicated.

For starters, the sailboat Foy had sent to Jamaica, *Beyond Time*, had too deep a draft for the shallow canal behind the rented house, so its keel was in danger of getting stuck in mud. To remedy this, Foy ordered his hired crew to sail *Beyond Time* to the Bahamas, where they would transfer the pot to him aboard a powerboat. The problem was, he didn't have a powerboat, and acquiring one large enough to hold six thousand pounds of pot was more difficult than he'd imagined. After some searching, Foy and Riley found a suitable sportfishing boat in Fort Lauderdale, although the owner was reluctant to lease his pleasure craft to two long-haired men who seemed to be up to no good. Before letting it go, he demanded references.

Foy and Riley scratched their heads. The up-and-coming drug smugglers were flush with many things in their twenties, most notably confidence, sex appeal, and bravado. They were, however, critically short of references, and the assorted smuggling runs they'd made to Jamaica weren't exactly the career accomplishments one listed to establish professional credibility, either. Desperate, they turned to Pogo Hartman, a wild South Carolina lawyer who was visiting the men in Florida and lending a hand with their venture. Happy to do them a favor, Hartman promptly tapped into South Carolina's good ol' boy network, putting the boat owner in touch with a South Carolina judge who vouched for the sterling characters of Foy and Riley.

"Oh yeah, them boys are fine . . . Go ahead and give them that boat," said the judge in a telephone conversation. "I just hope Pogo is a better boat driver than he is a lawyer in my courtroom."

The judge's words seemed to satisfy the boat owner. After hanging up, he issued a stern warning to the men.

"Listen, let me tell you all something. There's a lot of guys out there that are hauling drugs. You gotta be on the lookout for them," he said. "They might want to capture you, they might want to talk you into doing something. Just remember: It's against the law. You all aren't doing anything illegal, are you?"

"Hell, nooooo," Foy replied. "We've got girls down here. We're on vacation."

"We'd *never* do anything like that," added Riley, turning on the charm.

Handing over the keys somewhat warily, the man asked who was driving. Foy and Riley pointed at each other, the awkwardness of the moment broken when Foy gave in and volunteered to captain the boat. He took the wheel, and he and Riley soon cruised away from Florida, doing their best to look like a pair of weekend warriors hoping to haul in a tuna, or, if they were lucky, something even bigger. Decades earlier, writer Ernest Hemingway had fished nearby waters as a resident of Key West and Cuba. He revered the water off Florida and in his books depicted it as a scene of constant struggle, whether between man and beast, as in *Old Man and the Sea*, or between man and man, as with the desperate characters of *To Have and Have Not*. In hard times, the plot of the latter novel showed, fishermen and smugglers could often be one and the same.

It took considerable strength and skill to haul in sailfish, marlin, sharks, and swordfish from the water off Florida. In the 1970s there was a prize more easily reeled in from those seas—the so-called square grouper. A stray, floating bale of pot was a godsend for any hard-luck fisherman or hippie sailor. Tossed overboard by nervous or distressed smugglers, the bobbing bale could allow its finder to take a month's vacation or pay off a heap of debt. Lucky beachcombers were ecstatic to find this special type of seaweed—sun dried and stale on top, soggy and sea soaked on the bottom, but still perfectly capable of getting you high.

The frequent discoveries of stray bales were a testament to the incredible amounts of marijuana coming in each week to South Florida. Lucrative profits and the promise of a leisurely lifestyle lured many a hopeful smuggler to the Sunshine State. They were men, and occasionally women, whose eyes were as bloodshot from smoking joints as they were starry-eyed from dreams of striking it big.

Another clue to the overwhelming amount of marijuana smuggling were the scraps of pot Riley found wedged between cushions in the sportfishing boat's cabin. He and Foy had nearly died laughing when they pulled away from the marina, repeating the man's warnings about smugglers. Now they laughed even harder upon discovering stray weed throughout the boat. They obviously weren't the first to use his boat for illicit purposes, a fact that perhaps eased any guilt they may have felt as they cruised toward the island of Bimini in the Bahamas, clearing room in the cabin for their expected cargo.

If the men had an easy rapport, they owed it in part to the similar trails they had blazed in their short lives. Each grew up in South Carolina's capital city, Columbia, and wasted little time in leaving that hot and humorless hellhole just as fast as he could. Foy, twenty-three, and Riley, twenty-nine, dropped out of college in the Palmetto State in the early 1970s, independently striking out for South Florida, but embracing different means for making a living. In Key West, Riley cut grass. In greater Miami, Foy smuggled it. The income gap between their respective businesses was stark: What Riley could make in a decade, Foy could clear in a night. Riley wasn't too strongly tied to his lawnmower business, however, and the rolling waves felt much better beneath his feet than thick sod. Should he strike out on his own, he knew, he'd never have to step in dog shit and fire ant mounds again.

When Les Riley first moved to Key West in 1971 or so, money didn't matter as much as freedom. Operating the Green Acres landscaping company with his friend Larry "Groovy" Gray, he mowed lawns for $5 a pop. On a good day Riley and Gray might make $20, which was enough to cover living expenses, including the $75 Riley owed each month for a downtown house he shared with his beautiful, blond hippie girlfriend, Suzanne. She had thumbed a ride down from Columbia, carrying little more than a backpack and a pet iguana in a box.

Key West was a haven for drifters, malcontents, and assorted misfits. Many stayed in the town simply because they could go no farther, creating a population of artists, old salts, the occasional outlaw, and lots of hippies, most of whom seemed to drive Volkswagen vans. There were few tourists in town, and fewer rules. Locals felt comfortable sunbathing nude on beaches and cruising around town on bikes, dragging on the joints that dangled between their fingers. No one much cared, including the police. Riley felt the vibe on Key West was so cool he regarded it as the Haight-Ashbury of the East.

Among Riley's landscaping clients was playwright Tennessee Williams. Among his friends was aspiring songwriter and musician Jimmy Buffett. Many fellow South Carolinians landed in Key West, too. Some, like Riley and his girlfriend, came from the University of South Carolina, either as dropouts or recent graduates. Others were part-time residents of the Conch Republic, who came to fish, following the shrimp populations that migrated south from the Carolinas in the wintertime. Riley worked on shrimp boats from time to time, hopping on board for a week and, if things went well, making a few hundred dollars. With this cash in hand, he and Suzanne would take off for monthlong visits to Haiti, Jamaica, or islands off Nicaragua, where they lived with locals on the beach and subsisted on bread, honey, and peanut butter. They swam in the ocean and smoked lots of pot. One day, the couple dreamed, they would own their own sailboat and cruise the Caribbean, living an existence close to that of Adam Troy, the fictional sailor and adventurer Riley idolized from the short-lived television show *Adventures in Paradise*.

Riley had first visited Key West his senior year of high school with a classmate from the Bolles School, an all-male academy in Jacksonville, Florida, on the banks of the St. Johns River. At Bolles, Riley mingled with the scions of Florida's wealthiest families, most of who headed off to Ivy League colleges. Riley was not destined for similar prestige. Bolles was his third high school in four years, and Riley, though bright, was not a model student. He was amazed Bolles let him in and even more amazed the boarding school let him out to graduate.

Riley was born to straitlaced parents in Columbia, South Carolina, on October 11, 1945, the second of three sons. His family lived in one of the city's wealthier neighborhoods, across from basketball courts in tiny Mays Park, and a few miles east of the University of South Carolina, the State House, and downtown. Riley's upbringing was a traditional one for the South, with an emphasis on family, sports, hunting, fishing, and social graces. The family would sometimes retreat to their farm outside Columbia, and Sunday was filled with church activities. Riley's father, who worked as an executive for the Havertys furniture chain, didn't drink, and was fairly strict with his boys.

Riley worked as a teenage lifeguard at Myrtle Beach and ran through the local girls. He escorted his fair share of debutantes and hunted with their fathers on family land. In Myrtle Beach he exhibited some of the first signs of his unique business instincts that would later flourish—instincts defined by considerable entrepreneurial ability and questionable ethics. Sitting on the beach with beautiful bronze skin, he hawked bottled concoctions of motor oil and English

Leather aftershave to beachgoers, labeling his product Riley Tan. For best results, apply liberally.

As he got older, Riley went through phases, most of them rebellious. First Les was a beach bum. Then he rode motorcycles. Then he became a hippie, growing his hair long. Sometimes, the teenaged Les would come home drunk, infuriating his parents. Les taught his younger brother Roy to play poker, and he gave him his first beer, when Les was fourteen years old and Roy just seven.

In the fall of 1963, Les enrolled at the University of South Carolina, studying business. His education was frequently interrupted, once because he moved away to sell pot, and another time due to military service. He joined the Sigma Alpha Epsilon fraternity and became one of the university's most popular students, frequently seen in Maxcy Gregg Park by the tennis courts or hanging out with cute girls. He was long on charm, laid-back, and low-key, known to take his dates up to the top of the nearby eighteen-story Cornell Arms apartment building to watch the sunset and smoke a joint.

Riley's good looks and mellow manners went a long way, enabling him to enjoy opportunities and good fortune that passed other people by. He also got away with things no one else could. When he was a kid, his family moved to Memphis for a brief time, and Riley met a young Elvis Presley, who lived nearby. In the military he earned promotions despite doing his best to skimp on his domestic service. At the University of South Carolina, the skinny athlete briefly joined the rugby team and fed everyone LSD before one match. They raged like lunatics across the field.

During his final year of college, Riley began making regular road trips to Key West. From Columbia the drive was considerable, especially since Interstate 95 had not been completed. Riley enrolled in only one course his last semester, and he'd leave after class on Thursday in his 1964 Volkswagen Beetle, arriving early Friday morning to work the weekend as a doorman at the Anchor Inn. Monday afternoon he'd leave to drive back north, making it to class on Tuesday, although he'd sleep through it. Come Thursday, he'd do it all again, taking friends with him, among them Ashley Brunson.

On this fall day in 1974, it was Brunson that Foy and Riley were going to meet in the sportfishing boat, due to rendezvous off Orange Cay in the Bahamas, a spot they described to him as the first rock south of Bimini. The men didn't have to wait long before Brunson and *Beyond Time* arrived. He and his crew dropped the sailboat's anchor and hopped aboard a dinghy, cruising over to see the rented boat and enjoy a few beers with Foy and Riley. As the time passed and darkness came, the tide slowly changed, subtly spinning their boats around and disorienting the men, though they failed to realize it. A few hours later, when they set out to find *Beyond Time* and transfer the pot, they headed in the wrong direction. The sailboat and the six thousand pounds of Jamaican marijuana inside it were nowhere to be found, sending the men into a mild panic. They cursed themselves for being so stupid, second-guessing whether they even dropped the anchor, imagining the sailboat drifting toward New England without a crew, their massive payday floating away in the dark. Only at dawn did they see the sailboat was just a few hundred yards away, on the opposite side of where they expected it. Making up for lost time, they quickly transferred the pot and parted ways.

Cruising home, Foy and Riley entered Biscayne Bay through Stiltsville, the community of wooden homes built on pylons just south of Key Biscayne. Driving into the canals of nearby Gables by the Sea, they docked the sportfishing boat at the rented dock behind the vacant home, making sure to lock the boat's cabin door to protect the pot. Seeing a party at the house next door, Riley warned Foy not to say anything to anyone. The warning was pointless. Minutes later, Riley heard Foy talking with a partygoer who had seen the fishing poles in the back of the boat.

"Y'all have any luck?" asked the partygoer.

"Oh yeah," said Foy. "We caught some fish."

"Oh, we'll be over in a few minutes to look at them," came the reply.

Riley and Foy did not wait around for the visit, making a hasty escape to the Coconut Grove Hotel to meet their friends and discuss plans for unloading that night.

Foy, Riley, and the men in the hotel had already made significant preparations, clearing out a stash house up the road, shooting out a streetlight near the dock with a BB gun, and renting a Ryder truck. Some details, though, were unfinished, and Foy, Riley, and their cohorts disagreed on how to execute the operation. Everybody seemed to have an opinion on the best way to unload the pot and avoid attention from the neighbors. As they argued into the evening, Foy finally had enough. It was his load of marijuana, after all, and the only one giving orders would be him. He held up the large, long silver key that opened the sportfishing boat's cabin.

"I got the key," said Foy to a hushed audience. "We're gonna do it my way."

In the beginning things were always done Barry Foy's way. The brash, upstart smuggler did not have colleagues or partners, but followers and employees. He was younger than almost all his smuggling peers, yet he had figured it all out much more quickly, finding a Jamaican connection and moving hundreds of pounds of marijuana across the Caribbean before any of his former classmates at Newberry College earned degrees. The secret of his success was a truth he divined through his remarkable criminal intuition: Nice guys finish last in the smuggling business. Accordingly, Foy muscled his way into as many deals as he could. While his perceived greed created a few enemies, his confidence inspired more admirers.

"We thought he could do anything," says one smuggler's former girlfriend.

"He could tell his crew to shit in a post office, and they'd shit in the post office," says Tommy Liles, a smuggler who grew up with Foy in Columbia.

Foy was tall and athletic, with a curly head of hair that added a few extra inches to his height. His massive ego and swagger made him intimidating, and when it came to striking deals, he was unapologetic about demanding the largest cut, unafraid of bruising feelings. Even friends who resented him for his avarice felt powerless to stop him. They rationalized his dominance, figuring they were making a lot of money, and Barry was just making a little more.

"If you got one thousand pounds, Barry's getting six hundred, you're getting four hundred, just because Barry figures that's the way it's supposed to be," explains Ken Smith, a smuggler who attended the University of South Carolina before moving to Florida. "Call it a character flaw—I don't know what it is. It's just Barry."

If men occasionally became angry with Foy, they were mollified by the fact that his aggressive actions weren't malicious, but natural. It didn't take a licensed psychologist to understand Foy couldn't help his wicked ways.

"He was destined to be huge," says Smith. "There was nothing else Barry could do."

Foy, born March 31, 1951, grew up not far from Riley in a neighborhood of brick ranch homes and big yards surrounded by nearby golf courses and lakes. He worked often as a kid and teenager, channeling his abundant energy into paychecks. He delivered papers, as well as eggs. He worked construction jobs and pumped gas. He worked at the *State* newspaper's printing press on the paper-cutting machines. In time, he'd be making the front page of the Columbia daily, although not for reasons of which his parents would be proud.

Foy's father was a banker and his mom a registered nurse who put aside her career to raise Foy and his four younger siblings. To Foy's recollection, he committed his first crime in high school, when he was at a party and everyone was out of beer—and money.

"We'll be right back," he told his friends, before driving off in his 1952 pea green Chevy to a local pool hall, which had already closed for the evening.

Driving behind the building, Foy backed the heavy car into the pool hall's rear door, smashing it open. He and two accomplices carted out all the cases of beer they could find and returned to the party as heroes. The next day, he returned to the scene of the crime, and while Foy was shooting pool, the theft was discovered. He suppressed a smile and continued his game.

"Started me down the road to bigger and better things," he says of the burglary.

After graduating from Dentsville High in 1969, he went to study and play basketball at nearby Newberry College. He lasted just one semester. Returning to Columbia, he enrolled at the University of South Carolina, but soon dropped out there, too.

"Some people are blessed and know exactly what they want to do in high school and they get out and go to college and know exactly what to major in, exactly what direction they're going in," says Foy. "Shit, I was all over the place. I had not a clue.

"Shortly thereafter, though, I started to find what might work," Foy says. "Drugs were everywhere, all over the place. Everybody had them. Everybody was doing them. Everybody wanted to buy them. Weed was the least, probably the least harmful for lack of a better word. That's the kind of direction I went."

The best market for Foy was Columbia's Five Points neighborhood beside the university. Foy sold pot out of his truck and in front of a Five Points head shop, acquiring his merchandise from a local hippie. He made additional money dealing at a bar called the Campus Club South, just two blocks south of the steps of the South Carolina State House. Soldiers from nearby Fort Jackson would flock to the bars, clubs, and restaurants in downtown Columbia, eager to spend their monthly Army paychecks. Foy waited for them with a leather satchel, reaching in and grabbing a bagged ounce at a time. On a good day, he'd sell up to forty ounces.

Eventually Foy's reputation around town caught up with him, and he was arrested in 1973 after police found pot in his trunk. He escaped significant punishment, although the authorities did not forget him. Years later, while checking in for a flight to New York from Columbia's Metropolitan Airport, an airline employee matched Foy's name to a watch list. While processing Foy's ticket, the employee quietly called security. Minutes later, as Foy walked toward the airport gate, he was approached by a policeman who called him by name and asked to speak with him for a moment.

"Right then," says Foy, "I knew this is not the right time to have any conversation with this guy."

Handing the officer a piece of luggage to distract him, Foy bolted for the terminal doors, a briefcase full of "party favors" in his hand. Foy raced across the parking lot outside as the overweight policeman chased him, his belt jingling with assorted equipment.

"Halt, I'm going to shoot! Halt, I'm going to shoot!" shouted the policeman, losing ground to the thin, athletic Foy.

"Nah, you can't shoot because I ain't done nothing!" Foy shouted back, turning around to face the cop as he ran backward.

Turning forward, Foy sprinted harder, crossing a field and a road, and then running into the woods. He paused to catch his breath, convinced he was safe for the time being. To his dismay, he watched a vehicle pull to a stop on a nearby road. The big letters on its side read SLED, the acronym for South Carolina's State Law Enforcement Division. Foy could see there were hounds inside the car.

Foy started running again, crossing another road and through more woods before reaching a cornfield. By now it had become dark, so Foy laid down between the rows of corn to let the night pass. As soon as dawn broke, he walked to a nearby store, picked up a pay phone, and called his sister to come pick him up.

Eager to straighten his legal troubles out, Foy turned to two Columbia lawyers who suggested a bribe might help clean up his record, which included the 1973 arrest for being in a car loaded with pot, as well as parole violations from a 1971 conviction for possession of methamphetamines in a coastal South Carolina county. Foy says he gave the lawyers $30,000 or so and was instructed to plead guilty and meet with narcotics officers to supply them with a certain amount of false information about a drug transaction. In exchange, the lawyers said, Foy would be given probation.

"Some name they gave me and some date and some fictitious bunch of bullshit," Foy says he told the narcotics officer. "It was just to cover everybody's ass. Sure enough, that's how it went down."

The favorable treatment did not escape notice. The *State* newspaper of Columbia reported how Foy received six months probation and a $250 fine after allegedly cooperating with Drug Enforcement Administration (DEA) agents. The problem, the newspaper noted, was that no members of the DEA could confirm such cooperation, and prosecutors and defense attorneys could not get their story straight, offering varying accounts of what information Foy provided, with one saying he tipped police off about a deal in Mexico or Texas, another saying it was Florida, and yet another attorney mentioning

Jamaica. A note in Foy's case file mentioned him giving information about a drug deal in Columbia, South Carolina.

The chief of police at the Columbia airport later wrote to a prosecutor with concerns about Foy's prosecution, noting "this case was postponed so Foy could deliver evidence to federal agents. I have checked with all federal agencies and no one is working with the subject Foy. It is my belief that this is just another way to stall prosecution on this subject."

As the case against Foy fizzled in Columbia, he was making a name for himself in the underworld of South Florida. In 1971, Foy had moved to a beachside hotel in the Sunshine State's city of Hollywood, eager to get in on the ground level of drug trafficking. A number of gangsters frequented the same hotel—men who gambled, sold guns, stole jewels, and dealt drugs. Naturally, Foy gravitated to them, and he soon learned the gangsters had a connection in Jamaica. They offered to pay Foy and another hotel guest named Jimmy to take Jimmy's twenty-six-foot sailboat down to the island and load it with pot.

"We said, 'Well fuck, let's go,'" says Foy.

It was Foy's first time sailing offshore, and, after departing Fort Lauderdale, it took days for him to find his sea legs. Rough seas tossed the small sailboat, and he became seasick. While Jimmy cooked, sang, and sailed, Foy lay on the floor of the cabin, vomiting and sleeping.

"He's all happy because we on some big-time adventure," says Foy. "I'm just dying thinking, 'What in the hell am I doing down here?'"

When Foy recovered enough to assume his watch, he found the sailing slow going. There was little wind, and the sailboat was equipped with an underwhelming ten horsepower motor. They ran the motor often, to little effect, reaching Jamaica in ten days. By comparison, that same year, a racing boat set a record by sailing from Miami to Montego Bay, Jamaica, in less than three days and four hours.

On the island things went much more smoothly, as men loaded their boat with about four hundred pounds of pot. The modest load filled much of the cabin, owing to the bulky size of the hand-pressed bales of marijuana. Jimmy and Foy slept atop the pot and carved out a niche near the sailboat's stove to cook up canned food. On the return voyage they stopped to refuel in the Bahamas. It was critical to have the motor available when they brought the boat into Florida; they would be foolish to rely on sail power alone when they were most vulnerable to being spotted and intercepted. The last thing they wanted was to be dead in the water and stuffed full of bales.

Despite the importance of gasoline, Jimmy did not want to risk refueling with drugs on board. He beached the sailboat on a cay about ten miles from a Bahamian fuel dock on another island, and he and Foy tossed the fifteen or so bales onto the beach, moving them behind a rock. Then Jimmy left for fuel while Foy stayed behind on the cay, surrounded by ocean and not much else. In the distance he could see another cay. It was also uninhabited.

"I hope to God he comes back," thought Foy, "because I'll starve to death."

Hours passed. Darkness came. Mosquitoes began their feast of Barry Foy. Soon it was pitch-black, but the mosquitoes still found him with ease. He waded into the water to escape, submerging his body up to his neck. The insects were relentless, buzzing around his head and tormenting him. About midnight, Foy heard the familiar whine of the ten-horsepower motor. For so much of the journey the sound of the engine—*nyaaaaaaaaaah*—had been a grating noise. Now it was music to his ears. Jimmy returned to the cay and helped Foy toss the marijuana back on the boat. Foy was elated and angry at the same time.

"You left me here, man," Foy yelled at Jimmy, once the joy of his rescue faded. "We ain't doing this again. Not this way."

The amateur smugglers made it back to Fort Lauderdale and pulled into an anchorage beside the Intracoastal Waterway. At about 2 o'clock in the morning, each bale of marijuana was ferried to shore and placed in a black plastic bag before being thrown in the back of a vehicle brought by the gangsters.

"It looked like loading bodies into a truck," recalls Foy, an activity in which the gangsters might have had considerable practice.

In recognition of their success, the gangsters asked them to return to Jamaica, this time to pick up one thousand pounds of pot. Foy, Jimmy, and a third crewman sailed down to Jamaica in a forty-foot trimaran. Foy was not particularly pleased with this vessel, either.

"It was fiberglass and it was plywood and it was a piece of shit," says Foy.

What's worse, it leaked.

On the return voyage, sailing through the Windward Passage between Cuba and Haiti, the trimaran took a beating from rough seas stirred up by wind passing between the mountainous islands. Foy and his crew were constantly bailing water out of one of the boat's three hulls. The trimaran, which lacked a keel by design, was not sailing into the wind well, either, and the crew took four days to sail a distance normally traveled in one. After sitting off the coast of Cuba for days, they decided to turn the leaky mess around.

"I was afraid it was going to fall apart. We didn't have a dinghy aboard, we didn't have a life raft, nothing," says Foy.

The irony of the moment was not lost on the young smuggler.

"As far as I know," he says, "I'm one of the few guys that's ever taken pot back to Jamaica."

Such hardships might have driven the less determined away. Not Foy. With some of the proceeds he earned from his first venture, he purchased a sixty-five-foot fireboat he had found for sale on the Miami River. It had been used by the Coast Guard in the 1940s and closely resembled a tugboat, though with a nozzle on top to spray water and douse flames. Foy found two crewmen and set off for Jamaica again, glad to have a more substantial vessel and its diesel engine taking him south. Yet this trip, too, would have its share of hiccups.

As they rounded Cuba, Foy was lying on a bench in the pilothouse. Suddenly, he heard a loud scraping sound as he was thrown to the floor

"Stopped dead in the water," says Foy. "Ten knots to nothing. Oh my fucking God."

Looking over the side of the boat, Foy saw they had run aground on a coral reef. He and the crew used a rowboat to set an anchor astern of the boat, and then winched themselves off the reef with the help of a rising tide and engines running full throttle in reverse. Set loose, they discovered the hull's wooden planking had been split. They were taking on water so quickly the bilge pump was overwhelmed, unable to expel the incoming sea. Foy did not abandon hope. For the next two days to Jamaica, he and his crewmen used milk cartons to toss seawater out of portholes. Upon reaching Jamaica, they had the boat dry-docked and repaired.

Coming back home, disaster loomed again, this time when the crew ran out of drinking water. The men gazed with hope at the occasional rain clouds on the horizon, hoping they'd pass over and release a shower. When they did receive a burst of rain, the men gathered with open mouths under the tugboat's scuppers. These channels along the edge of the deck and pilothouse normally diverted spray and rain off the boat, back into the ocean, much like a gutter does for a roof of a house. This time, the scuppers routed water into parched mouths, nourishing the sailors who waited below the pilothouse's dripping spouts.

Nearing Florida, Foy and his crew stopped in Bimini to transfer the drugs to a faster boat. No one showed up to meet them. Riled, but now with drinking water, they sailed to Florida and anchored off a pier in Hollywood, then rowed to shore and rounded up the gang.

"It looked so out of place. There was this ugly-ass tugboat-looking thing anchored out by the pier," says Foy. "Back then it didn't matter. Nothing was going on enough for anyone to pay much attention to it."

Jan Liafsha, Foy's girlfriend at the time and his eventual wife, remembers getting a call from him when he returned, instructing her to walk down to the beach and look for the boat. To her surprise, she saw it anchored offshore in plain view. That night the men unloaded the pot in a state park. In celebration, someone danced on top of a picnic bench. Despite all the miscalculations, misfortune, and near calamity, Foy had landed his first major load.

The trips put Foy on the map, earning him instant stardom among the pot smokers of South Carolina, which, in the 1970s, was a considerable portion of the state's youth. Foy's feats were nothing short of astonishing to a crowd used to obtaining no more than a few pounds of marijuana at a time. It didn't hurt, either, that Foy was a talented salesman who touted his hard-earned marijuana as superior, even if others begged to differ. One friend recalls complaining to Foy about the prevalence of sticks in the pounds of pot he purchased.

"Sticks?" said Foy, incredulously. "You gotta take the good with the bad."

"The good with the bad?" replied the friend. "There is no good."

No matter if the highs were mild and the buds few and far between, people wanted to buy Foy's pot. They also wanted to smuggle with him, eager for a bit of adventure. What could be better than leaving the stultifying South behind for days on the deck of a sailboat, headed for Caribbean isles, with return trips spent getting high and sleeping on a mattress of marijuana? Sweet dreams, indeed.

Among those eager to cash in was Ken Smith, who was selling small amounts of pot around Columbia and helping smugglers in St. Petersburg, Florida, unload shrimp boats full of marijuana. He was astounded at how much marijuana could be put on a boat, and more impressed by the money that could be made on each deal. He was determined to find a connection in Jamaica, even if it meant working with Foy, whom he held a grudge against. Though Foy disputes this happening, Smith says Foy gave up his name after getting arrested in Columbia as part of the deal to save his own skin. Regardless, if it happened, nothing much came of it. They did a deal anyway.

"I was upset with him, but I mean, I was so desperate to get this deal," says Smith. "Barry was at the cutting edge of this stuff . . . there ain't no doubt. And I wanted to do it. And the only way for me to do it was with Barry. So I even actually put that aside."

The men agreed Smith would sail to Jamaica, where Foy would load the boat. Upon its return, Foy would arrange for its unloading and distribution. As for the other crew members, they turned to Les Riley and Larry "Groovy" Gray, persuading them to put away the lawnmowers in 1973 and hop aboard a boat. Foy and Riley had mutual friends in their hometown, and Foy had paid a visit to Riley with one of those buddies, impressed by how his fellow South Carolinian thrived in Key West. When Riley wasn't working a shrimp boat or tidying yards, it seemed he was smoking joints and engrossing himself in the newspaper, taking the occasional break for a jaunt on his bicycle through the streets of the sleepy town. It was hard to get him and the rest of the Key West crew to do just about anything, says Foy, but when the prospect of taking a trip came up, Riley conceded marijuana smuggling would pay him much better than his land-scaping business ever could, no matter how many million lawns he mowed. He agreed to help crew the boat, and so did Gray. A Jamaican joined the crew, too.

The trip had inauspicious beginnings. They traveled to Miami and purchased a thirty-six-foot Gulfstar sailboat, *Merry Chase*, which

Smith promptly crashed into another boat while trying to dock. Coming into a slip under power, Gray, sitting on the bow, instructed Smith to "cut it back," or slow the boat's brisk forward momentum by reversing the engine. Instead Smith, a novice boater, turned off the engine. The boat continued to cruise and plowed into another vessel, requiring repairs for the *Merry Chase*. It was of little consequence, as Gray, Riley, and Smith intended to make considerable preparations and repairs anyway for the upcoming voyage. Since Smith had a background in construction, he created a punch list for the boat, having his crewmates cross off tasks and equipment as they were completed and purchased. Such work did not sit well with the impetuous Foy, who was eager to get the boat to Jamaica.

Inspecting their progress one day, he expressed his impatience by snatching the punch list out of Smith's hands.

"You and your fucking lists," said Foy. "Every time I turn around you're making fucking lists."

"Barry, my ass is on the line here," said Smith, taken aback by Foy's perceived disregard for their safety. "You're gonna get your pot."

"Fuck that, let's go," said Foy, hustling them along. "We're going, we're going."

The *Merry Chase* set sail for Jamaica on Thanksgiving, and the four men aboard soon learned why Foy was eager to outsource this part of the smuggling operation. Tall seas, fierce winds, and bad storms tossed the boat unmercifully. The crew discovered that the placid-seeming Caribbean could blow quite hard and that their Gulfstar sailboat was not the ideal blue-water boat.

"That's the time of the year in South Florida where you get your first backdoor northwesters. You start getting cold fronts kicking down here, and they kicked our ass . . . We didn't really know that the Caribbean Sea . . . blew a steady fifteen to twenty (knots). We were used to ten to fifteen sailing in the Florida Straits," says Riley. "It was a little bit rougher than we thought, and the boat really wasn't built well enough to handle those conditions."

After eleven days of atrocious weather, they finally spied the Blue Mountains of Jamaica in the distance. Smith suddenly dashed down into the cabin. Twenty minutes later, he emerged freshly showered, shaved, and sporting clean pants and a shirt. Eager to make a good impression on the Jamaicans, Smith fastened on a fancy wristwatch and put a big smile on his face. Riley says that if Smith could have blow-dried his hair, he would have. The problem with such grooming and a snazzy outfit was that they were still more than a day away from docking. Gray and Riley ribbed Smith, explaining that at their speed of four knots, and with their port of call on the opposite side of the island, they wouldn't be stepping off the sailboat anytime soon.

As they neared Jamaica, they were supposed to radio Foy, who had flown to Jamaica to meet with his suppliers. Foy preferred that the sailboat stay out at sea and receive the drugs offshore, and that Smith and his crew never meet any Jamaicans. Otherwise, the next time Gray, Riley, or Smith sailed down, they wouldn't need Foy to broker the sale and could cut him out of the deal. An engine problem, however, forced the men to dock in Montego Bay for repairs. It was just the excuse Smith was looking for, and he exploited the landfall and made his highly sought connection.

"Barry kept holding everybody at arm's length with Jamaica, and rightfully so, 'cause that's all I wanted—that guy in Jamaica," says Smith. "Everybody in this business makes a career out of jumping you."

Still, for the remainder of this trip, it was Foy's deal. Days later he signaled the *Merry Chase* with a fire on the beach. Boats came out with bales of marijuana, and the sailboat was soon headed back toward Florida, rounding the western edge of Cuba through the Yucatan Pass. The return trip was not much better than the first leg. A Cuban patrol boat fired on them when they strayed close to the Cuban shore, and vicious storms threw them off course and made life miserable. The sailboat handled even worse with all the marijuana stuffed inside, and they were without reliable navigation equipment. At one point an exhausted Smith said he didn't care if they were caught so long as they made it back to land.

"We basically relied on a compass and dead reckoning," says Riley. "By the grace of God, we made it back."

Arriving home two days before Christmas, they anchored off a Girl Scout camp near Big Pine Key, Florida. The crew, who had been sleeping on wet pot for a week and stunk to high heaven, then went to shore, entered an inn, and called down to Key West, advising Foy and his hired hands the boat had made it. That night, Foy and these men drove motorboats and trucks up from Key West to unload the sailboat, but they were thwarted halfway through the job when they discovered a canal was not fully dredged to the ocean, preventing the pot-laden motorboats from reaching the waiting trucks parked along the canal's edge. Adjusting plans, they piloted the motorboats and trucks thirty miles south to Key West, deciding to bring the pot straight into the town shrimp docks. It was now approaching dawn and raining as the smugglers cruised toward Key West with bales stacked to their noses. Approaching the docks, one of the motorboats nudged a sailboat, prompting a man aboard to wake from slumber, pop out of the hatch, and ask in an irritated tone as to what the hell was going on. Foy bounded aboard his sailboat and silenced the man by seizing him by the collar.

"We smuggling reefer motherfucker, and you better shut the fuck up," growled Foy. "Now help us unload this pot."

"Far out!" answered the man, helping hoist bales into the waiting trucks. Afterward, as the trucks left for Foy's and Smith's houses, the smugglers let him keep the scraps that fell to the ground. He was ecstatic.

Despite the hiccups, hassles, and slapdash nature of these early trips by Foy and Riley, smuggling was undeniably thrilling work, and the men's adventures did not go unnoticed by their peers. When it came time to assemble boat crews and drivers, Foy and Riley suffered from no shortage of volunteers. Friends from South Carolina joined them in Florida to participate in the intoxicating work, eager to transport pot and have their pockets stuffed full of cash. These neophytes, at least one of whom was still in high school, had never seen so much marijuana and money.

Foy took charge of some of these eager hands, who just hours earlier had watched from the hotel penthouse as Foy and Riley motored into Miami from the Bahamas. Assembling in Gables by the Sea under the cover of darkness, he ordered the men to take up stations outside the vacant home and docked sportfishing boat. Foy himself squeezed deep inside the boat's cabin, pulling out bales and throwing them to a man standing on the deck. This man passed them to others on shore who ran the pot to the rented truck. They moved quickly, spurred by fear and the adrenaline coursing through their bodies. There were scores of bales tucked inside the boat, and, despite the exhilaration, it seemed to take forever to pull them all out.

"We got a little bit more," Foy repeatedly intoned to the off-load crew. "We got a little bit more."

When they finally finished, the men piled into cars and the rental truck and headed for a nearby stash house. Halfway there, while cruising down the road, the men following the rental truck watched in horror as the cargo door flew open, exposing the bales of marijuana packed into the vehicle. The truck traveled the remaining miles to the stash house flashing its leafy load.

By the next day, the stash house was empty again, the pot packed into assorted cars and trucks headed for various points along the East Coast. Riley, who was paid with one hundred pounds of pot, and Foy returned in a pickup truck to check on the boat. Along for the ride was Foy's brother, Pat. As they cruised by the vacant house with the dock, Pat asked a question: "What's that on the side of the house, against that tree?" Easing up on the gas, Barry was seized with fear.

"Oh, shit. That's a fucking bale," he said. "We forgot it."

The brothers and Riley looked around nervously, expecting police to jump out of the bushes at any moment. Foy peeled off. It must be a setup, he thought to himself, circling the block and trying to make sense of the situation. There was no way such a huge bale of pot could have escaped the attention of the neighbors and construction workers.

Coming around again, though, he found the street empty. Barry's confidence surged, and the men formulated a plan. Pulling up to the driveway, Pat jumped out of the car and ran to the garage, grabbing hold of the bale by the strings that wrapped it. Barry and Riley watched him drag it down the driveway and throw it into the bed of the truck before sitting on top of it. Barry hit the gas.

Speeding away in broad daylight, Pat was giddy. His brother had previously forbid him from smuggling, reasoning that one felon in the family was more than enough.

"Damn! That was cool, man," Pat yelled to his brother from his pot bench, the wind in his hair. "We pulled it off."

Barry looked back at his sibling in disbelief.

"Dude, that was one bale!" said Barry. "There was about 150 to 200 of them last night we were running around with. You should have been there then."

"I got to do one, man."

"You ain't getting involved in nothing," said Barry. "That was your one deal. Your one-bale deal."

Chapter Two

It takes an exceptionally unreasonable person to smuggle drugs by boat for a living, someone who ignores or scoffs at all the things that could, and should, go wrong when sailing tons of drugs across entire seas every couple months. Someone who is unafraid of being stranded far from land, plying waters patrolled by the world's largest navies, and transacting with foreign underworlds and associated militants. This person has to be a top-notch seaman, able to navigate a large boat along unfamiliar coastlines at night should their employees prove unable. He has to be tough as nails and wild as hell, and it helps if he is a little bit crazy. Above all, he has to be absolutely oblivious to consequence. Barry Foy and Les Riley fit the bill, but so did a few other men, and it wouldn't be long before they joined forces, striking up partnerships that served to increase each other's prestige and earnings.

The more capers Foy pulled off in Florida, the greater his reputation grew, enabling his acceptance by veteran smugglers. His notoriety was enhanced by the many nicknames he attained. Some knew him as "Boy Wonder." Others called him "Raul," in reference to a prominent terrorist judged to be similarly dangerous. Yet others called him "Clone." How else to explain how Foy could be in so many places at once, with his hand in so many deals? He must have a duplicate.

The most frequently used and enduring moniker attained by Foy, however, was "Flash." Given his bold crimes, big mouth, and ability to command attention, it was the perfect handle for the youngster, aptly describing his ability to narrowly escape police custody and live ostentatiously. Foy favored fast cars and fashionable clothing and gold jewelry, looking more like a rock star than a pot smuggler. People could not help but notice the tall and intimidating Southerner who looked so young to be brimming with such confidence.

"He walked in, man, the room changed," says smuggler Buddy Ray "Fish Ray" Griffin Jr. "Fucking energy in the fucking room changed."

To complete his look, Foy kept company with a slender brunette he had brought down from South Carolina. Foy says he first met Jan Liafsha when she was a high school senior in his hometown of Columbia, South Carolina, but he moved to Florida before they could get serious. Despite the distance between them, Foy could not shake the fond memories.

"I was loving on her, man. She was five feet, ten inches, and 120 pounds of smoke," says Foy. "She was hot."

One day in 1973 he pursued her with the same determination he reserved for smuggling pot. Foy borrowed a gangster's Cadillac and drove up to South Carolina, hoping to steal Liafsha away from another boyfriend.

"I pulled up in the Eldorado with the top back, went up and knocked on the door, and said, 'Look, it's now or never . . . I came here to get you.'"

When Liafsha protested that she already had a boyfriend, Foy was not deterred.

"I don't care who you're living with," said Foy. "It's time to go."

Foy left without an answer, and a few hours passed before he received a call telling him to come and get her, that she was packing her belongings. Foy pulled up again in the Eldorado, threw her suitcases in the trunk, and sped off to Hollywood, Florida, where he and Liafsha rented a small apartment. There, they lived a quaint existence, removed from the rough-and-tumble action of Foy's frequent smuggling episodes.

"We were young and simple in life, the sophistication was yet to come," says Liafsha. "He taught me how to make a proper egg sandwich and we played cards."

Soon after moving to Hollywood, they hopped aboard the old fireboat and headed to Stock Island, just north of Key West, making themselves a new home. The change in scenery suited Liafsha just fine.

"I loved living on the boat; it was made from huge timbers, had a captain's cabin, and a double bunk in the main room," says Liafsha. "We were tied off at the end of the dock, and I used to get up early and go look into the clear water at the sea creatures just below."

Along with Liafsha's stunning looks came a ferocious temper. Foy could upset her, and the two were forever fighting, according to other smugglers, then making up again. Nicknamed the "Mad Albanian," she had the distinction of being the single person in Florida who could scare Flash.

"When Jan got mad," says smuggler Bob "Willie the Hog" Bauer, "Barry got out of town."

Ken Smith remembers trying to visit Foy in Key West after the two had a disagreement over the pot brought in by the *Merry Chase*. Foy was not home, but Liafsha was, making breakfast. She came to the door in a white slip, her hair freshly brushed, looking like Lauren Bacall. Upon seeing Smith, the angelic-looking creature became profane, cursing him for daring to challenge her boyfriend. Smith just stared at her and smiled, unaffected by the vitriol.

"What's so fucking funny?" she asked Smith.

"You are so fucking hot," he replied, unable to help himself.

"Fuck you, man," said Liafsha, before calming down. "Really?"

"Jan, right now, you're the hottest looking girl in the world," said the utterly smitten Smith as he turned to leave. "Just so you know it . . . You are something else"

Liafsha and other smugglers' girlfriends might not have been clueless as to how their men made money, but they weren't heavily involved, either, excusing themselves when business was to be discussed. Even though marijuana smuggling was a pervasive activity in 1970s South Florida, men tried to be discreet when projecting their power. Smugglers typically masked their ambitions with a cool demeanor, and their actions betrayed a sense of fear that their good fortune could dry up in an instant if they weren't careful. They were socially aloof and often told strangers they were in the real estate business. One exception was smuggler Mike Abell, who tried to have a sense of humor about his occupation. When he was asked what he did for a living, he coyly told a woman he was "an importer of tropical plants."

For the initiated, others' guarded conversations, fancy cars, and vague explanations of their livelihood were dead giveaways. So when Foy and Bob "The Boss" Byers met on the docks of a Coconut Grove marina one day in 1975, it didn't take long for the men to size each other up as smugglers. About every other boat at the marina belonged to a scammer, Foy says, and the men kept identical forty-five-foot Columbia sailboats in adjoining slips. But the smugglers' similarities more or less ended there.

While Foy had enjoyed a relatively privileged upbringing, Byers's childhood was marked by an alcoholic father. As a young adult, Byers left behind family tumult in Minnesota to strike out on his own down South. Byers's transcendence of his troubled youth and his eventual ascent as a marijuana smuggler gave him a keen eye for the qualities needed to succeed in Miami's crowded drug underworld. No doubt he was impressed with Foy. As his Porsche and sailboat attested, Foy had already amassed a small fortune moving marijuana and had done so before the age of twenty-five. Foy had made money the hard way, too—by smuggling Jamaican ganja, which sold for much less than Colombian marijuana. Byers, five years Foy's senior, was impressed. He was drinking in his sailboat with two women when he called out to Ashley Brunson, who he had seen walk by with Foy.

"If you guys are up to what I think you're up to, tell that guy you're with to come see me," Byers told Brunson.

Byers's proposition was intriguing: "Let's take a trip to Colombia," he said to Foy, "and do a deal together, choosing our supply first-hand from mountainside marijuana farms—I'll show you how to make some real money." The pair soon flew to Santa Marta, a coastal town at the base of the Sierra Nevada de Santa Marta. The mountain range, separate from the Andes, rises dramatically along a portion of Colombia's Caribbean coast, running from Santa Marta to Riohacha before petering out to the arid Guajira Peninsula. The peaks of Cristobal Colon and Simon Bolivar both stand nearly nineteen thousand feet above sea level.

To most people in the world, and, indeed, even to most Colombians, Santa Marta, Riohacha, and the Guajira were insignificant locales. They were underdeveloped, remote, and not particularly beautiful, at least compared to other wondrous areas of South America and the Caribbean. But to marijuana smugglers, Riohacha and Santa Marta were as renowned as Amsterdam, Hong Kong, New York, or Shanghai. Successful marijuana smugglers forged relationships with the area's Colombian suppliers who could load boats punctually and with an agreed-upon amount of drugs. American crews regularly sailed along the shore, made appropriate radio contact, and then waited as Colombian Indians left the shore to meet them in their long marijuana-laden canoes, which were powered by outboard motors.

During Foy's first trip to Colombia with Byers, he made the mistake of drinking river water. Severe thirst had caused him to ignore warnings that upstream, in the hills, peasants used the rivers as baths and sewers. Foy was laid up in Santa Marta for a week, sick as a dog.

On a second trip with Byers, their suppliers took the men into the foothills by Jeep, riding over rough, pitted roads and passing military checkpoints without incident, ostensibly because their hosts paid bribes to the soldiers. When the roads ended, they switched to burros, riding up narrow paths that hugged mountainsides and fell off to cliffs. Their journey ended at a camp beside a cold mountain stream. There, the men were provided meals and given lodging in a hut. Chickens wandered across dirt floors in the camp buildings.

For days Byers and Foy entertained visiting farmers who led burro trains loaded with marijuana bales. Each bale was a sample from their nearby fields, and the farmers offered assorted bits of their crop to the Americans, who carefully examined the product. Foy and Byers stared hard at the marijuana, preferring to see more buds than leaves, twigs, and seeds. They rolled it between their fingers, feeling how sticky or dry the marijuana was. They smelled it deeply, and then, as a final trial, they smoked it.

As Foy and Byers sucked the smoke inside and their minds lightened, the farmers waited anxiously for a thumbs-up or smile from the men. If the kingpins were pleased with the pot, the Colombian suppliers arranged a wholesale purchase and paid the farmers. If Foy and Byers rejected a sample, the dejected farmer would leave, oftentimes slitting open his burlap bags and dumping the baled pot into the stream, unwilling to carry the inferior product any farther in the rugged terrain. It paid for Byers and Foy to be discriminating. Back home, top-shelf Colombian marijuana would fetch $250 a pound when sold by the ton to their distributors, which was double the price of Jamaican weed. Santa Marta Gold was regarded as the best pot available at the time, though one still had to be particular when attempting to procure it.

"That's their culture. They'll show you the worst stuff, and if you'll buy it, they'll sell it to you," says Abell, the self-proclaimed importer of tropical plants, who made buying trips to Colombia for Byers.

Bob Roche, a longtime friend to Byers, confirms this. He recalls traveling to Colombia for the kingpin and smoking pot at a stash house. Soon his neck stiffened and he grew uncomfortable.

"Fuck. Nooooo. This isn't what it is supposed to do," Roche recalled thinking. "It was crippling. It was the wrong kind of high. It sent you into rigor mortis."

That experience was one of many uncomfortable moments during Roche's trip, which was typical of what any American might encounter when venturing to coastal Colombia in search of pot. Before heading into the mountains to meet farmers and pick a load of marijuana, Roche stayed in a stash house in a seaside city. During the day he was required to stay inside, lest he be arrested and his handlers be forced to pay a bribe for harboring the obviously American visitor. His bathroom was filthy and smeared in excrement. Walls surrounding the house were topped with broken glass bottles, cemented into place to discourage burglars. Should Roche have to flee the house in the event of a raid, he was advised to throw a mattress on top of the wall to avoid cuts when scaling it.

His meals were provided to him, though he quickly tired of the food. He found little relief in the area restaurants he patronized after dark. At one place he excitedly ordered a Chateaubriand steak. Out came a plate with a tiny piece of ham topped with a pineapple ring.

When drivers picked him up for a long trip into the mountains on badly maintained roads, he was told to sit between the two men on a bench seat in the four-wheel-drive Ford Bronco. A stack of tires sat in the rear cargo area; they were gradually consumed as the wheels rumbled over the rutted road, suffering flats. Each time the Colombians changed a tire, Roche was required to hide behind nearby brush so as not to be seen by soldiers in passing military Jeeps. As he lay down in the sand of the desert lowlands, thoughts of snakes and scorpions crowded his mind.

Upon reaching the mountains, Roche traveled to ravines lined with marijuana plants and caves crammed with harvested pot. He sampled the drugs and indicated which crops he preferred, making up a purchase list of close to thirty thousand pounds. Later he visited other stash houses in the mountains, including one with a pool and a view of the ocean. Here he enjoyed the company of hookers. Together they hugged the floor when someone mysteriously began shooting into the house before being chased away.

Despite his handlers' precautions, they did run into a military patrol, which extracted a bribe. The military could often be bought in Colombia, and soldiers frequently supervised the loading of marijuana on beaches after a burro train had brought pot down from the mountains. On the beach the pot might be loaded into wooden shakers to sift out rocks, sticks, and stalks. After that, a compressor squished it into bales. Soldiers, too, advised Roche when Colombian patrol boats were away and when to cue the smuggling boat to come in toward shore for a rendezvous with the canoes.

Cooperation from the police and military was never guaranteed. Some soldiers had no tolerance for the drug trade, and some took pleasure in making an example out of the smugglers they caught. A number of American drug smugglers died in Colombian prisons, often because of brutality. Roche remembers meeting one smuggler in Colombia who was released from prison after his partner allegedly died from being sodomized by a military officer's greased arm.

Despite these dangers, the superior quality of Colombian pot enticed Foy and his fellow smugglers to cease making trips to Jamaica. Besides, among other drug enforcement support, the United States had started leasing helicopters to the Jamaican government in 1974 for marijuana eradication. It was wise for Foy to avoid Jamaica, too, considering the number of men he had stiffed, failing to return and pay for the marijuana they fronted him. One former South Carolina smuggler says that when he picked up his own shipments on the island, he was routinely thronged by Jamaicans who demanded, "Where's Barry? Where's Barry, mon?"

Foy had figured out one easy way to maximize his profits as a kingpin: not pay people what you owe them. Such a tactic was to be used sparingly, as a spurned business associate might tip off the police or retaliate with violence. Calculations scribbled on a paper cocktail napkin—the kingpins' answer to a spreadsheet—revealed there were only two reliable ways to significantly increase your profits on a deal: bring in more drugs or sell the load for more. In a country awash with marijuana, the only way to sell your product for more was to bring in primo pot, hence Foy's and Byers's jaunts to Colombia.

The basic business plan for smuggling pot is straightforward. For every deal, a smuggler must coordinate three parts: the purchase, transport, and distribution of marijuana. On paper the tasks seem manageable, so long as a kingpin and his employees possess an adequate amount of moxie. But many an amateur smuggler has made a go of bombing in a load only to become bogged down by the inevitable mishaps that occur when inexperienced sailors pack a boat to the bursting point and try to cross the Caribbean. When these amateurs stumbled, they called established kingpins in to help, sacrificing a healthy amount of profit to salvage the load.

It's clear from smugglers' accounts that kingpins like Foy and Byers rose through the ranks not by smuggling differently from others, but by smuggling well. It was the crafty and capable kingpin who could recover from a missed connection in Jamaica, a crew that quit right before loading, a conked-out engine, or crippling weather. It was the seasoned smuggler who recruited discreet and reliable men to execute each venture and paid them enough to keep them loyal. On a typical operation a kingpin's payroll normally included a boat captain, two crewmen, and a handful of others who stayed behind to unload and distribute the marijuana, splitting duties as lookouts, radio operators, bale lifters, and truck drivers. Then there were all the other costs.

"People involved heavily in the drug trade, particularly on the importation side, have a lot of overhead expenses: purchase of boats, airplanes, paying vessel captains and off-loaders, purchase/rental of stash houses, attorney's fees, etc. Plus, when they spend all of that to bring in a load and it gets seized by the government, they have to absorb the total loss; they can't report it to their insurance company," says former DEA agent, Jim Mittica, a veteran of marijuana investigations. "Even so, if they are even mildly successful smugglers, they stand to make a lot of money."

To mitigate some of those potential losses, kingpins obtained marijuana on consignment from their Colombian supplier and paid the bulk of their debt once the marijuana was successfully smuggled and sold in the United States. Should the shipment be intercepted or lost at sea, the supplier would absorb the costs of the load, provided a smuggler could produce proof of law enforcement's interference, whether in the form of arrests or a newspaper article reporting the drug seizure.

It was a logical arrangement. On account of the low prices suppliers paid farmers for each pound, lost loads were of relatively little expense to Colombian drug lords. The marijuana attained value only upon successfully reaching the shores of America. Prior to that, it was just an inexpensive and plentiful crop in Colombia.

Given all the overhead costs associated with smuggling, American kingpins with any sense ordained that if the pot didn't get sold, no one got compensated. A bust canceled everyone's payday, no matter where someone might be on the drug-running food chain. Money was managed very carefully by those in charge, as evidenced by the 1983 testimony of a frequent partner to Foy, Virginia-based smuggler Julian Pernell, who worked for years as an accountant before trafficking drugs: "Our [purchase] costs would run $40 a pound, and our transportation costs would run anywhere from $30 to $40 a pound, then our off-loading crews and so forth, maybe an additional $20. So if we could keep our costs down to $100 a pound and sell it for three, we would make three to one on our money."

Critical to every operation was finding an isolated spot to unload the drugs. The best sites featured a dock close to the ocean, the absence of neighbors, and proximity to major highways. The savvy smuggler scouted several potential sites to unload drugs in case the preferred location was unsafe to use the night a boat came in. In South Florida, where much of the coast was urbanized, finding back-up locations could be tricky. Increasing law enforcement patrols in the 1970s also began to make Florida a riskier location to import drugs, motivating smugglers to explore other states.

"When Florida got warm, everyone was looking for spots," says Foy. "[We said] let's go somewhere they ain't."

For Foy it was logical to look back home on the coast of South Carolina, where there were more than 180 miles of coastline and so many rivers, inlets, and creeks it'd take a lifetime to explore them all. An assortment of media—movies, beach novels, and hotel pamphlets, most notably—portray the South Carolina coast as the perfect place to find serenity or romance, what with the soft sand, palmetto trees, gentle night breezes, and breaking surf. Such depictions are not untrue, though they give short shrift to South Carolina's extensive wetlands. On the coast, looking inland, just beyond the beaches, it's marsh that stretches on for mile after mile.

Marsh boardwalks, platforms raised just a few feet above gooey pluff mud, offer extraordinary vistas of cordgrass and creeks. Live oaks sit twisted atop small bluffs, and Spanish moss trails delicately from the oaks' gnarled branches. Tidal creeks twist into the mainland. The salty marsh air can be exceptionally pungent. It is a repulsive smell, but one forgivable for its uniqueness.

Small sandy islands dot the vast marshes, covered with cedar, pine, and palmetto trees, as well as more oak. The land looks exotic, or prehistoric even, fit for dinosaurs. In his tale of treasure seeking, *The Gold-Bug*, Edgar Allan Poe described the South Carolina marsh as a "wilderness of reeds and slime."

At low tide, mudflats covered with scurrying fiddler crabs are exposed. Herons walk the creek beds, pecking for food. Pairs of dolphins surface in the shallows, and rays glide in inches of water. Raccoon tracks are imprinted in the pluff mud, and exposed oysters spit seawater. As the tide rises, periwinkle snails inch up the cordgrass, clinging to the last bit poking above water. Below, blue crabs shake the stalks with their claws in hopes of dislodging their dinner.

The Europeans who laid eyes on the South Carolina coast in the sixteenth and seventeenth centuries must have approached the shoreline with wonder, staring into the dense pine forests abutting the beaches. The coast is absent landmarks, save for the mouths of rivers. Anything and everything in this part of the New World was contained beyond or within the trees.

What was beyond the trees of South Carolina? For Foy and other marijuana smugglers, there was isolation and rural roads. Rural roads led to highways. Highways led to the interstate. And the interstate led to big cities: Atlanta, Chicago, Indianapolis, New York, and Washington, D.C., where there lived legions of waiting customers.

In the marshes, off-loaders stomped through muck to pull bales off boats, trying to avoid oysters, whose shells pointed upward like small alabaster daggers, threatening to ribbon skin from unprotected feet and legs. Off-loading in South Carolina creeks was vastly different from tossing bales in the condo-lined canals of Florida. Working under cover of darkness, smugglers agonized over the dangers of the marsh, home to alligators and poisonous snakes. They quickly learned that insects and mites could collude to make life miserable. Mosquitoes bit exposed skin, chiggers snuck under clothing to attack legs and groins, while no-see-ums swarmed faces and crawled through hair. One smuggler from Indiana was so terrified of chiggers, he religiously dusted his socks and shoes with sulfur before daring to work in the marsh.

Navigation in the marsh could be extremely challenging, too, especially on moonless nights. The area's eight-foot tides restricted operations, as a boat, already sitting low in the water because of its heavy load of drugs, could easily catch its keel or hull on a sandbar or the mud bottom. In places, South Carolina's marshes spread for a few miles offshore, and the creeks that wound through them split continually, like capillaries, dwindling into dead ends. As the smugglers discovered, it's much easier to enjoy South Carolina's coastal landscape by looking across it, than working in it.

Despite the challenges, smugglers were eager to exploit the sleepy South Carolina coast, especially as law enforcement patrols in Florida became more frequent. Julian Pernell, the Virginia kingpin, testified that he and his partner, Barry Toombs, conducted fifty-two smuggling operations in eleven years, forty-five of which were successful. Pernell, who forfeited about $7 million to the government, estimated about half of his smuggling operations came through South Carolina: "I had some in McClellanville, I had some in Edisto Island, some in Hilton Head, some in Charleston, some came into Georgetown, Conway, up and down the South Carolina coast," said Pernell.

"Is [South Carolina] a pretty good place to drop off marijuana?" asked a defense lawyer.

"One of the best," said Pernell.

Among those smugglers most intrigued by the South Carolina coast was Byers, a native Midwesterner who'd spent little time in the Deep South. The almost unspoiled coast of South Carolina would serve him well, and so would its people. Within a few years he'd work closely with no less than five South Carolinians the federal government would classify as marijuana kingpins, including Foy. Born in Minneapolis on October 12, 1945, Karl Robert Byers Jr. spent his childhood in Minnesota, shuffling back and forth between households after his parents divorced when he was twelve. He was an average student, he later told his South Carolina lawyer, Gedney Howe, and had a paper route as a kid. In the summertime he learned to sail on Lake Harriet in Minneapolis with his buddies Bob Roche and Bill Thompson, whose parents had a boat. On weekends they volunteered at the lake to crew sailboats in regattas. Byers's passion for sailing proved an enduring one. In time he'd own some of the world's finest boats.

Before his parents split, he and his siblings watched his father mistreat their mother. Nevertheless, when he was sixteen, Byers ran away from Minneapolis to find his father in Portland, Oregon.

Life was not better on the West Coast. His father had remarried, but the relationship was crumbling. Byers's stepmother, who had children of her own from a previous relationship, treated Byers as second-rate. Byers and his father moved out, but Karl Robert Byers Sr.'s drinking didn't stop.

"He was an alcoholic and I was subject to his abuse, and he was never around," Byers said. "He really wasn't much of a father."

Absent supervision, Byers began skipping school and stealing cars. After a 1962 arrest for boosting a new Ford, a judge asked the seventeen-year-old if he'd rather be released to his father or go to a state reform school. Byers chose the latter, and he attended MacLaren School for Boys for six months, wrestling and playing football and baseball.

"I thought it did me a lot of good," Byers said.

After being released from MacLaren to his father in January 1963, however, the lessons from reform school were quickly forgotten. Byers was jailed in Portland for operating a car without a license and speeding. He moved in with a friend's family while he finished high school. In February 1964 he married. His wife, Karen, waited tables while he worked at a furniture company.

"I had a pretty, you know, torn-up childhood, and her childhood was pretty much the same as mine. Her parents weren't divorced but they were constantly breaking up and separating," Byers later explained. "I think we sort of found some sort of a common denominator of the two of us."

It was not, however, enough of a bond to ensure his fidelity. Within a few years, he cheated on Karen with her friends and even members of her own family.

"When we got married, both of us being Catholics, she agreed—we agreed—that she was going to take the pill. About a month or two weeks before the marriage, one of her Catholic friends got into her ear and told her that wasn't the right thing to do to take the pill. So discretion or better part of valor or whatever, I went ahead with the marriage," said Byers. "She became pregnant immediately after we were married, which was against, you know, my better judgment and everything like that.

"The first kid came along and she wasn't taking the pill, so I was having extracurricular marital activities because I didn't want her to get pregnant again and I didn't want to have any more kids because we were only eighteen years old and to be tied down by that sort of thing. That went on for a while, and I decided the best thing to do would just be to give up the relationship because she still wouldn't take the pill.

"So I left and went my way, went back to Minneapolis, and was working out there. She flew out to see me and we tried to reconcile our relationship, her still not being on the pill, and she ended up pregnant again. So that's where it ended."

Although his parents had since reunited—they rekindled their love on the occasion of Byers's wedding—Byers's father did not stop drinking. The elder Byers's debauchery reached a boiling point in 1967, after he and his son had separately moved back to Minnesota.

"I went to blows with him one day and put him in the hospital," Byers said. "After that one of my brothers did the same thing about a year later, kicked him out of the house. After we made up over that fight, we got along pretty good."

With an ex-wife and two young daughters left behind in Oregon, Byers traded Minnesota for Miami, where he worked for two years as a soft drink deliveryman along with Roche, his childhood friend.

Byers was also building his criminal résumé at this time, though the petty crimes he was accused of were a poor preview of the future misdeeds he'd commit as a kingpin who'd make the U.S. Marshal's most wanted list. In 1970, Miami Springs police charged Byers with buying, receiving, or concealing stolen property after finding him with a television, telephone, and liquor that had been taken three days earlier. He received probation. In 1972, according to Byers's friend and fellow smuggler, Mike Abell, Byers was no more than a small-time pot dealer who drove a Volkswagen.

Byers's underwhelming rap sheet and a succession of blue-collar jobs obscure the fact that at some point in the 1970s he started making a fortune selling marijuana. Beyond buying the prized Columbia sailboat, Byers lived on a houseboat on the Miami River and owned a Porsche and cigarette boat that he towed across the country. Foy says he and Byers would take the overpowered motorboat, capable of speeds upward of sixty miles per hour, and jump the wakes made by cruise ships off of Miami. Cruise passengers would watch with delight as the cigarette boat went airborne. They'd holler when Byers and Foy's female passengers removed their swimsuit tops.

Roche remembers even more debauchery, with a woman lying on the hood of the speedboat's engine, accepting more than one sexual partner at once. Another time, Abell and Roche say, Byers's passengers mooned marine law enforcement officers patrolling the Intracoastal Waterway and then hightailed it to Bimini in the Bahamas. Byers ran the boat hard, and the cigarette boat was in fact a replacement for his former boat, which broke in half after being used by Byers at high speed in rough seas. Byers was passionate about researching the quality of his equipment and putting it to the test, says Roche. Similarly, he put severe stresses on his body. One friend, Bob "Willie the Hog" Bauer, said that when others were doing half a quaalude, Byers would take two.

Bauer, the sulfur-sock dusting native of Indiana, first met Byers in a Miami apartment complex, finding the Minnesotan staggering on walkways after he had consumed a number of downers. Bauer worried Byers might stumble off a third floor balcony, so he walked with him until the depressants' effects lessened. Quaaludes were popular in Miami in the early 1970s, and Bauer, a connoisseur of illicit substances, nominates the Rorer 714 Quaalude as the world's best drug and quaaludes in general as a fine aphrodisiac. A number of airlines had stewardess training programs in Miami at that time, so the apartment complexes were flooded with attractive, adventurous young women, much to the budding drug dealers' delight. The quaaludes were so effective at disarming these women that the men nicknamed the drugs "instant pussy."

"You could have been with the Virgin Mary," Bauer says of the quaalude, "and her drawers were coming off before the night was over."

For any of the men, a life peppered with drugs, sex, and sunshine was enough, at least for the short term. Beyond pleasures of the flesh and getting drunk and stoned, regular diversions included motorcycle rides, golfing, boating, and waterskiing. For Byers, it wasn't enough. So one day, Roche says, Byers persuaded a friend to fly him in a private plane from Florida to Colombia. The plane landed on a beach, refueled, and took off again, flying low to avoid radar. Left behind was Byers, with a single backpack. He hiked into town and then traveled into the mountains, intent on finding someone to supply him premium marijuana. It wasn't long before he established a golden reputation among the farmers, paving the way for future visits by his lieutenants and friends, including Abell, Roche, and Foy. In other words, he left Colombia with what he came for: a connection.

That even this much is known about his kingpin beginnings is surprising given Byers's propensity for secrecy. Among his favorite sayings was, "loose lips sink ships," and he would not discuss the smuggling business openly. Accordingly, he chose friends and employees carefully. Before Bauer began driving vans full of drugs for Byers, the kingpin required him to rub down his cigarette boat so Bauer could demonstrate his work ethic. With other employees, Byers entrusted them with suitcases full of cash, returning months or a year later to retrieve it. Of course he expected every dollar to be untouched.

Byers's hiring practices reflected the discipline with which he approached the drug trade, and he often emphasized he "hired the needy, not the greedy." Roche calls Byers a thinker, and says although the two friends were renegades, they didn't consider themselves outlaws, but rather businessmen. At times, despite his own occasional binges, his tolerance for frivolity and overindulgence could be limited and his temper short. He was the "sweetest, kindest person in the world," said friend Liz Kennedy, "but you did not want to be on his bad side."

Byers dated Kennedy's roommate for some time, so she saw the kingpin often and sometimes joined him on his sailboat. To her, Byers seemed to be wary of abusing drugs and alcohol. She remembers him smoking pot often, but only snorting a single line of cocaine before putting it away. Kennedy was not capable of such restraint, she says, and she recalls once asking him for another hit. Byers's response was sharp.

"You've had enough to last a lifetime," he snarled. "Have a beer."

Working with the young and freewheeling Foy, Byers was careful to keep him in line. When Foy was short some cash for a deal they were doing, Byers insisted he take possession of Foy's Porsche as collateral. Foy fumed over the lack of trust, but Byers cut him no slack.

"Barry," Byers said, "business is business."

Whether Byers knew it or not, he and Foy were contributing to a rich history of illicit activity on the Carolina coast. For the past three hundred years, the area's expansive marshes and isolated inlets had been used by pirates, Civil War blockade-runners, and rumrunners. In the seventeenth century, English buccaneers followed the example of French and Spanish pirates and frequented the area's waterways. There, sheltered in inland rivers and creeks, they could refit and repair their ships in safety before returning to the Atlantic or Caribbean to terrorize merchant vessels. English colonial leaders welcomed the buccaneers' attacks on Spanish ships and the booty they brought back to sell and trade. In return, pirates appreciated Carolina's agreeable customers and unobtrusive authorities.

In response to complaints from ship owners and the governor of Jamaica, Carolina's leaders passed stricter antipiracy laws in 1685, diminishing the influence of pirates at the turn of the century. But by 1715, with the colony's military resources pushed to the frontier to combat Indian tribes, pirates repopulated the coasts of North Carolina and South Carolina, which had become separate colonies three years earlier. The most outrageous attacks were led by the infamous Edward Teach (or Thatch), otherwise known as Blackbeard. The appearance of Blackbeard struck fear in the hearts of merchant sailors, and for good reason: Prior to boarding a ship, Blackbeard was said to have hung weapons across much his body and set fire to cannon fuses tied in his beard and tucked under the brim of his hat.

In 1718, Blackbeard blockaded Charleston Harbor with *Queen Anne's Revenge* and three other ships, seizing a number of merchant vessels and holding their passengers ransom for a chest of medicines. South Carolina Governor Robert Johnson, without a warship at his disposal, acceded to Blackbeard's demands. Three months later, Johnson was less accommodating, sending an expedition from Charleston to capture another notorious pirate holed up in the Cape Fear River in North Carolina, "Gentleman Pirate" Stede Bonnet. A former Barbadian militia officer, Bonnet had left behind his family and a small fortune to become a pirate and associate of Blackbeard. After his capture he was brought to Charleston to be tried, though he soon escaped, perhaps by bribing a guard or by disguising himself as a woman. The Gentleman Pirate's escape would be echoed more than 250 years later, when a notorious marijuana smuggler would also manage to slip away from a Charleston jail.

Bonnet was soon recaptured on Sullivan's Island, across Charleston Harbor, and publicly hanged. By this time an expeditionary force from Virginia had killed Blackbeard in North Carolina. The deaths of Blackbeard and Bonnet more or less marked the end of piracy on the Carolina coast, but not the area's utility as a site for illicit commerce. Rumrunners had a short heyday two decades later, when Georgia prohibited the importation of rum and brandies between 1735 and 1742. Opportunistic South Carolina smugglers sailed south to secluded Georgia beaches and unloaded spirits.

More than a century later came the blockade-runners. In April 1861, a week after Confederate forces fired on Union troops at Fort Sumter in Charleston harbor and started the American Civil War, President Abraham Lincoln, intent on starving the Confederate Army of supplies, ordered a naval blockade of the South. Seven months later the Union Navy captured Port Royal, South Carolina, sixty miles south of Charleston, and used it and nearby Hilton Head Island as a base for the Atlantic blockade, which massed many of its ships around the ports of Charleston and Wilmington, North Carolina. The blockaders faced long odds in stopping the Confederate runners. In 1862, for example, a mere eight steamers and four sailing ships were assigned to patrol a thirteen-mile arc around Charleston Harbor, as well as an inlet to the south, and the port of Georgetown, South Carolina, sixty miles to the north.

Still there was danger in trying to slip by the stretched Union Navy. Fortunately for the Confederacy, many men were willing to try. Blockade-runners, steam-powered supply ships adept at evading Union warships, regularly crept along the Southern coastline, waiting for darkness and the chance to make mad dashes for the mouths of Confederate harbors. Within the harbors the crews of blockade-runners could breathe easy, knowing Union ships would not pursue them for fear of being shelled by Confederate forts.

The typical blockade-runner was approximately two hundred feet long, had an iron or steel hull, and was powered by steam engines that turned side-mounted paddles. Most steamed across the Atlantic from Nassau, Bahamas, or St. George, Bermuda, to deliver sorely needed cargo in the dead of night. They left the southern ports in darkness, too, bound back for the Bahamas or Bermuda with cargoes of cotton bales piled high below and above deck. The cotton bales were so closely packed "a mouse could hardly find room to hide itself among them," wrote Charles Hobart-Hampden, the British captain of the blockade-runner *Don*.

While the Confederacy deployed some enlisted crews on blockade-runners, most crewmen were entrepreneurs hired by British supply firms. Accordingly, many of these men were more interested in making money than helping the war effort. Meat, for example, was sometimes left to spoil on wharves in the islands so a crew could pack a ship with lighter luxury items like medicine, liquor, and silk. Should a blockade-runner's captain become fearful of being caught at sea, he'd order lead tossed overboard, lightening the ship but depriving soldiers of material to make bullets. During the war, ships departing Bermuda for the South had manifests showing cargoes that included cigars, soap, pepper, coffee, whisky, bonnet frames, sherry wine, hams, cheeses, and wire frames for hoop skirts. It was not until March 1864, nearly three years after the Civil War began, that the Confederacy began to regulate blockade-runners, forbidding the importation of luxury goods and curbing war profiteering by requiring half a ship's cargo be devoted to freight at fixed prices.

The substantial riches collected by blockade-running crews helped convert Nassau and St. George into dens of vice. As Samuel Benjamin wrote of Nassau in an 1878 travel guide:

During the Confederate years the little town actually swarmed with Southern refugees, the captains and crews of blockade-runners, cotton brokers, rumsellers, Jews and Gentiles of high and low degree, coining money and squandering it as if they owned the secret of transmutation of metals . . . The shops were packed to the ceilings; the streets were crowded with bales, boxes and barrels—cotton coming in, Confederate uniforms and pills of lead and quinine to pepper patriots and patients, going out. Semmes and his bold boys twisted their mustaches at every corner, danced involuntary reels and hornpipes from groggery to groggery. They were also often seen on the waxed floors of Government House, where they were always sure of a cordial reception, along with other guests from the Banshsee, and Alabama—bully chappies who brandished their revolvers in the faces of Union men, whose lives were too uncertain to insure thereabouts in those rollicking days.

Nearly one thousand miles north, the scene was much the same, according to James M. Morgan:

In Bermuda these men seemed to suffer from a chronic thirst which could only be assuaged by champagne, and one of their amusements was to sit in the windows with bags of shillings and throw handfuls of the coins to a crowd of loafing Negroes in the street, to see them scramble. It is a singular fact that five years after the war not one of these men had a dollar to bless himself with.

Some things never change. More than a century after the Civil War, South Carolina's marijuana smugglers spent the bulk of their money on women, or on drugs to get women, says smuggler Oliver Mayfield. While Nassau was the site of some carousing, it was more commonly visited for the purpose of making bank deposits. Marijuana smugglers preferred to keep their sailboats, and occasionally raise hell, on other islands, including the fashionable St. Barts. Even during visits to less glamorous, and downright dangerous Caribbean ports, the smugglers made the most of their time. Mayfield recalls sailing into Colon, Panama, to pick up needed cash and visit a brothel with a crewman. After he finished with his own woman, Mayfield waited in a bar downstairs for his friend to join him.

And waited.

And waited.

He's falling in love up there, Mayfield thought to himself, nervously eyeing the increasing number of Panamanians streaming into the bar. Colon had a reputation as one of the most dangerous cities in the Western Hemisphere, and the $5,000 wad of cash in Mayfield's pocket seemed to be more and more conspicuous as the bar filled with intimidating men.

Finally Mayfield struck an idea and summoned some courage.

"That was the best pussy I ever had," he yelled across the bar, the American slang apparently understandable to the Panamanians. "And with my last $20, I'm going to buy everyone a round."

Carefully peeling away a single bill from within his pocket, Mayfield bought the drinks and made new friends—brothers bonded by an appreciation of female anatomy. He and the crewman soon left, unmolested, and made it back to the boat.

Like their blockade-running predecessors, South Carolina's marijuana smugglers eschewed violence as passionately as they pursued sex. Not only personally distasteful, violence was often impractical.

"It must be borne in mind, that the excitement of fighting, which some men (inexplicable, I confess, to me) really love, did not exist," wrote Hobart-Hampden. "One was always either running away, or being deliberately pitched into by the broadsides of the American cruisers, the slightest resistance to which would have constituted piracy; whereas, capture without resistance merely entailed confiscation of cargo and vessel."

Much more thrilling was slinging illegal cargo at midnight, sneaking in lead bullets or marijuana bales right under Uncle Sam's nose. As Englishman Tom Taylor, a cargo supervisor aboard the blockade-runner *Banshee*, described evading Union ships to deliver needed Confederate Army supplies in Wilmington during the Civil War:

> *Hunting, pig sticking, steeple-chasing, big-game shooting, polo—I have done a little of each—all have their thrilling moments, but none can approach "running a blockade" . . . perhaps my readers can sympathize with my enthusiasm when they consider the dangers to be encountered, after three days of constant anxiety and little sleep, in threading our way through a swarm of blockaders, and the accuracy required to hit in the nick of time the mouth of a river only half a mile wide, without lights and with a coastline so low and featureless, that as a rule the first intimation we had of its nearness was the dim white line of the surf.*

More than 120 years later, after running the same rivers, Mayfield put it much more succinctly than the Englishman: "Pussy wasn't even fun after that."

The conditions that had made Carolina so attractive to swashbucklers—isolated backwaters, poverty, and sparse settlement—were still intact three centuries later. In the 1970s, South Carolina's waterways were lightly traveled. The state was still poor and relied heavily on its textile industry. It was also still sparsely developed. Compared to Florida, the South Carolina coast was virtually untouched, save for Charleston and the hotel-lined Grand Strand of Myrtle Beach.

Most important for smugglers, law enforcement in the state was weak, at least along the coast. In 1973, upon the formation of the Drug Enforcement Administration (DEA), only one U.S. Customs officer from South Carolina, Harold Stein, was transferred to the DEA. His territory stretched more than three hundred miles, from the border of North Carolina and South Carolina to Brunswick, Georgia.

"Needless to say," Stein says, "it took a lot of cooperation from state and local law enforcement agencies to develop cases."

From the outside looking in, it can be difficult to understand the division of responsibilities when it came to drug smuggling interdiction in the 1970s. Before the DEA was formed, U.S. Customs had jurisdiction over drug smuggling cases. After the DEA was formed, U.S. Customs lost that responsibility, and Customs reorganized, forming an additional branch, the U.S. Customs Patrol. The uniformed officers of the U.S. Customs Patrol served to apprehend suspects they physically caught in the act of smuggling, but could not investigate cases based on clues, leads or informants. When they made an arrest or received a tip on any illegality, they turned the case over to special agents in the U.S. Customs office of investigations. The exception was information on drug smuggling cases, which was handed over to the DEA. The bureaucracy could easily complicate anti-smuggling efforts with overlapping jurisdictions inspiring rifts between law enforcement agencies.

"There was always the undercurrent of turf war, conflict, whatever, everybody wanting the stats," says Lionel Lofton, an assistant U.S. attorney in Charleston from 1971 to 1983. "I spent half of my time refereeing turf wars between Customs and DEA."

Beyond jurisdictional distractions, patrol officers suffered from a lack of equipment. The Customs Patrol office in Charleston didn't acquire its first boat until 1975, says Mike Bell, a former patrol officer. It was a boat seized from a suspected drug smuggler. Customs Patrol offices in Savannah, Georgia, and Wilmington, he says, didn't have boats until a year later. In fact Bell can't remember many local law enforcement agencies having boats at that time, just game wardens and the U.S. Coast Guard. Like many Customs officers at that time, Bell had joined the agency as an air marshal in the early 1970s. In 1974, with the introduction of X-ray baggage screening, the need for air marshals declined drastically, resulting in their reassignments to other posts, including coastal patrols.

Without boats, patrolling for drug smugglers was done on land, with agents driving on island roads in the dead of night. Given the number of islands and waterways south of Charleston, a thorough patrol by automobile was nearly impossible.

"Most of the time you'd be by yourself," recalls Chuck Pittard, a former special agent for the South Carolina State Law Enforcement Division, or SLED, who was detailed to U.S. Customs Patrol in the early 1980s. "You used the stars and the moon and everything. But you'd have to go down there with your lights out because they could see you."

Using tips from informants, Customs supervisors would select specific areas of the coast to concentrate the patrols, sending a handful of Customs officers to Hilton Head Island, for example, with support from state police officers and the local sheriff's department.

"If you saw something, you would call, call for help," says Pittard. "[Of] course you'd have the old primitive radios. Nobody was on the same frequency. Charleston County had one frequency. Customs would have a frequency. SLED would have a frequency."

The most intensive smuggling patrols occurred each holiday season, from Thanksgiving to Christmas, to coincide with the harvesting of marijuana in Colombia. State police officers from South Carolina's capital city would bolster the patrols, staying in motor homes or motels for a few days at a time while working night shifts. Pittard remembers keeping busy and working night after night until three or four o'clock in the morning.

"There wasn't a whole bunch of Christmas shopping you were doing," he says. "You weren't going to a bunch of parties."

Despite the long hours, the nighttime work could be enjoyable. It was certainly different from traditional police work.

"I use the word *fun time*," he says.

If you were intent on catching crooks, though, it could be disappointing. The majority of patrols did not yield arrests. Without help from an informant, the searches were stabs in the dark. The agents used a phrase to describe their often-fruitless pursuits: "goat fucking"; or, in polite company, "goat roping."

"We would be out there working and you ain't gonna catch nothing, ya know," Pittard explains. "You're just a wasting your time, but you out there doing it."

"What kind of goat fucking we going on tonight?"

Half a century earlier, fellow South Carolina law enforcement officers expressed similar exasperation in trying to intercept smugglers bringing booze into the marshes during Prohibition. South Carolina had relatively few of these smugglers in the 1920s, though, with the bulk of the nation's rumrunners sailing to the Northeast and New York City. There they'd park along Rum Row, joining other spirits-laden ships bobbing in the ocean, just beyond the territorial waters of the United States. Speedy motorboats would rush out to meet the motley flotilla, get loaded, and shuttle the alcohol back to shore. When the Coast Guard initiated pursuit, the motorboats went to great lengths to thwart arrest, using decoy boats, smokescreens, and other ploys, all in the name of fun and money.

The Prohibition rumrunners in South Carolina were not so bold, preferring to avoid confrontation with authorities. They'd hide among barrier islands and unload liquor at remote boat landings. In a memoir, Sheriff J. E. McTeer recalled the trouble he had patrolling Hilton Head Island and the surrounding area:

> *Beaufort County with its hundreds of islands, three large sounds and miles of rivers and creeks was a perfect port of entry for smuggled whiskey. An army could patrol constantly and still fail to see a carefully guarded barge as it slipped through an obscure creek to run aground at the foot of a little used road. There trucks could unload tons of liquor and transport it throughout the country under the cover of darkness.*

As if they were taking cues from these rumrunners, marijuana smugglers in South Carolina avoided urban centers, preferring to unload in rural areas like McClellanville, a fishing village thirty miles north of Charleston. Billboards along coastal highway U.S. 17 boasted McClellanville was the shrimp capital of South Carolina, and the title was a badge of honor for the town. Though the crustacean may not be the most magnificent of sea creatures, shrimp occupy a special place in the hearts of South Carolinians, and, when fried, a special place in their stomachs. In McClellanville, shrimping was an important livelihood.

Many villagers spent months away from home, dragging shrimp nets off Florida in colder months before moving north to South Carolina for the summer and fall shrimping seasons. On the way home some shrimp boats made a detour, heading south all the way to Colombia to bring home a product that fetched a much higher price per pound than shrimp. Even better, it didn't need to be kept on ice.

U.S. Customs agents were not unaware of the marijuana coming into McClellanville, and Customs officers occasionally patrolled the waters outside the village at night, hoping to make a bust. Wary of being compromised by eavesdroppers, and in a nod to the billboards, Customs agents referred to the village as the "Capital City" when discussing their patrols on the radio. Thanks to Foy, it wouldn't be long before they considered McClellanville the state's marijuana smuggling capital as well.

The hamlet and its tranquil surroundings suited Foy's needs just perfectly. Despite the village docks being just a short cruise from the Intracoastal Waterway, the prime spots to smuggle were a few miles north of McClellanville, on the banks of plantations that lined the waterway. The land belonged to wealthy, unsuspecting out-of-town families who seldom visited their coastal estates. Any chains around the properties' gates were easily removed, allowing a small convoy of trucks to rush in and head toward water's edge. Most of these trucks were provided by new business partners Foy had made in 1974—the pair of talented distributors from northern Virginia: Pernell and Toombs.

Pernell and Toombs had met years earlier in The Place Where Louie Dwells, a Washington, D.C., restaurant. Toombs was a cook; Pernell did the taxes, as his father-in-law owned the place. At that time Pernell, a native of North Carolina, worked as an accountant, negotiating loans for small businesses. He also ran a gambling house, taking bets on ball games and organizing poker and craps games. He was busted in 1972, but escaped conviction because police executed search warrants illegally. Toombs marveled at Pernell's ability to break the law, and claimed that if Pernell was offered $100,000 to tell the truth and $10,000 to lie, he'd lie because it was more enjoyable.

Toombs was born in Vienna, Virginia, and, after high school, was drafted into the Army for sixteen months, serving much of it in Vietnam as a helicopter gunner in the 1st Cavalry Division. Coming home at age twenty-one, he gambled and hustled at Virginia pool halls for three years. The experience was instructive: He learned not to fear losing everything he had.

Though he didn't care to smoke pot himself, his friends in the pool hall did. Toombs began selling it, and soon started driving out to Arizona three times a month for Mexican pot, motoring for two and a half days each way. He didn't fear getting caught, but the drive was a grind, no matter the cargo and the money it would make him.

"You get an adrenaline rush, but you get through that," recalls Toombs. "Everything basically comes down to work when it's repetitive. It's a job."

Five years after Pernell and Toombs struck up their friendship, Toombs's connections in Arizona had dried up. Both men were eager to discover new sources of pot, so Pernell asked a friend in Key West, Florida, for help. The friend arranged an introduction to Foy in the Coconut Grove Hotel in Miami, where Foy offered Pernell the chance to invest in a boat he'd be sending to Colombia. Pernell declined.

Three months later, however, Foy called Pernell and advised him the boat was returning. Would he like to buy some of its cargo now? This time, Pernell said yes, and Foy instructed him to drive down from his home outside the nation's capital to McClellanville, the shrimp capital.

Without the help of local watermen, smuggling into McClellanville was a nearly impossible endeavor. It was difficult to navigate the shallow, serpentine creeks that separate the Intracoastal Waterway from the Atlantic Ocean, especially at night. To avoid disaster, Foy usually required the large sailboats and trawlers he loaded in Colombia to wait offshore when they reached McClellanville. Once the skippers radioed in, local men would pilot small boats out to meet them and transfer the pot. Despite Foy's best intentions, things rarely went smoothly.

One time shuttle boats got caught by a falling tide, leaving the crafts stranded in dry creek beds and forcing panicky smugglers to stash marijuana bales on a marsh island until they could be removed the next night. Another time, Foy didn't have enough trucks to cart off the marijuana, so they stuck thousands of pounds of pot in the woods for a few days and covered the bales with a tarp. It looked like a marijuana mountain. Another time the boat arrived from Colombia four days earlier than expected, forcing Foy to scramble his off-loaders and unload the drugs. No matter how much practice and preparation, every deal was a potential disaster.

"All that was so unorganized and haphazard and crazy the way it happened," says McClellanville shrimper and smuggler Billy Graham. "The communications and all were always fucked up and backwards."

Foy, however, was a master of improvisation, able to pull off each caper in McClellanville without attracting the attention of the authorities. It may not have always been pretty, but Foy resolved whatever problems came his way, pulling ten thousand pounds of pot off boats at a time and quickly getting it on the road. Within a few weeks any frustrations felt by his hired hands washed away when he handed out paper bags stuffed with cash.

Chapter Three

Despite being born more than a hundred miles inland, it wasn't until he was at least a day's sail away from shore that Les Riley felt at peace, finding rhythm in rolling waves and ocean winds. He was a restless man and discovered early in his adulthood that a sailboat was the perfect place for him to call home. A sailboat meant freedom, and escape was always available through a few tugs. Just yank up the anchor and the sailboat was loose. Just yank up the halyard and the mainsail rose and filled with wind. Then the sailboat would move wherever Riley pointed it.

Thanks to the success of his early ventures with Barry Foy and others, Riley and his girlfriend, Suzanne, were able to buy a sailboat to call their own. They purchased a thirty-five-foot wooden Cheoy Lee sloop about 1975, named her *Whisper,* and lived aboard as they cruised the Bahamas, snorkeling, swimming, and fishing. Theirs was a simple existence in which they stretched the money Riley made from smuggling pot, going without comforts like air-conditioning or refrigeration. All their clothes, Riley says, could fit in a single suitcase. He kept their sailboat orderly, with each belonging assigned its proper place.

Suzanne became pregnant aboard *Whisper,* and in 1975 she gave birth to daughter Leah in Nassau. About this time Riley started making more money by organizing his own smuggling ventures, quietly earning a small fortune. He met businessmen in the Bahamas who steered him toward investments, such as gold and securities. The day's interest rates were high, giving Riley a good return on his money. His wealth would have surprised most of his friends from college and Key West, who had dismissed Riley as too laid-back to ever work seriously at anything.

Wealthy or not, living aboard a sailboat with a small child had its hassles. A year or so after Leah was born, Suzanne pleaded with Les to move back to the United States. Riley acceded to her demand, but only on the condition they find a home "no further north than

Charleston, no further west than A1A or Highway 17." The young family settled on sneaker-shaped Hilton Head Island, South Carolina, and purchased a home in the fashionable Sea Pines Plantation subdivision. On one side of the gated community stretched the beach and ocean, where Riley bought a house. On the other side, along the back of the island, were tranquil marshes that lined Calibogue Sound. On this side, too, sat Harbour Town Marina, where shops and restaurants surrounded boat docks. A small lighthouse served as the marina's landmark.

Developer Charles Fraser had started Sea Pines Plantation in 1957 on timberland owned by his family. The graduate of Yale Law School sought to build luxury homes there without disrupting the natural grace and beauty of the island. Just years earlier, Hilton Head Island residents went without paved roads, telephones, and a bridge to the mainland. The development of Sea Pines changed all this. Fraser developed approximately five thousand acres in Sea Pines, but sought to leave at least 25 percent of the land undisturbed.

By the mid 1970s, many more people than just the Rileys discovered Hilton Head. The island's sleepy pace of life gave way to an energized atmosphere trucked in by developers and tourists. Tennis courts and golf courses started to appear, with Sea Pines hosting prestigious professional tournaments for both sports. Businessmen carved other resort subdivisions on the island. There was a belief, though, especially among those associated with Sea Pines, that residential development could be accomplished while maintaining the serene setting. People had big ideas about how Hilton Head could be made different than other spoiled paradises. Among them was Wally Butler, a former executive with the Sea Pines Plantation Company who moved to the island in 1958 and bought a house on Calibogue Sound. After leaving the company, he sold real estate in the area and engaged in a legal fight with his former employer regarding the development of nature preserves in Sea Pines that he argued were supposed to be protected.

A recovering alcoholic who chain-smoked to help stay sober, Butler's odd sense of humor earned him the nickname "Weird Wally." But more than weird, he was an affable man and an excellent fisherman. Upon being introduced to Riley, he became the smuggler's fast friend, even though Riley was about fourteen years younger than Butler. Butler encouraged his new friend, whom he understood to be a Florida yacht broker, to invest in real estate on the island. Residential lots in Sea Pines could be purchased for a few thousand dollars, and Riley scooped up land, including a piece of waterfront property just down the street from Butler. Riley saw great resale value in the land and figured he'd made enough money from smuggling to live comfortably for the rest of his life, so long as he invested wisely. There was nowhere else he wanted to be.

"Hilton Head had the Montessori schools. They had the bike paths—it was beautiful," says Riley. "No streetlights or stoplights or anything like that. Great place to raise a family. So I basically retired and Wally and I fished."

Two years after delivering daughter Leah, Suzanne gave birth to a son, Justin. Riley would take the kids down to play on the beach, just a short walk from their home. Almost every day, Riley could be found catching a tan on the sand, reading newspapers, or doing crossword puzzles. As the day wore on, he held court at the nearby tiki bar.

Coming back from a fishing trip one day with Butler, Riley cruised toward the Harbour Town lighthouse, ready to call it a day. On the dock were two men, one of them flashing a big grin. Riley greeted the smiling man, a college friend who'd just served time in prison. He invited him to jump down into the boat. The men cruised back out into the sound and started to catch up. As Riley would later write to a judge, "This was the biggest mistake of my life."

The Harvey family of Alexandria, Virginia, operated a service station on Fort Hunt Road and had just about as many kids as gas pumps. Seven boys were born to that family, and by the time each was a teenager, he helped run the family business, rotating tires, pumping gas, or performing some light mechanical work. Dad paid them a buck an hour, which the boys regarded as big money at the time.

The oldest was Butch, born in 1947. A year later came brother Lee. A year after that came Tom. After taking a break, the next Harvey boy, Michael, came four years later and was followed by the birth of the other siblings. The boys attended parochial school until the eighth grade, and it was Lee who gave the nuns the most grief. Even when he wasn't causing mischief, recalls Tom, Lee would often get blamed.

"Lee always had a smile that said, 'I'm guilty,'" he says. "He had kind of a crooked grin."

The smile served him well in high school, where Lee was voted the best looking in his class. He never had a problem getting dates with the cutest girls and was a good student and athlete. He could be regarded as quiet, but was extremely outgoing, his brothers say, and loved to read and engage in conversation.

"Intelligent, good looking, unbelievable charisma," says Tom. "People were just drawn to him."

Conscious of his appeal, Lee took great care in his appearance, staying neatly groomed and wearing preppy clothing. He required his mother to iron his boxer shorts, and if he got oil on his uniform at the service station, he promptly took it off and changed into another. It was at the service station where he practiced his charm, doing his best to earn nickel tips from customers. At home he was the same way with his brothers, hoodwinking them into deals with lopsided returns and convincing them they were making out like bandits.

"Lee started a lawnmower service where he made all the money and I did most of the work," says Tom. "We'd get paid $2.50 to do a yard, and I'd get 50 cents . . . [but] you would walk away thinking, 'Man, he's a great guy.'"

"Yeah, he was real good at that," says Michael.

"If you wash and wax my car for me, I'll give you a ride over to Timmy's house," he recalls Lee saying.

"Great," replied Michael. "It's a whole block away!"

If he sometimes leveraged his age and smarts, other times he was genuinely nice. Michael remembers his older brother teaching him how to throw a baseball and coming to his baseball games to support him. Oftentimes he'd stop by on a Saturday night before meeting friends, just to tell Michael he was proud of him.

"He didn't stick around long, but he would always come by and encourage me and help me," says Michael. "He was a great brother, just a super brother."

In 1966, when Lee was about seventeen, his father passed away after suffering a series of heart attacks. Lee then left for the University of South Carolina, where he studied business, joined a fraternity, and dated more pretty girls. One of them, Cameron Currie, remembers going to a football game and party with Lee. He dated her roommate for a while, too. All the girls at the University of South Carolina had a crush on Lee, she says, and he stood out as preppy, known as the first boy on campus to wear a pink shirt.

As Lee was finishing college, his older brother, Butch, was killed in Vietnam along with fourteen other Marines, including a highly decorated colonel, William Leftwich. On November 18, 1970, Butch boarded a helicopter in heavy fog to rescue seven soldiers surrounded by an enemy division in mountainous terrain. After the rescue team extracted the men by dangling a rope ladder from the helicopter, the chopper banked and crashed into a mountain, killing the entire crew and all the rescued soldiers. A Marine chaplain and honor guard knocked on the Harvey door days later to break the news. Lee, now the oldest male in the family, had to identify his brother's body. The charred corpse was almost unrecognizable, a far cry from the handsome, athletic, and fearless man who went off to war. Years later, Lee confided to his brother Tom that, "I'd wish to God I'd never seen him."

"Things like that really set you back," says Michael. "When there's something going on in the country that you absolutely despise and hate like that freaking war in Vietnam and somebody that you love and admire comes home in a box. It just, it does something to you."

After graduating from the University of South Carolina with a marketing degree, Lee Harvey enrolled a year later at the university to obtain a master's degree in business administration. His graduate schooling would be interrupted, however, by his arrest in 1974 for certain extracurricular activities: Harvey had acquired hundreds of pounds of marijuana for a northern Virginia drug ring. He was convicted of conspiracy and interstate travel to facilitate an illegal act, and sentenced to three years in prison.

Fortunately for Harvey, federal prisoners in the 1970s often served a third of their time, earning early release dates through good behavior and parole. After leaving prison, he called up a college buddy and asked for his help. Harvey told the old pal he was trying to get in touch with a fraternity brother from the University of South Carolina, Les Riley. Did he know where he could find him?

Yes, the classmate answered, offering to drive Harvey to Hilton Head to see Riley. He even loaned his friend money for a hotel room. They arranged to meet Riley on a dock near the Harbour Town lighthouse, just as Riley returned from fishing. Standing on the dock, the classmate watched Harvey climb into the boat with Riley and exchange greetings. The reunited friends motored off into the sunset while the classmate yelled after them, reminding Harvey he needed to pay him for the hotel bill. The message went unheeded, and the former classmate didn't see Harvey for another six months.

"He was gone," he says. "He stiffed me."

Lee Harvey's friends say that he was determined to move beyond the family gas station, unwilling to live life as a grease monkey. When he was arrested and developed a criminal record, though, his hopes of being a legitimate businessman were dashed. He viewed his conviction as a stain he could not remove, no matter how many times he changed his shirt. To pursue a conventional career, too, would deny his God-given criminal talents.

In college Harvey had sold some pot and hash oil, but he wasn't thought to be nearly as devoted to peddling drugs as someone like Barry Foy. Most classmates remember that Harvey was always grinning, a habit that earned him the nickname "Smiley." Riley remembers Harvey for the way he could snag a date with any woman he wanted.

"He was a good guy," says Riley. "Fun to be around because all the girls liked him, so you could pick up his leftovers."

Harvey's purpose for meeting Riley was not to reminisce about their glory days, but to re-create them. He told Riley he wanted to learn the smuggling business and become his partner. He tried to make the offer enticing, explaining he knew people who wanted to buy any marijuana they could bring in.

"I've got people, and you'll teach me the business," Harvey told Riley. "You don't have to do anything, except show me what to do."

As he would realize years later, Harvey's appearance marked a crossroads for Riley. Seven years earlier, he'd dropped out of college to crew boats and cut lawns in the Florida heat, scrounging together any cash he could to rent shacks during island vacations. Now he owned slices of a resort island, including a beachside home. He had a wife and young family, and a fat bank account, too. Any crimes he had committed were long forgotten; the marijuana he smuggled already smoked. The worst thing he could imagine happening is some problem with the IRS. It was nothing that couldn't be fixed.

But Riley was a little bit bored in his paradise, and itching to travel again. He agreed to take his insistent friend on as a partner, and explained to Suzanne that if she wanted to keep on living as they were, she'd need to permit him some freedoms. He might need to leave home from time to time, Riley said, and he might miss the occasional holiday. It was critical for him to take care of business when it needed to be done.

That Harvey could lure Riley out of retirement was no surprise. Like almost everyone else in the world, Riley was susceptible to Smiley's charms. Harvey could exert a pull on people whether they were strangers or loved ones, friends or foes. When his brother Tom was pulled over for drunk driving in Jacksonville, Florida, after a day at the beach, Harvey stopped the car he was driving to talk to the cop, persuading him to let his brother go and continue driving a half-mile more to his hotel. After his first stint in prison, he prepared for a visit by his parole officer by taking Tom's two- and five-year-old daughters across the street from the family service station for ice cream. When the parole officer stopped by the garage and flashed his badge, he advised Tom he was here to see Lee.

"He'll be right back," Tom said.

Glancing out a window moments later, the parole officer observed Lee crossing the street, flanked by two cute little girls. Each had a hand held tight by Lee as they watched for traffic. The other hands clutched ice-cream cones.

"Oh my God," muttered the parole officer. "I can see where this is going."

When dealing with friends and smuggling associates, who were essentially one and the same, Lee Harvey could be similarly transparent yet somehow able to get away with it. Barry "Ice Cream" Toombs began to work extensively with Harvey after discovering the Virginia natives had mutual friends and business partners in South Carolina. He could cajole you like a used-car salesman, says Toombs, but was exceedingly sophisticated.

"He was a charmer. He could lie to you and you'd like it," said Toombs. "He had the gift. I mean, a serious gift."

It was with Toombs and his partner Julian "Doc" Pernell that Harvey and Riley tried their first deal together. While Riley had extensive experience using boats to smuggle marijuana, Harvey convinced him to use a plane to get some Colombian pot. Against his better judgment, Riley agreed, accepting responsibility for refueling the plane in the Bahamas and bribing Customs officials to look the other way. Although they planned to be picking up only thirty-six hundred pounds of pot, it was good marijuana and would fetch high prices. Plus, a plane could make the trip much faster than a boat, and the pilot they hired was known to make more than one trip to Colombia in a day.

On March 6, 1978, Harvey, Pernell, Toombs, and others waited on the ground in Sylvania, Georgia, for the loaded airplane to arrive from the Bahamas. Minutes after the plane landed at about ten-thirty at night, they began moving the marijuana into waiting trucks, which sped away. A minute after the trucks left, the smugglers found themselves in handcuffs.

For months, it turned out, they had been meeting with an informer and undercover federal agents posing as smugglers. The agents had tricked the smugglers into thinking the airport was a private Georgia airstrip, when in fact it was the municipal airport for the town of Sylvania. Police sprang from the woods and stopped the speeding trucks, seizing the marijuana. As an appeals court decision later boasted of the sting, "No ambush was ever more successfully laid or executed."

The smugglers flew down lawyers from Alexandria, Virginia, to arrange for their bail. Meanwhile, Riley sweated it out in the Bahamas, unsure if his name had been mentioned to authorities. To his relief, it hadn't. After posting bond, Harvey eventually called his panicked friend and said he wanted to try another deal. This time, though, they'd use boats.

Despite it being a violation of his parole, the Georgia arrest didn't faze Harvey. A couple thousand pounds of pot was not large enough to warrant major punishment under drug laws at the time. If he had been caught in Florida, where drug running was rampant, he might not even have been prosecuted. In fact the likelihood of receiving nothing more than a five-year prison sentence, of which a convict might serve only a third, was a major reason so many were willing to smuggle marijuana. For Harvey's most recent arrest, he predicted a light punishment he could endure with ease.

"They're gonna give me two years," he told a friend. "I can do that standing on my head."

Marijuana use was of course exceedingly common among the youth of the 1960s and 1970s, with pot often smoked in public. Despite laws against its use, marijuana was not overwhelmingly condemned by the public, and many Americans favored regulation over prohibition. In 1978 eleven states did not consider possession of small amounts of marijuana a criminal offense, and President Jimmy Carter urged for reduced punishments of marijuana users. Paradoxically, that was the last thing smugglers wanted to hear. Heaven help the smugglers if marijuana was legalized—then they wouldn't make any money.

Punishment was also minimal for drug runners like Bob Byers, Foy, Harvey, and Riley because they refused to carry guns or traffic cocaine. Although they all enjoyed snorting a line or two (or more), the men opted not to smuggle cocaine, despite its potential for enormous profits. Disturbed by the emergence of automatic weapon-toting cocaine cowboys in Florida, they thought cocaine smuggling brought "bad juju" and was an invitation for violence.

When the Colombians tossed a few keys of cocaine on board a boat loaded with marijuana, an angry confrontation often ensued, with smugglers demanding they take it off. When someone carried a gun to a deal, they were shamed, as the presence of a firearm put a chill on the deal. How could you trust someone who might shoot you, they asked? Why would anyone ever shoot someone, anyway, when there was so much more money to be made? If there's a problem, they reasoned, we'll just make it right next time.

Given their aversion to violence, refusal to participate in the cocaine trade, and partially completed college educations, the marijuana smugglers of South Carolina and their partners earned the label "gentlemen smugglers." The authorities charged with catching, prosecuting, and punishing the smugglers considered them fairly civil, at least compared to other drug-related criminals. Defense lawyers felt the same way. These were men they felt comfortable taking home to dinner, they said, and some might even be allowed to date their daughters, though there's no doubt they'd break the poor girls' hearts.

It wasn't a label totally embraced by the men. Self-deprecating smuggler Skip Sanders writes: "as for that tag . . . 'gentleman smuggler' . . . total front. Total bs. 'chicken shit smuggler' would have been more appropriate."

Among the men unshaken by consequence and previous drug smuggling convictions was Christy Campbell, a young boat captain born into a prominent family who lived on a plantation outside Beaufort, South Carolina, north of Hilton Head Island. After high school Campbell finagled subsequent jobs as a captain in South Florida for two wealthy New York clothing industry executives, despite having no experience piloting yachts. During a trip to the Bahamas with one of his employers, he bumped into Riley, an old acquaintance, who said he might be able to use a boat captain. Campbell quit his job and sailed boats for Riley and Harvey, making a number of runs from Colombia to Cape Cod, Massachusetts, where'd they unload at a house owned by Riley's friend, Bruce MacDougall. Campbell's friend Kenny Gunn, a Miami lounge lizard who bore a resemblance to actor Burt Reynolds, often served as a crewman. Between the two and another crewman, they'd make $200,000 a trip.

The more trips Campbell did, the more he became known for his brazenness, which could no doubt be an asset when carting eight thousand pounds on each run, trying to zoom up the Gulf Stream in record time without getting intercepted by the Coast Guard. Yet his over-the-top personality irritated some colleagues. Toombs recalls Campbell arriving at Cape Cod and "bragging about how South Carolinians smuggle better than anybody else and how he was always on time." When Riley and Campbell began to have differences, Riley was happy to let his new partner, Harvey, interact with the brash captain Riley had nicknamed "Captain Crunch." Riley believed Campbell could be reckless and provocative. On the other hand, Campbell would sail wherever he was asked, with no hesitation.

"Christy was Lee's boy," said a fellow smuggler. "All he had to do was point and Christy would go."

In November 1978, Campbell, Gunn, and Ashley Brunson were sailing past the Bahamas one evening, loaded with pot, when it turned dark. A Coast Guard cutter was nearby, and Campbell decided to leave the boat's running lights off. The Coast Guard spied the sailboat *Love Affair* anyway and soon busted the crew, hauling them back to Miami. It was another hiccup for Riley and Harvey, but one they could tolerate. The sailboat crew was released without being charged. More important, plenty of their other ventures had been successful. They were making millions.

Chapter Four

To hear Skip Sanders tell it, the best seats in the house were by the window. There, regulars at downtown Charleston's 82 Queen could see the cars that rolled by and the women that stepped in. The restaurant was a popular hangout for area marijuana smugglers, and the initiated were well aware that Barry Foy owned a share in the fashionable eatery. Such ownership was inspiring to small-time smugglers, an indication that drug running could be a stepping-stone to legal and lucrative business. Unlike Foy, most smugglers did not have the heart to lead a full lifetime of crime.

Sanders's position among South Carolina's smugglers was unique. His grandmother owned a 325-acre plantation named West Bank on nearby Edisto Island, and its defining features, at least from a smuggler's point of view, were not its marsh views, ample farmland, or the nearby antebellum plantation house, but rather the remains of a deepwater dock and its proximity to the Atlantic Ocean.

Sanders had noticed smugglers using his grandmother's isolated property since 1973. One morning he'd raked up twenty pounds of pot left behind from the previous night. If they could afford to leave behind twenty pounds of top-notch pot, then they could certainly afford to pay a price for safe passage through his family farm. The Sanders family already leased acreage to tomato farmers. In November 1979, Sanders began offering one-night leases of the bluff to men who sold another type of crop.

"The first one, I went from deadass, flatass broke, to being handed a briefcase a week later containing eighty large," Sanders recalled. "Hello. It was on. I quit college and became a professional 'spot' salesman."

In Charleston, Sanders enjoyed a certain harmless notoriety, though he kept some clear-headed perspective on the depth of his involvement. He maintained a reverence for the men he believed to be the real entrepreneurs. Foy, or Flash, particularly impressed Sanders, not only for his boldness and success, but for his wit. Sanders thought it was brilliant that Foy referred to money as "dust," because it accumulates all around him.

In letters from prison filled with curious punctuation, Sanders reflected on 82 Queen's significance:

> *"see there?" this is why we sling weed. for a secure life down the road. this guy has a business. the Queen gave us hope some risks could [be] overcome. the QUEEN was argument whenever the girlfriends would all ask, "why not quit?" can't, liquor lips. need more dust to buy one of these . . .*
>
> *the Queen was youth and health and easy dust. leggy gals. and not dumb asses either. one day, i had a 911 parked outside and the prettiest sonofabitch in the place sittin' there all starry eyed at me. i thought, "how the fuck did this happen?" . . . we all had chunks-o-dust. sacks-o-blast [cocaine]. bottles-o-dom. when i think how many bottles i sucked back in the Queen? if i said a hundred, i'd probably be off. as in not enough. . . .*
>
> *sometimes, the godfather, FLASH, would breeze up in his. but his was different. it was a turbo, special import from Germany. flash gave me my lesson on Porsches one night just after I bought my first one, a 924 turbo. pure junk. he was at my house one night and we went to town . . . he said, let's take my turbo, you drive. well, getting on the interstate, flash had me redline that machine. incredible. seems like it was 70-80 mph in first gear, 100-110 in second, and about 135 in third. . . .*
>
> *later that night, i gave the girlfriend the 924 and bought a real one [a 911] a week later. there is nothing like 'em. it ruined me for life.*

Foy owned no less than four Porsches in his twenties and early thirties, and his frequent automobile purchases made for some interesting interactions with car salesmen lucky enough to have him as a customer. Arriving in shorts and flip-flops to showrooms full of luxury cars, Foy would return the next day with a paper bag full of cash, dumping it unceremoniously on salesmen's desks as they scrambled to close the office door and drop the window blinds. Sometimes, though, he made them work for their money.

At a dealership in his hometown of Columbia, Foy once brought his father along to test-drive a Mercedes sedan. Father and son piled into the front seats as the salesman slid into the center of the back bench. Foy motored out of town, charging along a rural road. His foot grew heavy on the accelerator, and the speedometer needle climbed smoothly past one hundred miles per hour.

Foy glanced in the rearview mirror. The salesman appeared tense.

"How fast you going?" Foy's father asked.

"I'm testing it out," he replied.

The Mercedes crested a hill and, descending, approached a ninety-degree turn. Sand had washed into the road from recent rains, and Foy applied the brakes quickly as the car rushed over the hazardous soil, sending the Mercedes into a full spin.

"I saw it, but I was going a little bit faster than I should have been," recalls Foy, in a rare confession of poor judgment. "God almighty, it hit that sand and went SCRRRRRREEEEEECCHHH."

When the car slid to a stop in the middle of the road, Foy's heart was thumping. Looking over his shoulder, he stared at the car salesman. "The poor son of a bitch in the back," says Foy, laughing. "He was a red-headed dude, and he had kind of a reddish complexion to him. Well, buddy, he was so white I thought I was looking at a ghost. I'm not kidding, I could see through him."

More ridiculous than Foy's driving was the frozen, spread-eagle pose the car salesman had struck during the spin. "He had gripped both the handles on top of the doors on both sides. When we stopped, and I looked back, that's how he was . . . it was like he couldn't release," says Foy. "He just saw his whole career go down the tubes in one turn."

Such recklessness did not go unnoticed. In the late 1970s the business partners who became rich with Foy slowly began disassociating with the brash kingpin. For Bob "The Boss" Byers, it was Foy's unexplained disappearance in the middle of an off-load on Hilton Head that more or less severed their ties. Unloading the boat, Byers's crew begrudgingly stacked Foy's share of the drugs against a fence and covered the bales as daylight approached. Byers soon followed his own advice on the best way to get even with bad business associates: stop working with them.

For others, it wasn't so easy to walk away, or affect change. As Bob "Willie the Hog" Bauer says, "It's hard to tell some twenty-eight-year-old guy with $3 million in the bank what the fuck to do."

In many ways the character traits that made Foy a villain are what enabled his breathtaking success in the drug underworld. He was impetuous and took too many risks. He was flashy with his money. He had little regard for others' well-being. Foy was going to make a dollar, one smuggler said, no matter who got fucked.

In 1976, Foy was blamed, he says unfairly, for rushing an off-load in the Florida Keys that led to a lobster fisherman spotting the smugglers and contacting the police. As the smugglers scrambled, with Foy swimming between keys to escape, a few men were arrested and a sixty-five-foot sport fisherman with fifteen thousand pounds of unloaded marijuana was sent on autopilot in the direction of Cuba, never to be seen by the smugglers again. One imagines a Cuban beachcomber had the find of his life soon after that debacle.

Initially grievances against Foy could be satisfied with drugs, girls, money, and heart-pounding excitement, all of which were plentiful when Flash was around. After so many frustrations, though, the charm began to wear thin.

Upset that Julian "Doc" Pernell and Barry "Ice Cream" Toombs smuggled a load into McClellanville by partnering with another South Carolinian, Foy traveled to Washington, D.C., and demanded a $150,000 payment from the men, claiming he controlled half the South Carolina coast. They claimed to have told him to "buzz off," and didn't see him again. Not that Foy really cared.

"Foy was burning his bridges behind him," Toombs later testified. "There's a lot of people in the drug business that like to burn their bridges behind them. They accrue more money, and they have got the capability of making new friends quicker than they can burn out bridges, so it is profitable."

Among Foy's new friends was Tom Rhoad, a young lawyer from Columbia who, at first glance, wouldn't appear to be the best candidate to replace the savvy smugglers from whom Foy had split. The men met after Foy's lawyer friend, Pogo Hartman, had referred Foy to his colleague Rhoad for help resolving a traffic ticket. Foy entered Rhoad's office and approached the diminutive lawyer with wonder.

Behind the desk sat a man dressed in a pink shirt, green and blue tie, and chartreuse pants. Foy thought he was looking at a rainbow.

Perhaps the multichromatic assault on Foy's senses impaired his judgment, because he soon opened his briefcase to retrieve the citation and inadvertently exposed its other contents to Rhoad—$60,000 or so in cash. Waving the ticket in front of a seemingly catatonic Rhoad, Foy realized his gaffe and snapped shut the briefcase. Rhoad's eyes did not waver. Moments passed before he finally promised to take care of the ticket. Days later, Hartman gave Foy a call and told him Rhoad wanted Foy to know he was always available for legal work. In the weeks that followed, the two formed a fast friendship at Hartman's house, partying close to the governor's mansion.

The pair was an odd couple. Rhoad had spent his early twenties learning law, and Foy had spent that time breaking it. Foy took a hands-on approach to smuggling, while Rhoad began participating as a financier, rarely stepping foot on a boat or getting his hands dirty. They both attracted attention, but in different ways. Foy favored making a name for himself through smuggling exploits, custom Porsches, and full-length mink coats. Rhoad's style attempted to be more refined, with his preppy wardrobe and prized, powder blue classic 280 SL Mercedes convertible—the same car owned by Lee Harvey and Les Riley. His voice was nasally, and many regarded him as a prick, but others forgave his flamboyant fashion sense and particular habits because of his insatiable appetite for drugs, crude jokes, and loose women. As he became more involved with the East Coast's marijuana smuggling underworld, he earned a variety of nicknames highlighting the aspects of his personality sure to make his mother recoil.

Foy had his own nickname for his friend—"TT Rebozo," a play on the name of Florida banker Bebe Rebozo, President Richard Nixon's close friend and Key Biscayne neighbor. Others knew Rhoad as "Tommy Love" or "Kinky Tom," as friends had once discovered Rhoad in an apartment wearing a leather mask and little else. His girlfriend lay bound and gagged in a quite vulnerable position on a nearby bed.

He also had been spied prancing around a room with a woman leading him by a leash tied to his penis. Rhoad's buddies joked that he was so consumed by sex that one of his girlfriends constantly walked around with wires running down her legs, attached to a sex toy that vibrated and produced a stimulating electrical current. When Rhoad had an apartment in New York, he'd invite prostitutes and girls, Foy says, some allegedly as young as fifteen, to have orgies and freebase cocaine, cooking the drugs on his stove for days on end.

When it came to money, Rhoad could be stingy. Riley knew Rhoad as his "2 Percent Man." Each time Riley sold Rhoad some pot or hashish, Rhoad would complain about being shorted 2 percent or so in weight, and would pay slightly less than the agreed upon amount. After noticing a pattern of these complaints, and doubting their legitimacy, Riley stopped arguing with Rhoad and simply charged him more per pound to offset the expected loss.

Rhoad's most popular nickname, though, was "Rolex," and its origins are a bit ambiguous. Some surmise the nickname stems from his fondness for the expensive timepieces and the prominence they assumed on his narrow wrist. "He had this massive Presidential and, he's small, so the watch looked twice as big on him," says John Jamison, a former neighbor of Rhoad and an occasional smuggler. "It was the first thing you'd see."

Others say the catchy moniker was coined after he began giving away the watches as calling cards. "One night partying, I asked why they called him Rolex. And he whipped out a new Rolex and gave it to me," says Sanders, in a letter. "I said, 'Hey, I'm gonna like kickin it with you fuckers!'"

For all his eccentricities, Rhoad's upbringing was traditional. His parents owned a tobacco and hog farm outside the small town of Branchville, South Carolina, and, when not farming, his father delivered mail. His family attended a Baptist church, and, according to one former girlfriend, alcohol was not allowed to be consumed in the house, per Mother's rules. That didn't stop Rhoad and his brothers and father, however, from sneaking a drink in other buildings on the property.

Rhoad was the oldest of four children and a quarterback on his high school football team, playing in a state championship game. At the University of South Carolina he served as a manager of the football team and belonged to a fraternity. His football experiences came as a surprise to his smuggling buddies. They, of course, saw him as a sex-crazed dandy fond of inappropriate comments and bewildering expressions. One favorite he'd often mutter in that distinctive nasal voice: "It ain't no fun when the rabbit's got the gun."

Bauer, a man known as both "Willie the Whale" and "Willie the Hog" because of his large size and appetite for cocaine, respectively, was particularly baffled by his small friend's football glory days. Bauer and Foy were once at Rhoad's house on Hilton Head when they came across a photo of Rhoad in uniform, striking an iconic football pose, with an arm cocked back, ready to throw, and head up, surveying the field. They chuckled as they kidded Rhoad about the photo, but then nearly died from laughter as Rhoad played along, re-creating the pose for them and extending and retracting his fingers to match his words. "Tom Rhoad—number eleven on the jersey, number one in your heart," said Rhoad, hamming it up.

Rhoad and Foy lived in beachside houses a few blocks apart on Hilton Head, less than two miles up the beach from Riley. Wally Butler, in a flourish befitting the marketing mind of a Realtor, gave their community on North Forest Beach a name: DDOA, or Drug Dealers of America. By this time Riley's fishing buddy was well aware Riley was not a yacht broker, and he began working with the men to find suitable sites to unload drugs, including a dock behind his own house.

On Hilton Head, Foy and Rhoad lazed around their houses, hanging out almost daily, smoking pot, watching sports, and going out at night. Apart from a few frantic nights of preparations for an incoming load, their lives were full of leisure. They were awash in cash, often keeping tens, if not hundreds, of thousands of dollars around in bags and briefcases. It became a chore to keep up with so much money. It was only so often they mustered the effort to pay someone to pack wads of cash into their boots and pants and head to the bank in Nassau, or make the trip themselves.

Jamison recalls walking by Foy's house one day and seeing a hand-tooled leather attaché case sitting conspicuously in the back of his Jeep pickup—an attractive target for a beachgoer with sticky fingers. Doing the kingpin a favor, he grabbed the case and returned it to Foy, who answered the door looking disheveled and nonchalantly thanked him. Jamison, who was suffering from financial difficulties with his charter fishing business and the IRS, was amazed to learn the case was stuffed with money.

Rhoad was no better. The only time Bauer can recall getting angry with his friend was when he flew to Hilton Head on a chartered plane to deliver a million dollars. When the plane landed and Bauer disembarked, Rhoad was nowhere to be seen. The pilot soon became impatient, wanting to make the return leg of the flight. Bauer didn't know what to do. There was no sign of Tommy Love.

Bauer stewed. Rhoad eventually pulled up in his Mercedes, half-lit, his face decorated with earrings and a pair of shades. He greeted his friend, whom he affectionately called "Young Will." Bauer dispensed with the pleasantries, asking him what the hell took so long. "Did your mom die?" Bauer said, with some annoyance. "Did something happen to your brother?"

No, Rhoad explained, he had been trying to pick up a waitress.

Bauer was floored. As Rhoad vouched for her beauty and offered apologies—"Now, now, Young Will, I'm sorry, I'm sorry."—Bauer fumed, trying to comprehend how anyone could leave a million dollars, and a friend, sitting on a runway for hours while he flirted with a Hilton Head waitress.

Bauer also recalls taking a trip to Vegas to run an errand for Rhoad, only to find out Rhoad had skimped on the reservation and booked him at an exceedingly dumpy hotel. Bauer picked up the phone to complain. "What the fuck's wrong with you?" he asked the millionaire.

Another time, Bauer rang Rhoad from Vegas, only to have Rhoad end the conversation early, informing Bauer, who was doing him another favor, that "I gotta go, this bitch is gonna blow me in cowboy boots."

And yet another time, when Bauer had finally been booked in a reputable hotel, he spoke again to Rhoad, who giddily let him in on a secret, directing him to the third machine in a bank of pay phones. "You won't believe this. It's the *bonanza*," Rhoad told Bauer. "Lee [Harvey] found it. You can talk for twenty minutes. It gives it back!"

That drug kingpins celebrated a pay phone that returned quarters, and protected knowledge of its existence like a national secret, is perhaps slightly understandable when one considers how often they relied on the anonymity provided by pay telephones. Almost every drug smuggler in the 1970s kept a large container of quarters in his car or home, and it was always wise to take a drive and find a pay phone instead of talking business on the home phone, lest the government be tracing calls on that line.

Even in this mundane detail of the drug business did Rhoad stand apart from his peers. He allegedly bought thousands of dollars of quarters at a time, and kept $40 at a time in a European-style "fag bag," says Bauer.

Trips to Vegas, of course, included visits to high-end prostitutes, including one who appeared in *Playboy* magazine. Bauer was smitten with her, and so was Rhoad, who made it a point to detail the depth of his infatuation. "Will, she's so fine, I would take her home at Thanksgiving," Rhoad gushed, "and at Thanksgiving table tell Maw Maw and Daddy that I love her and that she's a prostitute."

Bauer found all this endearing. "I loved him like a brother," he says. "He was fucking nuts."

In July 1979, President Carter holed up at Camp David for ten days and invited a smattering of American leaders and citizens to meet with him and share their opinions on the state of American life. Carter was preparing to address the nation about America's energy woes, but, after listening to the sampling of constituents and some of his advisors, he decided to deliver a broader message. For the last decade, the country had slogged through Vietnam, Watergate, stagflation, and fuel shortages. These crises had taken a toll, Carter concluded, and the United States was suffering from a "crisis of confidence."

"It is a crisis that strikes at the very heart and soul and spirit of our national will," Carter said in a televised address from the Oval Office. "We can see this crisis in the growing doubt about the meaning of our own lives and in the loss of a unity of purpose for our nation . . . In a nation that was proud of hard work, strong families, close-knit communities, and our faith in God, too many of us now tend to worship self-indulgence and consumption. Human identity is no longer defined by what one does, but by what one owns."

The remarks became known as Carter's "malaise speech." Though his criticisms had broad application, they seem particularly insightful when applied to the case of the gentlemen smugglers. Indeed, their hedonism and avarice exemplified what Carter considered the very worst habits of modern Americans. They favored easy money. Family harmony was tenuous in the face of frequent substance abuse and cheating. Their community was loose knit, composed of a transient privileged class that moved between resort islands and beachfront towns. They worshipped money and were poster boys for conspicuous consumption, parading around in Gullwing Mercedes and Rolex watches.

The gentlemen smugglers were the epitome of an overindulgent lifestyle, and they were spreading it to whoever wanted to purchase an ounce. At least that's one perspective. They saw it differently; they exemplified true American spirit, courage, and capitalism by trafficking a natural substance on the verge of legalization, or at least widespread decriminalization. If they didn't pay their taxes, so what? Nobody got hurt.

Had any of the gentlemen smugglers appraised Carter's speech—an unlikely scenario, given their general disinterest in politics—they may have agreed wholeheartedly with his comments regarding America's diminishing value of hard work. As young men, each of the smugglers had toiled at jobs they found unfulfilling. Foy worked as a mason, Riley a lifeguard. Harvey was a mechanic, and Byers assembled furniture and delivered soda. Their earnings were entirely inadequate for their oversize expectations of life, a week's worth of wages easily dwarfed by earnings from a few small pot sales among friends. The smugglers saw little promise in the vocations that awaited them, following in the footsteps of their parents to become bankers, business executives, barbers, mailmen, or carpenters. There was simply no match for the excitement and income a night of smuggling could provide. As Byers told his hired hands while unloading twenty-one thousand pounds of particularly potent and pricey pot, "Remember, every bale is a BMW."

Such quick riches cemented any disaffection smugglers might have had with traditional work. Toombs said he saved every paycheck he collected during the sixteen months he spent in Vietnam as a helicopter gunner. Boredom defined much of his service, with the exception being the occasional firefight. His heart raced during those chaotic moments in which he dodged bullets and pulled a trigger, killing strangers he barely saw.

He made additional cash by volunteering for extra guard duty. Still, it didn't amount to much. When he was honorably discharged at twenty-one, he left with the conviction that collecting a regular paycheck doesn't get you too far. "Working hard doesn't necessarily mean you have money," says Toombs. "And saving well doesn't mean you have money."

Drug smuggling, of course, did make him money, which enabled him to pursue his own passions on his own terms, without having to clock in. "Money is only freedom," says Toombs. "It's nothing else."

If the gentlemen smugglers owned too many things, it was easy to understand why. When you're an exceptionally good smuggler, you're rewarded with excessive amounts of cumbersome cash. You're net worth can double, triple, quadruple, or more in one night. Money can quickly become a nuisance, though one that many people are glad to help you resolve.

You can do two things with money: save it or spend it. Saving was harder for the smugglers, requiring trips to overseas banks and hours of bill counting, or, alternatively, finding secluded spaces, such as a spare bedroom closet, to store it. The closet, though, could fill up quickly, and it wasn't the safest place to store hundreds of thousands of dollars. Foy was robbed once at his Hilton Head beach house, $10,000 or so snatched from a concealed closet safe he had left open. It was spare change to the kingpin, but it could have bought him a car.

Those who opted for sticking profits in foreign bank accounts or safe deposit boxes were running similar risks, counting on their frequently drug-addled brains to recall where they stashed their cash. It was easier for them to buy things, remembering where they parked their Mercedes or where they docked a sailboat. Spending was a requirement, too, for keeping up appearances in a violence-free underworld where power needed to be *projected* more often than proved. Sanders says he'd try to keep up with Jimmy Connors, comparing the tennis star's winning purses at tournaments to the money Sanders made leasing his grandmother's riverfront property a night at a time. Another smuggler, upon locking his keys in his convertible, used a pocketknife to cut open the car's cloth top and retrieve them instead of walking back into his apartment building and riding an elevator up to retrieve a set of spare keys. He'd rather replace the top than waste time.

The smugglers bought fur coats, cashmere clothing, and thick gold chains, otherwise known as Mr. T starter kits, after the heavily gilded member of the A-Team. They ordered the most expensive bottles of wine and champagne when dining out, but not necessarily the best. Sometimes they dined in, ordering one of everything off room service menus. One smuggler was said to have taken a date aboard the Concorde jet to Paris for dinner, then jetted back home that same night, just because they could. As a rule, Riley only flew first class, reasoning that you meet more interesting people that way.

Harvey earned the nickname "Lee Lear," given his penchant for traveling aboard a private Learjet. Harvey patronized the charter services of Fort Lauderdale, Florida-based pilot Harvey Hop, and the aviator's newly formed business Hop-A-Jet, allegedly persuading Hop to perform barrel rolls in his aircraft. One wonders if Hop ultimately appreciated the irony of flying Harvey and his band of fellow millionaire marijuana smugglers in the same aircraft he used to transport celebrities that included Nancy Reagan. The future First Lady and Harvey, who very well may have sat in the same Learjet seat, had opposite agendas in life. While Reagan would seek to decrease Americans' drug use with her "Just Say No" campaign, Harvey brought in drugs by the boatload, organizing a handful of deals at a time. It was Harvey who stepped into a Las Vegas hotel room one day, lamenting the latest news to Bauer.

"Hey Willie, I've got a problem. I just read in the paper today high school kids are smoking less marijuana," deadpanned Harvey. "We got to get those numbers up, it's bad for the market share."

Beyond Carter's claims that rampant materialism was poisoning America's soul, the perils of runaway consumption included attachment to objects. For freewheeling smugglers, forever looking over their shoulders and trying to stay three steps ahead of authorities, attachment could be problematic. If you bought a home, you've created a paper trail and public record, as well as a place where the neighbors will recognize you. If you bought a boat or plane, you're responsible for its maintenance, storage, and registration, which also creates a paper trail. With almost all things, including women, it was better to use it once and leave it behind. Not that anyone listened, but a smuggler named Diamond Jim once said, "If it fucks, flies, or floats, rent it."

Rent women they did, though they preferred high-end prostitutes as opposed to streetwalkers. The gentlemen smugglers referred to women as whores so often, one cannot be certain when that meant there was formal exchange of money for sex and when they enjoyed the company of loose women looking for a more causal receipt of excitement and drugs. When the smugglers did turn to prostitutes, they did it because they were sex crazed, not sex starved. None of the men had much trouble getting a date or a regular girlfriend, though they might have trouble keeping them from heartbreak due to infidelities. Some smugglers flew in call girls by seaplane and invited them aboard chartered yachts, where, for example, they nicknamed the stateroom the "Briar Patch." The girls pranced around the boat in bikinis, enjoying unlimited amounts of drugs while coquettishly cooing to the men, "Ooh, don't throw us in the Briar Patch."

They were thrown in the Briar Patch, and they got pricked.

Rhoad met a woman who would become one of his steady girlfriends in Key West in 1979, walking with Foy into a Duvall Street shoe store and picking out a few pairs of designer cowboy boots. While browsing, he flirted with the saleswoman and co-owner, Maura Mooney, and handed her a huge bag of cocaine. Mooney accepted the gift, ducked into the storeroom, snorted a line, and then returned the powder to Rhoad. He pulled out a wad of cash to purchase the boots and made plans with Mooney to go out that same evening, and then the next day, too.

"It didn't take long for him to open up at all. As a matter of fact, before he left town, which I think was three days, he had pretty much divulged himself to me. I knew exactly what he did," recalls Mooney. "Maybe he needed to be that way with somebody, I'm not sure."

She moved in with Rhoad at his home on Hilton Head Island, where she occupied her time by taking care of their dog, cleaning the house, and abusing cocaine. She soon got bored, unaccustomed to being without work. She frequently saw Foy, who was inseparable from Rhoad, and marveled at his cheating and the fact that his head-strong girlfriend never walked away.

"He also did a lot of screwing around. But they all did," says Mooney. "Shameless, absolutely shameless."

In summers, when the weather became hot, Rhoad and Mooney moved to his home on Nantucket, Massachusetts. When the weather cooled, they headed to St. Barts and rented a house next to the Rileys. Other smugglers had similar seasonal travel schedules. Wherever the smugglers went, says Mooney, they enjoyed smoking the finest pot and drinking the best liquors. There was usually a party somewhere, and she used cocaine daily.

Mooney remembers listening to singer Jimmy Buffett in a small St. Barts club with Suzanne Riley. During his performance, they both ducked into the restroom to snort some lines.

"Sue asked me if Tom had any coke," says Mooney, who thought the answer was fairly obvious. "I said 'Yeaaaah!'"

Buffett was popular on the island, and counted a number of the gentlemen smugglers as buddies. His close friend, Larry "Groovy" Gray, sailed with Riley and a handful of the South Carolinians, joining them on pot runs to Jamaica and Colombia. Buffett hauled a few bales himself, according to an article in the October 4, 1979, *Rolling Stone* magazine, and the singer lived in the smugglers' midst, the artist and criminals inspiring each other.

"St. Barts is a tiny, splendid island. Its populace is packed with sunbaked American and European hippies with lots of money and no visible means of support," wrote journalist Chet Flippo. "They sit around at places like the topless and sometimes bottomless beach over by the Hotel Jean Bart, drinking pineapple juice and greenies [Heinekens]. At night they slip their boats out into the opalescent waters to take care of business."

For as many smugglers that were on the island, there seemed to be even more beautiful, blond American hippie women. The women were not shy, and during Flippo's brief visit to see Buffett, the journalist had his pants unzipped in a bar and a pigtailed blonde advised Buffett to drink pineapple juice so as to sweeten the taste of his semen. One of Buffett's favorite haunts on St. Barts was Le Select Bar, where the regulars greeted him with a casual, "Hey, Jim, howzit?"

The bar, Flippo wrote, was "a real crossroads for smugglers and other exotic charlatans. It's a tawdry, open-air, whitewashed-stone joint with outhouses that would make a sewer rat gag, but the clientele makes the place, I suppose. Naked hippie children crawl across the floor, hard-eyed hippies whisper conspiratorially in English, French and Spanish at the bar, dogs wander in and out."

At night, discos raged in the hills, with tourists slinking out of clothes as they danced. Those who wanted a quieter night stayed aboard anchored sailboats, watching the moonrise. If sitting on a sailboat, signs of intoxication assaulted almost every sense, wrote Flippo. One smelled marijuana wafting across the harbor, saw glowing joints, and heard clinking glasses. It was undoubtedly paradise, and Buffett's tunes served as the official soundtrack.

"The local drug smugglers—Lord, they swear by the man and would no more make a run in their boats without Buffett cassettes on board than set sail without a few cases of greenies [Heineken beers]."

Both Foy and Riley owned homes on St. Barts, and the other gentlemen smugglers made regular appearances. Smuggler Freddy Fillingham, who rented a house above St. Jean Bay, writes of cruising in his motorboat and seeing Byers leaving St. Barts in 1979, bound for the other side of the world:

> As I was coming in the harbour this really pretty boat was coming out. Somehow he recognized me as I turned to run alongside and admire the boat. He said come aboard, didn't even slow down, so I pulled alongside, hopped aboard and towed my Whaler behind. He showed me all around. She was a light green . . . brand new Bowman 57 ketch. Really nice. I asked where he was going and he said "The Panama Canal" "and then across the Pacific." He had some party chicks on there and said "Come with us" and I might have if I had a passport.

Byers had decided to stop smuggling in the late 1970s, and instead traveled to England to supervise the construction of his yachts *Energy* and *Anonymous of Rorc*, both of which were fifty-seven-foot bluewater sailboats built by Bowman Yachts. Before he left to sail through the Pacific, including a stop in Fiji, he encouraged smugglers like Foy to include his friends in deals, hiring them as off-loaders and drivers. For as much time as the smugglers were spending away from South Carolina, they still returned to the Palmetto State often to conduct business, which was booming.

Among the successful ventures conducted by Foy and Rhoad, were the following:

- Eighty-five hundred pounds of marijuana onto Hilton Head in the spring of 1978,
- Twelve thousand pounds into McClellanville in the fall of 1978,
- Twelve thousand pounds onto Datha Island in June 1979,
- Eight thousand pounds onto Edisto Island in November 1979.

Riley and Harvey were just as prolific, bringing in, at the very least:

- Twenty-eight thousand pounds of marijuana near Conway in January 1979,
- Eight thousand pounds on Hilton Head in February 1979,
- Nine thousand pounds on Hilton Head in the spring of 1979.

Even with the lax drug patrols in South Carolina, that so many ventures could be accomplished successfully is a testament to the sophistication the gentlemen smugglers developed. By this time, the veteran weed runners had established routine procedures for each off-load. They would obtain Coast Guard "hit lists" of boats suspected of illicit activity, making sure to dispose of those vessels, or at least have them painted and renamed. At sea they flew a foreign flag to discourage the U.S. Coast Guard from boarding their boat. When entering American territorial waters, they would exchange the foreign flag for the Stars and Stripes in hopes of avoiding a Customs inspection, pretending to have never left the country.

Days before a sailboat arrived, kingpins would discern the location of local Coast Guard cutters and visit the U.S. Custom House in Charleston to see which undercover patrol vehicles were gone from the parking lot. Smugglers' radiomen tuned in to the frequency of every local law enforcement and public safety agency, including firemen and game wardens; set up equipment; and monitored the airwaves.

The night of an off-load, the kingpins, off-loaders, drivers, radiomen, and sentries would all gather. On Hilton Head, which had become one of the most popular off-load spots, they often brought marijuana in behind the Sea Pines home of Butler on an out-of-town neighbor's dock. As darkness fell, the men would gather in his living room with views overlooking Calibogue Sound. They relaxed and were friendly with each other, though they shied away from formal introductions and exchanging names. If the men worked enough loads, however, they started to put some names and faces together.

As the night passed and the boat was raised on the radio, they started to work. One man disappeared into the nearby forest with a walkie-talkie in hand, serving as a lookout. Another monitored radio frequencies inside Butler's house. Others tended to the vehicles parked in the backyard and garage, taping ready-made custom patches of cardboard and duct tape over the brake and taillights, allowing them to maneuver the cars in complete darkness. Parking the cars by the dock, they'd open the doors and load each vehicle with as much pot as it could hold, emptying the sailboat as they marched through the night, bales on their shoulders, like ants bringing food home to their mounds.

Most often, the men drove full-size vans or pickup trucks with camper tops, able to carry a few thousand pounds at a time in the rear cargo compartments, which were separated from the driver's bench by a partition. The men were particular about maintenance of the vehicles and often required them to be equipped with four-wheel drive. The smugglers had mechanics beef up the suspensions to accommodate heavy loads and installed extra fuel tanks. When the vans and trucks were not in use, they would keep them locked in garages or storage facilities, fearful of the vehicles being ticketed, involved in minor traffic accidents, or spotted with drug suspects inside. The vans and trucks were not daily drivers and came out only when it was time to work, ready to roll from South Carolina to any major East Coast city with tons of pot packed inside.

Despite all the precautions, things sometimes went awry. Bauer remembers driving away from Butler's house in a van they had packed with thirty-four hundred pounds, using a sledgehammer to pound in the last bale. Driving away, Bauer panicked when the fuel gauge read empty and the dashboard lights refused to work. He returned to the house, encountering a furious Byers, who demanded to know what the problem was. Crawling under the van, Byers tapped on the gas tank, determining it was full. Apparently, says Bauer, the weight of the drugs either crushed the van's electrical components or crimped its wiring, accounting for the malfunctioning gauges. He pulled away from Butler's house again, destined for an Atlanta stash house, but without a working speedometer.

There was always room for improvement. In the weeks between off-loads, Riley, Butler, and others would devise innovative methods to transport the pot from sailboat cabin to the dock. If the sailboat was small, and the tide high, there was no problem, as the boat could be brought alongside a dock and bales taken off with ease. But larger sailboats proved more difficult. Some were made to wait offshore, where they were met by speedboats and the pot transferred at sea. Sometimes the sailboat would anchor a few hundred feet from a dock, and small motorboats or dinghies would ferry the pot the remaining distance. Once, Butler and Riley constructed little barges made of Styrofoam to float the pot to shore.

There was always the chance of being seen by a neighbor, and the gentlemen smugglers went to great lengths to prevent this from happening, too. Butler uprooted trees and plopped them in holes he dug along his property line as a temporary cover, thinking the neighbors wouldn't notice a dying, leaning tree suddenly springing forth from a section of previously open lawn. He stretched netting between other trees to create a visual barrier, again unconcerned that this might prove more conspicuous. Another time, Riley fed a neighbor's dog a hamburger patty stuffed with quaaludes to prevent him from barking at any activity that night. Good night, poochy.

Such preparations took time, but there were other tasks for the smugglers to tend to, as well. When not physically handling the drugs, the aspiring or established kingpins, including Byers, Foy, Harvey, and Riley, concentrated on collecting their money, purchasing new sailboats, and concealing their cash and assets. Fake identification became an important consideration for the men, and they'd have associates scan obituaries, finding men of similar ages who had passed away. If only the good die young, they come back to life through men quite bad. The smugglers applied for assorted forms of identification to be reissued in the names of these dead men, but supplied pictures of themselves.

When buying cars, the men preferred using cash. When it came to banking, they sailed or flew to the Bahamas and opened offshore accounts to deposit their money, a few hundred thousand dollars per trip. Banking secrecy laws were also favorable in the Grand Cayman Islands and the Channel Islands off the coast of Normandy in the English Channel. In all these places, the smugglers could wire money back to the United States for the purchase of real estate and sailboats. They'd do so through shelf corporations, which were previously established companies with little more than a name to them, having no operations or corporate officers. These companies' incorporation paperwork would sit on a shelf until the company was purchased. Once the smugglers bought one of these offshore corporations, and listed their overseas lawyer's location as its place of address, they could use it to launder money and purchase assets, concealing their ownership. Property up and down the East Coast, including a number of residential lots on Hilton Head, were owned by overseas companies in the control of the gentlemen smugglers, such as Bahamas Leeward Ltd., Agora Properties Ltd., and Baachus Properties Ltd.

On Hilton Head, Butler was making a fortune leasing out his home for drug off-loads, but he was eager to find an even better spot for unloading larger amounts of drugs. Fortuitously, the real estate agent managed an abandoned oyster factory outside Hilton Head on nearby Sawmill Creek, just a few turns off the Broad, Chechessee, and Colleton Rivers. A small house was there, as well as a concrete structure where oysters were once shucked. The land stood on a twenty-foot bluff made entirely of discarded oyster shells and had a dock projecting into the creek. It was secluded, surrounded by dozens of acres of woods, marsh, and swamp. In other words, it was a perfect spot to unload marijuana, or even better, sacks of hashish. That's what was coming over next, Riley told Bulter one day. Everyone involved would be making double pay.

Chapter Five

Cold seafood, booze, and Valium: a sailor's feast. Christy Campbell had just returned to the *Second Life* in the sailboat's inflatable dinghy on the evening of June 9, 1980, dinners from Hudson's restaurant in hand. After sixty-one days at sea, fried shrimp was plenty tasty to the crew, even if it wasn't hot.

They had been drinking since leaving St. Martin in the French West Indies, and taking Valium with greater frequency the closer they got to the South Carolina coast. The cocktail responded to opposing emotions: the alcohol enhancing the ecstasy they felt at journey's end, the pills easing the anxiety over possibly being nabbed. God forbid they get arrested after coming this far—crossing an ocean and a sea. God forbid they lose thirty thousand pounds of hashish.

The Valium also dulled hangovers, which was good, since Captain Campbell and his six-man crew had just plowed through most of a $400 liquor purchase, staying up all night and dancing naked across the deck. For weeks they had been limited to the hash and Cisk beer, provisions obtained in Lebanon and Malta, respectively. Tons of hash and cases of lager would provide sufficient intoxication for most voyagers, yet on this boat was an exceptional collection of spectacular drunks, boozehounds, and bon vivants, each capable of truly impressive feats of debilitating debauchery. It took the liquor from St. Martin to restore morale on the ship after the long journey, creating, as one crew member put it, "One happy ship of crazies again."

The crew's raw nerves and desperate drunkenness were to be expected. Besides the threat of prison hanging over their heads, they had been starved of comfort for two months as they crossed the Mediterranean and Atlantic. Every return trip on a smuggling run is marked by the inconveniences the cargo of drugs create, and this one was no different, save for the extended length of time the *Second Life*'s crew sailed with sacks of hash stuffed into nearly every available space.

"It was no longer a boat. It was no longer a living quarters, it was no longer nothing," says Campbell. "The whole aft stateroom was full of hash. There was a forward forepeak, it was packed full . . . the only thing that was left open was the bathroom, the kitchen and the main salon."

Campbell had flown to Europe with his crew late in the winter of 1980. Just before taking off from Washington, D.C., on the Concorde, he was handed $15,000 cash and a scrap of paper that told him exactly where to find the *Second Life*— a seventy-one-foot double-masted racing sailboat docked in Mallorca, Spain. Among the world sailing community, the *Second Life* was famous, one of seventeen yachts to compete in the inaugural Whitbread Round the World Yacht Race in 1973. Three men died competing in that race, and sailors had respect for any boat that completed all four legs of the journey, as the *Second Life* had.

Campbell was friendly with most of his crew, having sailed with many of them on previous smuggling runs. Among this group was his reliable friend, Kenny Gunn. Despite being arrested with Campbell on the *Love Affair* fourteen months earlier, Gunn was eager to try sailing loaded across the Mediterranean and Atlantic. The rest of the crew was just as enthusiastic, no matter if they had little experience making long voyages on such a large sailboat.

The lone sailor unfamiliar to the rest of the crew was Kenny O'Day, a Virginian placed on the *Second Life* by kingpins Julian "Doc" Pernell and Barry "Ice Cream" Toombs. O'Day was there to help sail the *Second Life,* of course, but he was also tasked with keeping an eye on the sailboat's illicit cargo and protecting Pernell and Toombs's investment. The Virginia distributors had paid $500,000 as a down payment on their share of the load.

Once in Spain the crew spent two months in Mallorca, partying, prepping the boat, buying equipment, and installing new electronics. Campbell rented an apartment for his crew, and the seven Americans became quite popular in town, though no one seemed to know why they were there.

From Mallorca, the *Second Life* sailed to Malta, where they continued their fast lifestyle. The movie *Popeye,* starring Robin Williams and Shelley Duvall, was being filmed at the time, and a few of the crew crawled to the set on their bellies to try to catch a glimpse of the stars. The crew also organized a footrace through Malta, with Gunn tearing through the streets, shaking off his sea legs.

From Malta they sailed for Rhodes, Greece, and had their first indications that the trip would not be without obstacles when a mysterious military helicopter flew above them. The crew guessed it was from Libya. Then they encountered a wicked storm, with winds so powerful it spattered their faces with sand carried from Crete, miles away. Their navigation antenna was blown clear off a mast, into the deep. They'd replace it in Greece, where they stopped for more than a week, awaiting word to enter a war zone.

Lebanon was entering its fifth year of civil war in 1980, and the country was a hotbed of violence. Peace seemed implausible in the tiny nation, considering it was home to a handful of homegrown rival militias, militants from the Palestinian Liberation Organization, and occupying armies from Israel and Syria.

While the civil war and lingering violence ruined Lebanon's economy, it allowed a black market to flourish, especially the sale of high-grade hashish and opium grown in the country's Bekaa Valley. To protect their crops, farmers in the valley placed tanks and antiaircraft guns in their fields. The profits from drugs were so important to Lebanon's shattered economy that warring factions would regularly drop their guns to facilitate trafficking, so long as they received a cut of the money. At Lebanon's ports such cooperation was commonplace. Temporary ceasefires were negotiated when drugs needed to leave the docks.

Outside Beirut the *Second Life* waited offshore three days for the seas to calm. As in Colombia, the crew saw beaches and mountains while waiting to load. Unlike Colombia, the crew was not alone. Israeli jets flew overhead, at low altitudes. Large ships surrounded them in the harbor, waiting to enter the port. A trawler cruised by the *Second Life,* with intimidating armed sailors pacing the deck. Soon their American contact, whom they had met last in Mallorca, came aboard with a Lebanese militiaman who had suffered two gunshot wounds in his lifetime, including one to his heart. The man pointed to a German freighter nearby. It was allegedly full of weapons and would enter the port immediately after the *Second Life* picked up the drugs. The obvious implication, thought the crew, was that their hash purchase enabled the militia to buy arms.

Such a truth sat heavily with some of the crew. More troubling, however, was their fear. They felt vulnerable in the war zone, and weren't comforted by reports from their contact on shore, who said he had been close to gun battles in Beirut. He looked haggard from living on the edge for weeks.

Finally, in the middle of their third night spent offshore, the crew was instructed to come in and be loaded. The *Second Life* headed to shore on the northern side of the city, where Christian forces held control. The seas were still too rough to try to dock, so wooden launches piled high with hashish met them just off the shore, and tied alongside the sailboat. The crew of the *Second Life* could see a roadblock being enforced on the coastal highway, ostensibly so there'd be no interference. Militiamen in the boats beside them tossed bag after bag of hash up on deck as the *Second Life*'s crew scrambled to store it below. Each sack was wrapped in heavy black plastic. Inside, wrapped in more plastic, were oval-shaped bricks of hashish weighing a kilogram each. They were stamped "New Lebanon," and placed inside white or blue cheesecloth. In an odd but kind gesture, Campbell says, the Lebanese men applauded as the crew finished loading the drugs.

The crew set sail and headed west. Gunn put on a Bob Seger album. They were glad to be alive, even if they were saddled with awful beer for the long journey ahead.

They enjoyed exceptional winds across much of the Mediterranean and made good time. At night they witnessed a spectacle of lights around them, and they surmised ships in the distance were playing war games. At one point, a submarine popped up on their port side.

They traded shifts up on deck while also being responsible for maintenance duties. Two men cooked. One man was in charge of provisions, another maintained the boat's electrical systems. Two crewmen were responsible for the sailboat's engine. They used it sparingly, wanting to conserve fuel in case of an emergency.

As they approached Spain, they were almost flying, sailing the hash-laden championship racing boat as fast as it could go. Then disaster struck. Coming down a wave while sailing downwind, the boat unexpectedly jibed, it's mainsail violently flipping from one side of the boat to the other in an instant, snapping the thick aluminum boom with a crack so sharp one could have mistaken it for a firing cannon. The broken boom splintered off like a wayward helicopter blade. Fortunately, no one was hurt, though the crew despaired over the damage to the vital equipment.

They quickly made makeshift repairs. They reefed, or reduced, the mainsail and replaced the snapped boom underneath with the smaller boom from the mizzenmast. On the mizzenmast, they fashioned a boom from a log that had providentially been aboard and strapped to the gunwales. The boat could sail again, though it had been crippled.

The sailing became grueling. The crew spent four days trying to leave the Mediterranean, frustrated by a storm that kept pushing them back. In three days, they calculated, they had made a measly three-quarters of a mile. They were tempted to use fuel, but refrained. The going was absolutely tortuous.

Each time they went up on deck for their shift, the storm would soak them immediately, dampening spirits and clothes. They became demoralized, unwilling to enter a port and repair their boat because of their cargo, and they still had such a long way to go. Seeking to renew their spirits, Campbell ordered the boat to anchor off Spain for a good night's rest.

The next day, as they set sail again, there was a glimmer of hope. The boat received a visitor. He was short, just six inches tall, winged, and covered with yellow feathers. On his head was a spiked tuft of fluff. Since the bird shared a hairstyle with British singer Rod Stewart, they named their new friend Rod.

The crew figured the storm had blown Rod out to sea and he was desperate for a place to land. Their spirits lifted as they observed their marooned friend scurry around the deck. Perhaps, unconsciously, they realized their predicament was not as hopeless as poor Rod's, disoriented and stranded at sea. He stayed on board for four days before taking wing. Rod flew a hundred feet before being blown into the sea and swallowed by waves.

Those same winds that doomed the small bird helped push the sailboat through the Strait of Gibraltar and into the Atlantic. Here the crew had new reason to become anxious. They discovered a leak in the boat's water supply, meaning they'd be dependent upon bottled water as they crossed the Atlantic, and forced to ration. They sailed slowly through the Sargasso Sea, the light winds letting them travel at only a few knots. The *Second Life*'s spinnaker kept tearing, too, further hindering their speed as they struggled to harness the sea's faint breeze. Of course, with hundreds of miles still ahead, they were cautious about using fuel. If things got really bad, they joked, they could commit mass suicide with the handgun Campbell had bought from a man on the docks in Mallorca. There was only a single bullet, however, so they decided they'd have to stand side-by-side and take care when aiming in order to send it through all seven heads.

Despite the grim jokes, spirits remained high. When not on watch, the crew spent their time reading or listening to music. They exercised, doing push-ups on the deck and dips on the boat's handrails. They tuned in to news, music, or sports games broadcast by the BBC or Armed Forces Radio. One crew member particularly savored hearing Boston Red Sox baseball games while he took the midnight shift. He felt emancipated from the hassles of routine existence as he enjoyed the national pastime standing above a massive stash of potent drugs, skippering a world-class sailboat in the darkness through an empty and calm sea.

Girlie magazines were essential for morale on the boat, and a few women became favorites of the crew. If a man could not satisfy himself without a particular sweetheart's picture, he could be heard across the deck and through the cabins, ransacking the salon for his favorite lady's image.

"Who's got her?" he'd bellow. "She's mine!"

One slow-going day in the Atlantic, the crew devised a particularly zany game to amuse themselves. They began by tying one end of a one-hundred-foot length of rope to a cleat on the stern and the other end around a rubber fender. They tossed the fender in the ocean and let it trail behind the boat, bobbing in the waves. Next, a crewman stripped and walked to the bow of the boat, carefully stepping to the end of the bowsprit—the most forward part of the boat. He crouched, mustered the necessary courage, sprung hard, and dove deep into the ocean. Beneath the waves he kicked swiftly and reversed direction as he swam underneath the length of the seventy-one-foot sailboat hull and beyond. His fellow crew members watched from the stern in anticipation of a perfect performance, counting on their friend to gauge the remaining hundred feet to the target correctly and pop triumphantly out of the water, mouth open to capture air and arms spread wide to catch the fender and attached lifeline.

The water was exceptionally clear in that part of the ocean, giving the men a fair shot at seizing the target. Should they miss, they knew, they'd be bobbing in the middle of the Atlantic, without a life jacket, with thousands of feet of ocean beneath them. Swimming naked in the immense ocean, the transom of the *Second Life* steadily moving away, with no land in sight, was an overwhelming experience. One man said he felt like a guppy swimming in the water, waiting to be gobbled up. Treading water, he was without the protection of clothing, without hope of reaching land on his own, and dependent upon the goodwill of his crewmates to retrieve him.

No matter the diversions, progress was agonizingly slow. The crew had put their faith in the twenty-eight-year-old Campbell, and he was acutely aware of the tedium of the journey and that critical supplies were running low. He changed course and headed to St. Martin in the French West Indies to refuel and take on more water and food. Wary of the drugs being discovered, the crew anchored in a harbor and used their inflatable Zodiac raft to motor to shore. Campbell authorized the purchase of liquor, lifting the semi-enforced ban on alcohol he had decreed in Rhodes owing to one crew member's tendency to become so obliterated from drinkin' and druggin' he could hardly walk and talk, let alone satisfy his duties on the boat. On a boat full of drunken sailors, this man, nicknamed the "Gold Dust Twin," managed to consistently set new lows. Now his drinking seemed to be sanctioned again. What did it matter? They had crossed a sea and ocean without loss of life or cargo. It was time to raise a glass, or entire rum bottle.

Energized by their landfall, Campbell phoned Les Riley at his home on Hilton Head, shocking him with their location. Campbell told them they'd be to South Carolina within a week. The crew returned to the *Second Life,* but not before an old salt on St. Martin made a comment to them that their boat seemed to be sitting abnormally low in the water. They sailed north toward the United States, relieved to be in familiar waters with ample fuel, water, and food. Although they had tried not to dwell on their difficulties after leaving Lebanon, worry often pervaded their thoughts on the long voyage.

Owing to the broken boom, they had worried across half the Mediterranean: Would the repair hold? Then, more worries during the interminable crossing of the Atlantic: Would they go thirsty before making landfall? Now, as they approached Hilton Head, they worried again: Would they get busted?

The men drank to distraction on this final leg. Their minds were scrambled, and they wet their throats with Heinekens and booze. Tension, bottled up for the last two months, soon erupted. Such discord was common on long sea voyages, and the *Second Life* had been the scene of previous frustrations years before as it circled the globe. Then, ship physician Robin Leach spoke of the irrational grudges that could fester on the open sea:

> *One of three or four members of the crew would quite unannounced become the person to moan at for a few days. The issues were often trifling and that crew member had to take the abuse that was given to him until the needle was pointed to another. Trifling things became blown up at sea. Somebody had a perpetual sniff. One seat was always occupied by the same person. Somebody started reading a book before someone else finished it. Someone was late on watch again. The heads were blocked and no one admitted to being the last to use them.*

Such pettiness had more or less been avoided on the *Second Life*'s hashish trip, but it would not be avoided altogether. A day out of Hilton Head, the crew became rowdy and began horsing around on deck. Campbell started harassing a crewman and doused him with a bucket of water. O'Day took umbrage at his buddy being soaked and retaliated by clocking Campbell in the face, knocking him to the deck. The horseplay suddenly turned serious. O'Day had hit Campbell so hard he broke his hand, permanently dislodging a knuckle.

"You can't hit him, he's the captain," yelled another crewman, as Campbell recovered from the swift sucker punch.

Campbell's eye was cut, and he was enraged. With his head throbbing, he could think of one thing—the .45 caliber handgun stored below deck. He knew exactly where his souvenir from Mallorca was stashed.

"I had one bullet in there," says Campbell. "I wanted to kill him."

But the bullet stayed in the chamber.

Campbell's anger subsided, his eye was patched, and, with alcohol flowing, harmony was restored aboard the *Second Life*. Campbell chalked up O'Day's actions to the long journey and too many beers. "He was a pretty nice boy," Campbell says. "He just wasn't supposed to drink."

Campbell phoned Riley again through the radio. They were not ready, Riley said. Go back out to sea for a few days. Campbell was incredulous. "This has been two months and I'm not waiting anymore," he told Riley. "I'm coming in right now whether you like it or not."

Campbell sailed the *Second Life* past Hilton Head and into Port Royal Sound, disregarding Riley's instructions. They anchored the boat. Should Campbell have tried to take them out to sea again, they may have mutinied. "My crew was getting crazy. I was crazy, the whole thing was crazy," says Campbell.

He headed to shore aboard the Zodiac and purchased seafood dinners at Hudson's. Before returning to the *Second Life*, he phoned Riley from a pay phone. Between bites of shrimp, he told the kingpin he had anchored the boat right off Hilton Head and was preparing to sail her in behind the island. Riley was so shocked he could hardly speak. The off-loading boats were nearby, ready to meet the *Second Life* offshore, and Campbell was sailing her right along the island, unable to hide telltale signs of a long sea voyage, such as the boat's broken boom, its smell of diesel exhaust, and spots of rust. Riley handed the phone to Lee Harvey, who told Campbell to dock behind nearby Dafauskie Island. Someone would meet them that night.

Campbell's arrival and phone calls set off a flurry of activity. In Virginia, Pernell and Toombs phoned their fleet of truck drivers and instructed them to drive through the night to Hilton Head. When the drivers, Toombs, and Pernell arrived about midday on June 9, 1980, they were taken to rented houses on Hilton Head and encouraged to rest. Meanwhile, two boat captains readied the *Touch of Class* and *Hook 'Em Good*, two forty-eight-foot sportfishing boats that would be used to ferry the hash off the *Second Life* and to the abandoned oyster factory.

Trucks entered the property by turning off the highway to Hilton Head and onto a dirt road. Drivers passed through a gate, and, after traveling a mile or so through woods, came upon a clearing with a small house and a creek. At water's edge was a dock and a cinder block building, the spot where the oysters were once brought. The Atlantic Ocean was less than two miles away by water.

As evening approached, the drivers gathered, parking behind the house. A lookout sat at the gate, a walkie-talkie in his hand. Other men set up radios and antennas in the cinder block factory. The equipment was necessary to monitor law enforcement in the area, as well as communicate with the sportfishing boats. Surveillance was critical, and two other smugglers had already tracked the movements of a nearby Coast Guard cutter, satisfied it would not interfere.

At a hotel, Pernell and Toombs met a buyer from Virginia named Robert Reckmeyer, who agreed to purchase ten thousand pounds of hash. He handed over a down payment of $1.8 million. Pernell and Toombs took it back to the rental house and counted it with Riley. There were 180 stacks of $10,000 each. Some of the money was mildewed. Pernell suspected it had previously been buried.

A few miles away, at real estate agent Wally Butler's house, other men gathered. They piled into small motorboats alongside his dock and took off across the body of water behind Hilton Head, Calibogue Sound. In a twenty-two-foot Boston Whaler sat John Jamison and Kenny Floyd. They had been hired by Riley to run a decoy boat, which they had loaded with fishing poles and a carton of green phosphorescence in case they needed to lead one of the sportfishing boats to the oyster factory.

By this time, Campbell had sailed the *Second Life* around the back of Hilton Head and anchored her behind Dafauskie Island. The crew had continued drinking, and Campbell was zipping around in the Zodiac, annoying Jamison.

"He was going like a madman around the sound in this Zodiac," says Jamison. "I finally told him, 'Either quit it or I'm going to run over the boat, and that's going to be it . . . you're jeopardizing the whole operation.'"

The sun began to set behind Hilton Head. Everyone was in place. Men waited at the oyster factory to load their trucks. Decoy boats bobbed in the water behind the island. Sportfishing boats cruised Calibogue Sound, waiting to rendezvous with the *Second Life* under the cover of darkness. And the men aboard the sailboat were ready to finish their journey and toss off the sacks of hashish.

"That's when things started getting foggy for me," says O'Day, whose hand still ached badly from punching Campbell, and who was still very inebriated. "I started getting caught up in a drunk front."

At eight o'clock South Carolina wildlife officer Walter Baxter received a radio call from his partner, Tommy Simmons. Simmons said he was going to be late to that night's water patrol, and Baxter didn't see much point in waiting around the marina until Simmons arrived. He radioed back, "I'm going to go out in the sound, see what I can see."

Baxter motored into Calibogue Sound to begin his patrol alone. The shrimping season was starting the next day, and he and Simmons would be looking to catch any boats using the cover of darkness to get an early, illegal jump on the trawling. It could be a busy night.

In the middle of Calibogue Sound, a quarter mile south of the bridge leading to Hilton Head, Baxter shut off his engines and lights. He sat in his boat and listened. To the west came the sound of a motorboat, but it was running without lights. The engine became louder . . . and louder . . . and LOUDER.

Baxter quickly started his engine, afraid the two boats would collide. He also turned on his spotlight and illuminated a fast-approaching thirteen-foot Boston Whaler. There were two men on board. He ordered them to stop.

Baxter questioned the men and issued a ticket to the boat's operator, Les Riley, for running a boat without lights. As he wrote the citation, Simmons approached in his own boat, and advised Baxter he would continue the patrol farther into Calibogue Sound.

A few hundred yards away sat Jamison and Floyd, their eyes peeled and their nerves taut, looking for reason to spring to action and put the decoy boat beneath them to use. Throughout the evening they had seen the *Second Life, Touch of Class,* and *Hook 'Em Good* all cruise into Bull Creek. The men aboard those boats were surely in the middle of transferring the hashish as fast as they could, hauling each sack out of the sailboat's interior recesses, heaving them above deck, and then throwing them across the gunwales to the other boats tied along each side of the *Second Life.*

Jamison watched as an unfamiliar boat crept slowly toward the mouth of Bull Creek.

"I don't like that," he said to Floyd.

Jamison quickly flashed his spotlight over the boat. He was disappointed to see his suspicions confirmed. Standing at the wheel was Simmons, wearing the distinctive cap of a South Carolina wildlife officer. Jamison's mind flashed to the twin outboard motors mounted on his own craft's transom.

"Thank god we got a pair of seventies on this boat," he thought. "We can fly."

It was time for the decoy team to earn its money. Jamison once again turned on the spotlight and pointed the bright beam directly into Simmons's face, burning his eyes. Simmons gunned his engine and quickly turned his boat away from the creek and toward Jamison. The boat's blue lights were flashing. Jamison let Simmons come within twenty-five yards before gunning his own engines and heading south across the sound toward homes on the north side of Hilton Head.

Jamison soon learned he had underestimated the power of the game warden's motorboat. As Simmons pulled alongside, Jamison pushed his own throttle to the max, but it was no use, he couldn't outrun him. Desperate, he turned toward the docks along the backside of the island, trying to buy time as he plotted his escape. He knew these waters like the back of his hand, working for eight years in Hilton Head as a marina manager and charter boat captain. He had also fished a lot of trout off the docks that loomed closer and closer.

His next move was suicidal. In darkness and at full speed, Jamison steered the boat under the docks projecting from shore. The boat's radio antennas shattered as he and Floyd passed under the first structure. Wooden pilings and oyster beds passed by in a blur. Floyd went to pieces.

"John, don't get crazy, don't get crazy," he said.

Jamison ignored his pleas, but soon ran out of docks to dodge under.

Simmons again pulled alongside, close enough for Jamison to make out his face. As the two boats zoomed along the shore, Jamison feared Simmons would run his bow up over Jamison's stern, swamping the engine and stopping him dead in the water. He'd have to think of something else.

"Pull it back, pull it back," yelled Simmons.

"I can't stop. I hurt my leg on Dafauskie," screamed Jamison. "It's bleeding really bad."

As the chase continued, across the sound Baxter finished escorting Riley to a marina, where he ordered him to dock his boat for the night on account of having no lights. Baxter had seen Simmons in the distance turn on his blue lights to follow a boat. From that far away, it appeared Simmons was escorting the boat. But as Baxter reduced his throttle, he heard Simmons on the radio, pleading for help with a boat that would not stop. Baxter and took off, leaving Riley behind.

At the oyster factory, men listened to Simmons's transmissions, too. They grew restless, unsure if the wildlife officer was pursuing a decoy boat or one of the sportfishermen loaded with hashish. Some men were convinced the boat had been captured, others said the infrequent transmissions meant there had been no arrests. Harvey, doing his best to keep his trademark cool, stood next to his radioman, listening closely. Other men kept a close eye on the water, peering through a nightscope at the creek and the nearby Colleton River. Finally, they saw the sportfishing boats in the distance, coming up the river. They could hear their engines humming, and no police boats were in sight.

When Jamison saw Simmons speak into the radio, he realized he was running out of time. Backup would arrive soon. They sped past Palmetto Bay Marina, and Jamison suddenly turned his boat back toward it. Coming into the docks, he saw an available slip was filled with cordweed—a floating mass of dead spartina grass. He gunned the engines and ran the boat up on the flotsam, quickly jumping out with the bowline in hand. As Jamison stepped off the boat, he felt Simmons's boat nudge the stern of the Boston Whaler. He dropped the line and peeled off on foot, leaving Floyd behind to be arrested by Baxter, who had just arrived.

The wildlife officers called the local sheriff's office, asking for deputies to impound the boat and take Floyd to jail. The dispatcher questioned Simmons, unaware the smugglers were eavesdropping: "I thought you had two suspects?"

"Well," said Simmons, "that man hit the dock, and all I saw was elbows and smokin' sneakers."

Incredibly, officers Baxter and Simmons crossed paths with the smugglers twice more that evening. After Floyd's arrest, they patrolled together in the same boat and came across the *Second Life*. Half the crew was on board cleaning the boat, finding sacks of forgotten hash in the process. The wildlife officers knocked on the side of the hull, and a crewman popped his head above deck. His knees were shaking, and he felt like he was going to have a heart attack. The officers told him he needed to put on an anchor light, and then asked him where his captain was. Harbour Town, the crewman replied, eager to be rid of the men.

Baxter and Simmons soon found Campbell at Harbour Town Marina as the excitable captain and some friends left a waterside nightclub, piled into the Zodiac, and cruised into Calibogue Sound without running lights or life jackets. Simmons stopped Campbell and ticketed him back at the dock, provoking an inebriated Campbell to tell Baxter and Simmons they were dumb game wardens, that he could buy them both, and that Simmons was a son of a bitch. In turn, Simmons picked Campbell up by his collar and told him he was not a son of a bitch, and that he was now required to post a $300 bond. With the help of an attractive woman accompanying him, Campbell paid the money and left the dock for a nearby condo to get some sleep.

Meanwhile, the thirty thousand pounds of hash was unloaded at the oyster factory. The *Touch of Class* and *Hook 'Em Good* tied up stern to stern at the dock, and men formed a bucket brigade, passing sack after sack of hash into the factory and the backs of trucks. In the morning the trucks left at fifteen-minute intervals, blending in with construction crews driving on and off the island.

Weeks later Harvey reported to federal prison to serve a short sentence for his arrest in Georgia two years earlier. He'd just finished his first hashish venture with Riley, and he was already planning the next one. As Harvey's defense attorney, John Zwerling said, "He was incorrigible."

Chapter Six

The success of the *Second Life* hashish operation capped a remarkable run of drug-running ventures for the gentlemen smugglers. Ten years earlier they had casually sold pounds of pot around the University of South Carolina campus. Five years earlier, they nervously brought in hundreds of pounds of Jamaican pot before heading south for a few tons of Colombian Gold. Now the men were bona fide kingpins, coolly orchestrating regular shipments of more than twenty thousand pounds from Colombia and bringing hashish across the Mediterranean Sea and Atlantic Ocean. Each deal they did was designed to be more and more lucrative.

Such growth is natural to any successful business, and by this point in their illicit careers, the gentlemen smugglers were, first and foremost, businessmen. The kingpins no longer sailed the boats or piloted the off-loading vessels. Rarely did they get their hands dirty tossing bales anymore. Seeking to maximize profit and minimize risk, they shied away from investing their own money, and instead solicited investments from other partners and distributors, promising them generous returns, but of course keeping the bulk of profits for themselves. Their operations became complex enough for Les Riley and Lee Harvey to insure their smuggling boats with Julian "Doc" Pernell and Barry "Ice Cream" Toombs, and vice versa. If one pair of kingpins' boat got busted, the other kingpins would soften their loss with a payout.

As much financial sense as it all made, there were intangible costs to this evolution, with profits increasing at the expense of the fun and adventure that had once played an equal part in each smuggling operation. Greed increasingly overwhelmed camaraderie. The massive amounts of money to be earned made it difficult for many to walk away, no matter if the kingpins' charm had worn thin. Originally, many of the smugglers, especially those who didn't assume the status of a kingpin, reasoned they'd quit the business after a few years once they made themselves a nest egg. Yet the richer they got, the more smuggling they did.

"You can get out, you just don't want to," explains one smuggler. "How in the world can you go back and get a job after you've been flying around in Learjets drinking Dom Perignon at 50,000 feet, flying down to get on a yacht and go to the Bahamas? How you gonna compare that?"

Many marijuana smugglers knew no other way to make a living. It had become normal, and kingpins began to treat it casually. Smuggling ventures were scheduled so regularly that men couldn't help but integrate their illegal activities with the more pedestrian experiences that filled their days. If you worked nonstop as a smuggler, you had no other choice.

Toombs, for example, earned his well-known handle when leading a convoy of loaded trucks through South Carolina, each one spaced a mile apart from the other cruising up a highway. As his stomach rumbled, the short and stocky Toombs suddenly spoke into his CB radio, ordering everyone off the road.

"We gotta pull over," he said to the annoyed drivers hauling pot behind him. "I gotta get some ice cream."

For Toombs, it was more than the money; it was also the all-consuming rush of a deal that kept him working full-time, missing holidays and family events in pursuit of landing another load. He'd been excited before, in the jungles of Vietnam, shooting his way out of death, and in Virginia pool halls, routinely gambling his life savings, sometimes losing it all. Neither compared to the highs that pot smuggling could provide, where men adapted the same set of daredevil logistics to different-sized deals.

"You're caught up in the adrenaline, you're caught up in the fun, you're caught up in the women, you're caught up in all the money," says Toombs. "But what you do is you don't think. You're caught up in the moment . . . it's an adrenaline junkie's dream."

To enhance or merely sustain such highs, the smugglers abused drugs, including the one they would not traffic: cocaine. Toombs says he wouldn't smoke pot often, but instead liked cocaine, tequila, and young women, so long as they could all be enjoyed at the same time. Just as Toombs felt comfortable eating ice cream during smuggling operations, others became casual about snorting coke and drinking alcohol while killing time and waiting for a boat to arrive. A few smugglers took it too far, incapacitating themselves at critical times by freebasing cocaine. Especially notorious were Harvey and sailboat captain Warren "Willie Frank" Steele. Steele, an excellent and well-liked sailor, freebased so often that Wally Butler joked he was going to make him a harness so he could carry propane tanks on his back, always able to use a torch and heat the coke. Steele wasn't always so hooked. He went to college on a football scholarship, but quit school soon after his girlfriend broke her neck and died in a car accident.

"That was when Frank met drugs," said friend and fellow smuggler Tommy Liles.

Liles remembers Steele hopping in his five-speed BMW and speeding down Interstate 95 to Miami from his home on the Banana River in Melbourne, Florida. Fuzz busters, or radar detectors, were stuck to the front and rear windows. A big bag of cocaine sat on the floor. Cruising at one hundred miles per hour, Steele would dig down into the bag with his fingers, bringing heavy scoops to his nose.

Another time, John "Smokin' Sneakers" Jamison picked Steele up in South Florida, just after the boat captain had purchased an ounce of premium cocaine. Settling into the passenger seat, Steele opened the package and began to cut lines on a cassette tape as Jamison drove.

"You know," Steele said, "some people say I waste this shit."

The package then promptly spilled over, dumping the ounce of cocaine onto the floorboard, which was covered with sand. Steele closed his mouth and solemnly ground the coke into the sand with his shoe.

"Well," he said, "I guess it's true."

Harvey allegedly jeopardized ventures, too, by getting high or overdosing. One night on Hilton Head, he nearly died and had to be taken to the hospital from his rented condo. Toombs says Harvey would pass out and vomit from taking too many drugs. His eyes and body were yellow from jaundice, another friend says, and he became paranoid. Bob "Willie the Hog" Bauer says he remembers when Harvey called a tree surgeon to his home in Virginia, asking him to fell a tree. The tree surgeon protested, unwilling to cut down a beautiful old oak. "But the little people live in the branches," Harvey replied, referring to the hallucinatory Lilliputians that supposedly appeared to a number of smugglers and their girlfriends.

Harvey's brothers Michael and Tom disagree with such characterizations of their sibling's drug use. Like most of the smugglers, Lee did use cocaine, they say, and tried heroin after a girlfriend introduced him to it, though he stopped after two bad experiences, ditching the drug and the girlfriend.

"I was with Lee a lot. He never fell down, never vomited, never almost died in his own puke," says Michael, who said a culture of exaggeration existed among his brother's group of friends. "One thing that all those guys had in common was they liked to sit around late at night and talk. The lines are cut on the mirror, everybody's got a lot to say . . . Conversation changed to bullshit and goes to full-fledged lies by sunrise. Everybody just trying to one up the other, and 90 percent of what was said was just fabricated crap."

One thing all smugglers agreed on was that cocaine was a destructive drug, making fast lives even faster. The smugglers lament the hold cocaine had on them and their friends, especially those who freebased. Jamison later wrote a poem about his struggles with the drug. From "All Honey Isn't Sweet":

> . . . let her possess you, she'll strip you to bone
> Not just your body, but all that you own
> She'll peak out your senses, and keep you alert
> Then tease you and please you, she loves to flirt
> She has many names, to most she's their "honey"
> She's really Queen Bee, and her nest is your money
> Her sting can be lethal, or poison your brain
> It won't matter to her, cause you're all the same . . .

Between friends, drug abuse could cause rifts. Riley speaks with a combination of sadness and disdain about how his close friend and partner, Harvey, put most of his money up his nose and slept most of the day, only to rise and party into the night before sleeping again into the afternoon. Riley says he liked having a good time, too, but he also enjoyed being with his family, exercising, and spending time outdoors. On Hilton Head, he regularly fished and played basketball with Barry Foy. Although the men didn't work together all too often, they were friendly. Some people found Foy and his partner, Tom "Rolex"

Rhoad, exasperating, but Riley says he liked them, in part because he had learned what to expect from Flash and his 2 Percent Man.

Foy was fun, says Riley, and a good guy, though "he would be the first to leave when the shit hit the fan. But you accepted that with him, and some people didn't like it. It didn't bother me, but I said I'm not going to do any more business with him."

Many times Riley visited the Rhoad family farm to enjoy big meals of fried chicken and barbecue with the kingpin's family, and traded them seafood for bacon and pork. Some of Riley's family and friends failed to see Rhoad's appeal, finding him arrogant and nosy. One particular detractor of Rhoad marveled at how Riley could tolerate the man. Then he learned that Rhoad and Riley hunted together.

"No wonder you can put up with him," the man told Riley. "You had a gun in your hand."

The dynamic between Foy and Rhoad, or Flash and Flash Jr., as some liked to call them, could be intriguing, and their interactions were often over the top. Riley recalls the pair coming over to his home once to ask for his help on a deal. In typical fashion, Foy sent Rhoad off on an errand and then proposed that he and Riley work alone, cutting his buddy out. Riley sighed and explained to Foy that he doesn't tell on people, but that he would have to bring this up to Rhoad when he returned.

"Y'all are partners," he told Foy. "Come on."

Moments later Rhoad walked through the door and beat Riley to the punch.

"What kind of deal did he try to offer you?"

"I don't know," said Riley, smiling. "What kind of deal will you offer?"

Among the smugglers Riley had a good reputation for being honest and straightforward, though a few complained he had an ego and distanced himself from people he considered subordinate. During the unloading of the hashish off the *Second Life,* Toombs remembers getting into a confrontation with Riley and that it almost turned physical, which would have been a rare occurrence among the gentlemen smugglers. Harvey, he says, intervened.

"Les had a big, sort of control thing," says Toombs. "I like Les, but he rubbed me wrong that day. We didn't get along after that. I think that ended it."

When it came to smuggling, personality differences were rarely the cause of major disagreements, and people who didn't care for each other just opted not to work together. The root of almost all conflict was instead money. Paradoxically, the more money the men made, the harder it was to keep everyone satisfied.

Dissention in the ranks was often provoked by the so-called hillbillies of South Carolina. Although the terrain is, without exception, flat along the South Carolina coast, smugglers from other parts of the country referred to the Palmetto State smugglers as "hillbillies." The hillbillies, they said, could be particularly duplicitous members of the smuggling underworld. Among the top kingpins operating in South Carolina, none were immune from payment disputes, and their thrifty and shifty reputations began to precede them. When it came to broken promises of payment, the most egregious cheat differed depending on who one talked to. To some, like boat captain Steele, almost all his employers proved frustrating.

"Lee Harvey had problems paying . . . people. By nature of being Lee Harvey's partner, Les Riley had problems paying people. Bob Byers obviously had some problems paying people," said Steele. "Those would probably be the major offenders."

Others felt Foy was particularly unreliable and greedy, warning each other to keep their wallets close and their women closer when in his presence. If Foy was regarded as greedy, others felt Les Riley was stingy. Following his successful piloting of a decoy boat as the *Second Life* was unloaded, Jamison went to Riley's house on Hilton Head to be paid $10,000. As Riley handed Jamison the money, the kingpin remarked about a nightscope he had just bought his young son that cost just as much. Jamison bristled at the remark. If Riley has so much extra cash, he thought, why not share some with the man whose daredevil driving helped ensure the hashish was unloaded safely.

"To me that was a slap in the face," says Jamison "[I] kind of never looked at Les the same way again, you know, because I really felt like what I did was over, above and beyond . . . and that really ticked me off.

"Maybe he was high, I don't know, but I definitely took it wrong . . . and I feel like I could take it the only way it came to me. Like, 'Here's your ten grand, and I'm going to give my kid a ten grand toy to play with.'"

More notorious than Foy and Riley was Harvey. Although two of his brothers insist he was more than fair when paying his debts and never made much money because of it, others characterize him as manipulative and prone to avoiding payment. One smuggler labels Harvey an outright thief, and another recalls Harvey stringing him along until he finally made a visit to Harvey's farmhouse in Virginia. There, he said, Harvey came down from an upstairs bedroom, informed him he was on the phone, and tossed a bag of cocaine on the table. The diversion worked. The smuggler soon dived in and forgot his reason for visiting.

In similarly controlling behavior, Harvey once instructed smuggler Steve Ravenel to wait on a street corner in downtown Alexandria. He'd pick him up, Harvey said, so they could negotiate a price for thirty thousand pounds of pot they had just worked together to bring into South Carolina. As Ravenel waited, a car cruised up. Harvey was inside, with his brother Michael at the wheel.

"He picked me up, he handed me a slip of paper and said, 'This is what you're going to get, and I don't want to discuss it any further,'" said Ravenel. " . . . It was just a short ride around the block, and, before I could get into any discussion about it, I was out of the car. He popped the trunk, and I took the suitcase."

Such tactics were familiar to many of the men who worked with Harvey and his partner.

"This was what Les and Lee were famous for—'I never agreed to that,'" says Bauer, who counted Harvey as a friend. "Lee was one of them guys you had to pin down. Don't take nothing for granted."

The trick, Bauer says, was having the courage to confront these men to keep them honest. This could be a full-time job, but, as Bauer says, "It's on you to cover your ass."

"Basically, they were nothing but punks," Bauer says. "They were tricky to deal with, but hey, that's business. That's fucking business."

When men would come to Riley seeking payment, he'd often instruct them to go find Harvey, informing them that payment was his partner's responsibility. Many smugglers didn't buy it, feeling like Riley was passing the buck. Riley says he, himself, was shorted by Harvey, and that Harvey had problems collecting money they were owed, letting people slide.

When Riley agreed to take on Harvey as a partner, he outlined the basics of running a smuggling operation, which were straightforward:

- Pay your captain and crew first, because they worked the hardest.
- Pay your overseas suppliers next, so nobody gets killed.
- Then pay your off-load crew and drivers, so they stay loyal and want to work again.

Harvey, the business school student, had received different training when it came to making payroll, a lesson he once shared with Toombs.

"Barry, one thing they teach you in school: pay yourself first," said Harvey. "That's what a good businessman does."

Another paradox among the gentlemen smugglers was that as their operations became more and more sophisticated, they were increasingly controlled by men incapable of sailing a boat. Such lack of experience could be harmful, as those planning smuggling ventures had unrealistic expectations and did not appreciate the rigors of moving a sailboat across oceans, through hurricanes, and past patrols, all while loaded with tons of illegal drugs. These men wanted to do too much, too fast.

"People were looking for an easy, fast way to make money—it ain't easy," says Riley. "Let me tell you something, you pay your dues, whether it would be with weather, boats, conditions, [or] worrying about the possibility of getting caught."

Riley went out of his way to caution potential employees about the hardships and dangers of smuggling, including his own kid brother, Roy, who began to work security for Les's operations. If Roy did not have the same knack for smuggling as his older brother—he once fell asleep while guarding a gate—he was at least an exceptional athlete. In high school he played basketball, and, after graduating from the College of Charleston, he moved to Florida to work as a tennis pro at various clubs, even playing on the U.S. Tennis Association's Satellite Tour. Working at this level of athletics was fun, but didn't pay well. By the late 1970s, he fattened his wallet by helping his brother and moved near Cape Cod to help unload pot on boats sailed up from Colombia by Christy Campbell and others.

Also joining their older brother in illicit pursuits were Tom Harvey and Michael Harvey. Michael, in particular, was familiar with brother Lee's maneuvers, once accompanying him to an Alexandria, Virginia, diner where Toombs and Pernell passed a manila envelope containing $600,000 worth of rubies and diamonds to his brother as a down payment on a hash deal. After the *Second Life* landed on Hilton Head in June 1980, Lee came to be regarded as a mastermind, coolly planning five gigs at a time and taking orders while Riley stayed in the background, organizing crews.

With Harvey, the sky was the limit. He allegedly saw stunts on television or in movies and figured out how to incorporate them into a deal. Foy says Harvey believed in the power of volume, reasoning that if only 50 percent of the drugs he smuggled made it, he and his partners still stood to make a lot of money. His friends started to joke that his ego was as big as the world; that if his head got any bigger, it would explode. Nearly everyone liked him, even the people who complained he didn't pay, and even as he tried to outpace his partner and benefactor, Riley. He began working with other people, and contemplated even bigger hashish deals from Lebanon. If his ambition was excessive, it was all by design.

"Sometimes Lee Harvey had more partners than he knew what to do with. He was pretty slick," says Toombs, who regarded Harvey as the ultimate con man. "He had the charisma, and he had the stones. If you're a beautiful liar, things work pretty good."

The gentlemen smugglers were so wrapped up in deal making and their high-flying lives that they didn't realize, or didn't care, about their notorious reputations at home. On Hilton Head, the rumors were running rampant that the island was crawling with drug smugglers. IRS criminal investigator David Forbes finally decided to check it out in 1981, meeting with a man particularly convinced his neighbors were crooked, that the resort island was the home of a vast drug network. President Ronald Reagan had just taken office in the White House, and the man, like many other Americans, was suddenly convinced marijuana was Public Enemy Number One.

During his presidential campaign, Reagan appealed to conservative voters and families by attacking marijuana as "perhaps the most dangerous drug in America." This Hilton Head resident no doubt had helped Reagan crush Jimmy Carter in the previous November's election.

Arriving on the island, Forbes asked the man what clues he had of islanders smuggling.

"I just know," the man said.

"Have you ever seen anyone smuggling?" Forbes asked. "Ever heard anyone talking about it?"

"Well, no," the man replied.

Forbes walked away.

"What have I got here?" he said to himself. "A nut. A big conspiracy theory."

Forbes had been working money laundering and tax evasion cases for five years at the IRS, spending most of that time in Charleston, South Carolina. It was turf he knew well. The Holy City was his hometown, and he stuck around for college, graduating from the Citadel military academy in 1973 with a business administration degree. Seven years later, he had settled down to a cozy suburban life, living on James Island with his wife and two young kids, across the Ashley River from downtown Charleston.

The IRS had taught Forbes how to follow a paper trail. Because tax evasion was so difficult to prove, their criminal investigators spent time only on truly egregious cases, when the numbers didn't add up. When a man, for example, reported an income of $25,000 a year, but owned a Corvette, a swimming pool, and a big house. When Forbes saw a situation like that, he pounced.

He'd investigated cases against doctors, car dealers, and lawyers—cases that didn't make any headlines. He wasn't one for making a splash, anyway. Many law enforcement officers he worked with wanted to make big busts. Forbes preferred rifling through records before kicking doors down.

Soon enough, another call came in.

The caller sounded nervous. He didn't want to stay on the line, or give his name.

"You need to look into Les Riley," he said. "He's living high on the hog down here in Hilton Head, and he doesn't seem to have a job."

Click.

The veteran special agent wasn't getting his hopes up. Ninety percent of the tips Forbes received were bad—"kooks calling during a full moon," as he called them. Many of the callers had hopes for financial gain. The IRS promised tipsters a reward of 10 to 25 percent of any collected taxes or penalties assessed by the government should their information pan out. Such a payoff could motivate many a neighbor, or friend, to pick up the phone. Forbes had learned that you never knew when you'd catch a break. And you didn't catch suspected crooks by staying behind a desk. Forbes joked that he'd yet to have a criminal walk into his office and confess.

Actual drug busts weren't unheard of on Hilton Head, either. The year before, on February 5, 1980, a DC-3 airplane belonging to Island Aviation Service and loaded with five thousand pounds of marijuana landed in a pasture in Metter, Georgia—seventy-five miles west of Savannah. After a Georgia resident called to say a plane had crashed nearby, police converged on the plane, arresting two men in pickup trucks and seizing marijuana.

Immediately suspicion fell on the owner of the aviation company, Tommy Heyward, who called to report the plane stolen four hours after it landed in Georgia. In explaining the unusual timing of this call, Heyward said he had been suffering from back pain the last six weeks and was unable to visit the Island Aviation office and keep close tabs on his fleet, including the DC-3, which was used by Heyward to spray mosquito insecticide over Beaufort County.

Authorities didn't buy it, especially after discovering that the plane's insecticide tanks emptied into the main fuel tanks, ostensibly serving as auxiliary fuel storage during long flights to South America. One of Heyward's corporations, too, allegedly bought nearly twenty thousand gallons of fuel from 1976 to 1978 that was unaccounted for. Still, authorities ultimately dropped two sets of drug charges against Heyward and charged him with filing a false and fraudulent income tax return. These charges were the result of an investigation by Forbes and some colleagues, who traveled to Hilton Head often to review

Heyward's financial records and question him extensively following the seizure of the plane.

"At one time they had three or four agents in my office microfilming documents," one of Heyward's attorneys, Roberts Vaux, told the Island Packet newspaper after his client was indicted for the income tax violations. "One interview session lasted nine hours. I would estimate they've got 5,000 hours invested in this case."

Forbes's frequent trips to see Heyward and his associates had made him well-known on the island. During each visit, he endeavored to make new friends and overcome the negative reputation that dogged the nation's tax agency. He handed out his business card often, encouraging residents to reach out to him.

"Something funny," he'd say, "you give me a call."

Perhaps this most recent tip on Riley was the result of one of these introductions. And so he was off to Beaufort County again, but this time, with no clear sign, like a plane full of pot, that someone was smuggling drugs.

If nothing else, he'd have some pleasant scenery on his drive south to the Beaufort County Courthouse, which housed property records for Hilton Head Island. US 17 ran south from Charleston to Beaufort County, passing through the ACE Basin— 350,000 acres of wetlands and former rice plantations. The basin—named for the Ashepoo, Combahee, and Edisto Rivers—was popular with hunters stalking deer or duck. It was also home to creatures men preferred not to meet, including mosquitoes, alligators, and rattlesnakes.

From the road, though, it was just long-leaf pines and live oaks. Occasionally Forbes passed iron gates bordered by dilapidated brick masonry, the unassuming entrances to plantations that sprawled for hundreds, if not thousands, of acres. Behind many of these gates were oak-lined allées, the canopied, dirt lanes that sometimes stretched close to a mile, leading to historic plantation homes. Following the declining value of Lowcountry rice, indigo, and cotton crops in the 1800s, many South Carolina plantations were sold to Northern families in want of hunting retreats at the turn of the twentieth century. The new owners maintained the dikes and flooded the former rice fields, luring waterfowl flying south for the winter. In the early 1980s wealthy Northerners still owned much of the land in the ACE Basin, though they no longer arrived by rail but by private plane. And many spent little time there—perhaps the odd holiday or weekend—helping contribute to the basin's decidedly rural and isolated feel. There were a few communities of full-time residents down side roads off US 17, the largest of which contained no more than two thousand people.

Forbes drove past signs for these outposts: Bennetts Point, Green Pond, White Hall, and Wiggins.

But for the most part, there was nothing, save the occasional farm stand as he motored toward the Georgia state line and Savannah. Close to an hour into the drive, Forbes turned onto US 21, crossing over the Whale Branch River and into Beaufort, the county seat. Beaufort was South Carolina's second-oldest city, founded after Charleston. The little town's commercial district consisted of three blocks on Bay Street, which backed into a waterfront park and marina on the Beaufort River. Mansions lined another section of Bay Street, along a breathtaking bluff on the river.

Here, too, on the bluff, was the county courthouse, a white, two-story building built in 1884 and remodeled in the Art Deco style in 1936. Here were the county's property deeds and car registrations—what Forbes had come for.

Inside the courthouse Forbes started paging through the books, looking for homes or vehicles in the name of Les Riley—standard procedure for identifying assets. You started with whatever clues you had—in this case a name. Sometimes you'd spend hours in the courthouse and come away with nothing. But look hard and long enough, Forbes knew, and you could dig up the next clue. People had to own something: a car, a house, land. And people making money illegally, especially lots of it, had to spend that money somewhere.

But this latest tip wasn't panning out at the courthouse. Riley's name wasn't surfacing. Returning the books of deeds to the shelves, Forbes concluded he was at a dead end.

Chapter Seven

Upon release from federal prison for the second time, Lee Harvey had a choice to make, much like he had a choice after the first time he went to prison. One option was to clean up his life, start over, and maybe complete the master's degree he was close to finishing. Another was to organize international smuggling ventures again. He chose the latter, and, with the help of others, including Les Riley, began planning for a flotilla of boats to cross the Mediterranean and Atlantic, carting approximately 180,000 pounds of hashish from Lebanon. If that wasn't enough, he also planned for a freighter to travel back from Singapore at the same time, carrying Thai sticks or some other cannabis from Asia. In the autumn of 1981, more than a half-dozen ships would arrive off the coast of North America, dumping an astounding amount of potent pot into the hands of the gentlemen smugglers' east coast distributors. At least, that was the plan.

To pull off a caper of this magnitude, Riley and Harvey had to broaden their smuggling network, partnering with a handful of shadowy business partners, some of whom would never be identified by law enforcement. Barry "Ice Cream" Toombs claims Harvey made mafia connections when serving his second prison sentence, which gave him inroads to the Lebanese underworld and beyond, though Harvey's brothers deny that to be true. It's possible, too, that any number of people Riley and Harvey rubbed elbows with in the Caribbean, New York, Miami, or elsewhere turned them on to a source across the Atlantic—or that Lebanese men approached them, hoping to find able American traffickers.

Even with new partners, Riley and Harvey still made use of old friends. Since they required much more cash than normal to make down payments on the large shipment of drugs, Harvey solicited investments from some regular distributors, including $600,000 from Toombs and Julian "Doc" Pernell for a portion of the hashish. More significantly, Harvey was alleged to have earned important capital by defrauding the First National Bank of Chicago. In April 1981, a company allegedly controlled by Harvey and his partners obtained a loan from the bank's office in the Channel Islands, off the coast of Normandy, where banking secrecy laws were favorable. The money was to be used to buy yachts, and these yachts would be used as collateral for the loan in case of default.

Harvey and his partners did not buy any yachts, though they submitted false paperwork to the bank pretending they had purchased thirty-six boats, all of which were apparently fictitious. They did buy two refurbished North Sea fishing trawlers, though, paying about $450,000 in the spring of 1981 to Dutch shipyards for vessels they named the *Adeline C* and *Caroline C.* These boats would serve as motherships, carrying massive amounts of drugs.

Additionally, Harvey and his partners obtained use of the freighter *Sea Scout,* which would be another mothership. The boat was controlled by Mark Hertzan, a New York drug smuggler potentially bound for Hollywood fame. In 1979 he befriended actor John Belushi in a Manhattan bathhouse both men frequented and revealed to the comedian that he smuggled drugs in secret compartments of ships, as well as invested in horse-breeding operations. Belushi was mesmerized by Hertzan's double life and struck an agreement with him to make a movie based on the smuggler, called *Kingpin,* so long as Hertzan's identity was kept secret and Belushi could be the star. In 1979, Universal paid a screenwriter and Belushi for the rights to the proposed film, guaranteeing Belushi $100,000 if the movie was made.

Belushi pitched the project to director Steven Spielberg, who wasn't interested. He asked director John Landis, too, who also declined.

"You got this problem," Landis told Belushi. "You're going to make a fucking hero out of a drug runner. I don't like the idea of glorifying it."

"It's just marijuana in the screenplay," replied Belushi.

"No," said Landis.

In the late summer and early fall of 1981, the boats moved to the Far and Near East to be loaded with drugs. The least amount of information is known about the *Adeline C,* whose logs indicate that it stopped in Singapore, traveled back through the Suez Canal, crossed the Mediterranean and Atlantic, stopped in Florida, and then sailed north to

Halifax, Nova Scotia, Canada, where it was abandoned by a six-person crew, four of whom were supposedly female. Since portions of the $10.1 million bank loan were paid to an account in Singapore, and other portions were used to purchase waterfront property in Rhode Island, investigators speculate the boat was loaded with drugs, perhaps Thai sticks, in Asia, and unloaded in Rhode Island. No arrests were made.

As for the *Sea Scout,* it sailed from Lebanon in August 1981 with approximately eighty thousand pounds of hashish aboard. At about the same time, the *Caroline C* sailed into Tripoli, Lebanon, to pick up ninety thousand pounds of hashish. At the helm was Christy Campbell, who had sailed the *Second Life* across the Atlantic a year earlier with thirty thousand pounds of hash on board, and now was lured into a second hash load by the promise of a $1 million paycheck from Harvey. In the weeks prior, he and his crew— each of whom were promised $400,000 for their troubles—had sailed around the Mediterranean, meeting with Riley and rendezvousing in Cyprus with two other boats that would be accepting pot from their mothership. One was the *Anonymous of Rorc,* a fifty-seven-foot luxury sailboat owned by Bob "The Boss" Byers and sailed by Willie Frank Steele. The other was the *Meermin,* a ninety-foot steel-hulled motor sailer crewed by Europeans unknown to the South Carolinians.

When Campbell received the radio signal, he brought the *Caroline C* in toward the beach and Tripoli's harbor, where he said bullets were flying. On account of the trawler's arrival, he claimed, the fighting momentarily stopped, with enemies calling a ceasefire to facilitate the loading of the boat. The hashish was brought on board and soon filled every hold and cabin. Without any more room, the rest was stacked on the deck of the trawler. Militiamen escorted the *Caroline C* back out to sea and handed over a few AK-47 automatic rifles for protection against pirates. Of more immediate concern than pirates, though, was the foot of water that kept sloshing on deck. The boat was sitting perilously low in the sea on account of all the drugs aboard, and Campbell was afraid it might sink.

To the *Caroline C*'s rescue came the *Anonymous of Rorc* and the *Meermin.* The two sailboats pulled alongside the trawler, and all three vessels headed west on autopilot, set to a speed of approximately five knots. As the sailboats were tied to the side of the *Caroline C,* the assorted crews worked together to transfer the hash and lighten the trawler's load. Approximately thirty thousand pounds went aboard the *Meermin* and ninety-six hundred pounds of hashish went aboard the *Anonymous of Rorc* before they were untied.

The boats continued cruising west, slowly separating as they moved at different speeds. The *Meermin* was in the lead, followed by the *Caroline C,* which slowed its engines to keep pace with the *Anonymous of Rorc,* which was having engine trouble. The *Caroline C* soon steamed ahead, too, as the *Anonymous of Rorc's* crew decided to put up its sails, making slow but steady progress. Somewhere nearby, as well, was the *Sea Scout.* Each boat was told to head for the middle of the U.S. eastern seaboard. When each vessel got close, it'd be told exactly where to go.

Of the four boats plying the Mediterranean and Atlantic, Campbell's boat was among the fastest, its engines pushing it steadily westward. Before being loaded in Lebanon, the ship's adventure had been trouble free, save for crewman Kenny Gunn falling two stories off the pilothouse while trying to change a staysail. He was drunk, which at least made him feel less pain as he thudded onto the deck, breaking a leg. The crew stopped in Algeria so a doctor could set the bone, and they were forced to bribe a threatening Customs inspector with alcohol, cigarettes, and pornography. Days later Gunn got drunk again, stumbled around, and broke his leg a second time, requiring another trip to a doctor.

Now on the return voyage, Campbell and his shipmates encountered five hurricanes and were in danger of getting hit by a sixth as they bobbed 250 miles off the U.S. coast, out of fuel. They called in to friends for help, and, two weeks later, a boat captain was persuaded to bring them enough fuel to finish the voyage, supposedly at a cost of more than $250,000. By now Campbell had learned his point of entry: the Cape Fear River in North Carolina. They cruised toward its mouth, entering the river and steaming past Wilmington, North Carolina, in search of a private dock where they'd unload.

But the crew of the *Caroline C* searched in vain, eventually running aground. Campbell then hopped in a Zodiac raft and continued up the river, where he found a dock he deemed suitable to unload on, even though it was not the one specified by Riley and Harvey. He and his crew began stacking the hashish there in broad daylight, and somehow the off-load crew made its way to this dock and transferred it to a nearby plantation.

With the hashish off the boat and the tide high, the *Caroline C* was able to float again and head downstream, back toward sea. They soon ran aground again, this time in front of a Coast Guard station. Coast Guard officers came aboard and breakfasted with the crew, unaware that the trashed boat had just been unloaded of more than forty thousand pounds of hashish. When the tide rose enough again to lift the ship, the crew steered it out into the ocean and south to Savannah, Georgia, docking at Thunderbolt Marina. By this point they had been celebrating their homecoming for hours. As they docked the boat, the drunken men whooped and hollered, and some jumped in the water to take a swim. They tipped dockhands excessively, with half the crew driving into South Carolina and half the crew, including Campbell and Gunn, taking a cab to the Savannah airport. Before leaving the marina, they showed an AK-47 to marina employees.

As Campbell, Gunn, and another crewman waited at the airport to board a chartered Learjet, U.S. Customs agents scrambled to catch them. Minutes earlier, other Customs agents had discovered scraps of hashish aboard the boat at the marina during an inspection. A check of a U.S. Customs database found that members of the *Caroline C* crew, whose names had been left with an inspector at the dock, had criminal records for smuggling. A supervisor raised Customs agents across coastal Georgia on the radio, instructing them to cancel their patrols and head to the airport. The men must not be allowed to fly away.

Arriving first was Customs agent Rachel Fischer. Identifying the suspects, she approached the men wearing plainclothes. Gunn, the Burt Reynolds look-a-like who'd been starved of sex for two months, welcomed the woman's attention. He offered her a beer from a six-pack he was holding and gave her a peck on the cheek. In exchange, she placed him and his friends under arrest.

While the journey was ending at the Savannah airport for Campbell and two of his crewmen, the *Anonymous of Rorc* was still coming across the Atlantic, a few weeks away from landfall. It had been a long trip so far, to say the least. After flying to Europe and boarding the sailboat in Athens, the crew had cruised east between the Greek isles, Turkey, and Cyprus. At each stop they partied, often taking girls into the staterooms. Sometimes they watched movies aboard the sailboat on a small television.

The *Anonymous of Rorc*'s hull was painted a pastel yellow and featured teak decks and grab rails. The vessel was gorgeous—"one of the best-built boats in the world, at the time," recalled Kenny Brown, a member of the four-man crew. "Sailed like a dream, too."

"It didn't look like a boat to be used for what we were about to use it for," said his friend and fellow crewman, Ken Buckland. "God, it was like a yacht."

Both men were first-rate sailors from Florida, but neither was a veteran smuggler. In fact, this was Brown's first trip. But for a $150,000 paycheck, the sail maker was willing to try a new line of work. Plus, it was all fun before getting down to business, bedding babes and "sailing around, having a great time."

Brown and Buckland were the tamer half of the crew. Also on board was Bill Thompson, a friend since childhood to the boat owner, Byers. Thompson, also known as LB, was short and stocky, tough from years of playing hockey in Minnesota and serving in Vietnam as a distinguished helicopter pilot. Among other military awards, he received the Air Medal with V device, indicating a notable act of valor or heroism.

Despite Thompson's courage, Vietnam was said to have taken its toll on the man, and friends attributed his excessive drinking to the trauma of war. Day to day, though, he seemed to mask any psychological damage by inspiring hilarity. John "Smokin' Sneakers" Jamison, for example, fondly remembers a number of Thompson's inappropriate but amusing antics. There was the time they were on Tortola in the British Virgin Islands, outfitting a boat for a smuggling run, when a boy came by with a board piled high with mushrooms.

"My god, look at these magic mushrooms," said Thompson.

Jamison stared at the fungi—three or four dozen by his count. He had heard of their hallucinogenic powers, but had never tried them.

"Well, LB, how many are you going to get?" Jamison asked.

Thompson turned and looked at Jamison, giving him an incredulous look, like he was "totally wacko."

"All of them," Thompson said, as if there were any other choice.

Receiving the mushrooms, Thompson nibbled some first, to no apparent effect. Jamison then sliced a few, as if to top a salad, and plopped them down his throat. Thompson turned giddy, thinking Jamison was doomed. But, as the minutes passed, he was disappointed to see him remain sober. Concluding the boy had swindled them, they headed up the dock toward a bar. Somehow, someway, they would find a path to intoxication. That's when the mushrooms took hold.

Staring at the back of Thompson's head, Jamison noticed it seemed to be melting. He looked at Thompson in terror, motioning to his skull. Thompson raised an arm to feel his hair, but Jamison grabbed it and cautioned him.

"Don't do that, you'll mess it all up. It's like wax," Jamison told him in the most serious of tones, before both were cracking up, rolling around the dock with tears coming out of their eyes. "This psycho, the next day, I'm sitting in the cockpit of the boat, and this nice little family comes in on a bareboat charter, a forty-something footer.

"Dad's at the helm, just real careful, you know . . . coming in," says Jamison. "All of a sudden, just when they're about to the dock . . . there's this blood-curdling scream. I mean blood curdling.

"The dad locks up, just freezes," he says. "The boat goes careening into this concrete dock, destroys the pulpit on the boat.

"Guess who they all look at?" Jamison says. "I'm the only one there, right next to them on a boat. The kids and the wife are going, 'Well thanks a lot, you just ruined our whole vacation.'

"All I can hear was this snickering down below. I go down there, LB has got his head covered up with two pillows, laughing his nuts off," says Jamison. "He was psycho."

That bang up paled in comparison to the trouble Thompson caused in Vietnam.

"One of his favorites was, he would fly over an area where he knew there were friendlies," Jamison said. "Then he would call Saigon and ask for permission to open up.

"Saigon would come back and go 'Negative, negative. They're friendlies, they're friendlies,'" Jamison said, imitating their panicky tones.

"He'd go, 'Uh, Saigon, tower, you're coming in garbled and broken, do I take that as an affirmative?'

"They'd have, like meltdowns, and he'd laugh his nuts off. He thought that was the funniest thing in the world."

If Thompson's antics could be a bit disconcerting when trafficking massive amounts of drugs, boat captain Steele was no more reassuring. By this point in his smuggling career, his reputation for drug abuse preceded him, and even if it didn't, he unfailingly demonstrated to new acquaintances the depths of his addiction to cocaine. Buckland remembers once sitting in on Steele's crack-smoking sessions in a mutual friend's grandmother's house. Nude whores ran wild in one room while Grandma asked everyone to keep it down from another, complaining that she was trying to watch her soap opera. Steele would drive around after such sessions with Buckland riding shotgun.

"Scared the shit out of me," Buckland says.

For this trip, Steele had, of course, packed a propane tank and torch in his suitcase when he flew to Europe. Lucky for him, it went undetected by airport security. As he indulged his drug habit in Greece, it gave Buckland pause for concern.

"Jesus, man, this is our ringleader," he thought. "Our captain."

"That always bothered me about him," Buckland says, but "you untie those lines, man, he was sober."

When tying up to the *Caroline C*, Brown remembers counting 145 sacks of hashish being placed in the *Anonymous of Rorc,* the drugs filling the cabins and covering the comfortable beds and television room. The hash was stacked just a few feet shy of the ceiling, and only the galley was left open. The men were impressed with their new cargo. Each plastic-wrapped bale contained approximately fifty small cloth bags with drawstrings and stamped wax seals. Inside each cloth bag were two soles of blonde hashish—oval-shaped patties the size of dessert plates. Each was wrapped in plastic and weighed about a pound. The hash came so beautifully packaged it might have been sold on store shelves.

With the product loaded, the crew watched the *Meermin* and *Caroline C* disappear on the horizon. Steele and Buckland took turns navigating as they sailed through the Mediterranean, occasionally using the engine. Three days into the trip, the fuel pump malfunctioned and the engine conked out. The boat was so crowded with hash it was difficult to diagnose the problem. They anchored the boat off Fomenter, within Spain's Balearic Islands, where an Australian friend named Digger brought them a replacement part. It worked only briefly before failing, forcing them to raise the sails again in a treacherous area of the world—the Strait of Gibraltar. The crew labored for days to leave the Mediterranean, frustrated by weak winds that came from the west, nearly putting them in irons.

"We were tacking back and forth, all the way down, as close to the land as we felt comfortable," says Buckland. "We'd be sailing all day long and we'd maybe make a mile, two miles. We were going, 'God, can we ever get the hell out of here?'

"Sail down to Libya, sail back to Portugal," he says. "We just couldn't get out."

Complicating their maneuvers was the stream of humongous supertankers traveling through the strait.

"It's like a street trying to go through Gibraltar, it's only eight miles wide. They're just going back and forth, back and forth, and we're trying to go this way with the wind," says Brown, describing the perpendicular paths taken by their sailboat and the imposing ships. "It takes [the supertankers] five miles just to stop."

After finally exiting the Mediterranean, the crew decided to stop in the Canary Islands to buy another engine part and food. Unable to clear Customs because of all the hashish, they sailed the boat within ten miles of the shoreline and dropped a dinghy, putting Steele and Thompson aboard. The pair motored ashore at sunrise with plans to meet again in twenty-four hours back at sea.

Buckland and Brown sailed throughout the day and night, cutting back and forth, killing time. As the sun began to rise, there was no sign of the dinghy. Hours dragged on, and Buckland started worrying, wondering if Steele and Thompson had been arrested for entering the country without a passport. He knew he couldn't stay offshore forever without attracting suspicion. He didn't want to be paranoid, but considering the hashish was almost overflowing from the staterooms, it was hard to forget the massive amount of illegal drugs on board and the consequences it could bring.

"Well, it looks like it's you and me across the Atlantic, buddy," he joked nervously to Brown, his eyes scanning an empty sea.

Buckland remembers thinking, "You didn't want to leave them, but then again I don't want to keep sitting here with this thing full. What do you do?"

The sun climbed higher in the sky.

"We were really within minutes . . . I'm about ready to toss a coin . . . [then] *bzzzzzzzzzzzz*, I see this little dinghy," Buckland says. "Thank God."

Steele and Thompson climbed aboard and explained the delay. The men had arrived on shore safely, gone into town to shop, and returned to find their dinghy missing. The Canary Islands were notorious for thieves, and Steele and Thompson decided to take justice into their own hands. The former jocks marauded the small fishermen camps on the shore, beating men up until they were told where to find their boat. Upon finding the dinghy, they discovered that the outboard motor had been removed. So, they told Brown and Buckland, they had to fight a few more men to recover the motor.

The rest of the trip was still slow going but less dramatic. The engine remained disabled, requiring that they stay under sail across the ocean. The crew passed time reading spy novels and smoking hash. They played cassette tapes of Bob Marley, Jimmy Buffett, and classical music. Attempts to fish were unsuccessful. They had caught a tuna or shark every day in the Mediterranean, but had few bites on the lines in the deep Atlantic Ocean. The occasional storm stirred up trouble, and strong gusts tore a few sails to shreds, requiring replacements.

Halfway across the ocean, they were told over radio to change their course from New York and head to a back-up location in South Carolina. The crew concentrated on navigating south and fixing the engine. It would be difficult to maneuver the ship in the shallow creeks and rivers of South Carolina if they had to rely on sails alone. Once they had the engine working at a minimal level, they were nearly out of fuel, so they, too, arranged to have a boat meet them offshore to deliver large jugs of gasoline and groceries. Despite the engine problems and trying sailing conditions, the crew felt relaxed. On the other smuggling ships, men had formed cliques, started fights, and turned to drink to combat nerves and frustration. The crew of the *Anonymous of Rorc* kept themselves calm as they approached the mouth of the North Edisto River. After more than seventy days at sea, the trip was almost over.

The change in course for the *Anonymous of Rorc* was made for good reason. In New York, disaster had struck, eclipsing any anxiety Riley and Harvey may have had over Campbell's arrest. Scuba divers were now trying to rectify the situation, but it didn't look good.

Days earlier, the *Meermin* had arrived off the coast of New York City, ready to transfer the thirty thousand pounds of hashish it had on board. A fellow smuggler and paramour of Riley, Madeline Wasserman, had arranged for two wooden fishing vessels to meet the large sailboat, but they delayed departing on account of rough seas. As days passed, and the seas did not calm, the crew on the *Meermin* became impatient, suffering from a lack of water and food. They screamed into the radio, demanding to be met. On October 9, 1981, they got their wish, and the two wooden boats, the *Falcon* and the *Tanqueray*, left New Jersey to rendezvous with the mothership.

The smaller vessels cruised for four hours or so before finding the *Meermin* offshore. After dancing around each other for a few minutes, the *Falcon* pulled alongside the ninety-foot motor sailer, its crew tying them together and throwing aboard groceries. The weather was brutal, with heavy wind, rain, and fifteen-foot waves. Slowly, sacks of hashish came over the side of the *Meermin* and were stored below in the *Falcon*. The *Tanqueray* stayed nearby, ready to ferry most of the men back to shore once the transfer was finished, leaving a skeleton crew aboard the hash-filled sister ship.

After approximately ten thousand pounds had been transferred, an aft cleat busted loose on the *Falcon*, loosening the bond between the boats. Still tied together toward their bows, the two hulls, one wooden and one steel, started clapping violently together. The collisions cracked the *Falcon's* hull below the waterline, and the ocean began to flood the boat. The crews untied and pulled away from each other to inspect the damage. Some wanted to head to shore immediately, but others argued the leak was manageable, that the boat's bilge pumps would compensate for the flooding. A decision was made to keep loading the *Falcon*. The vessels were tied together again, and the rest of the hash was transferred. It was early in the morning when the *Meermin* sailed away and the *Falcon* and *Tanqueray* headed back toward New Jersey.

Twenty miles from shore, however, the *Falcon* could float no farther. The boat was going down, and the smugglers hastened its demise by opening the seacocks—valves on the hull below the waterline. They did not want the drug boat to be seen come dawn. As the *Falcon* slowly sank into the ocean, its few crew members jumped aboard the *Tanqueray* and headed to shore to break the news to Wasserman, Riley, and the other partners waiting in New York City.

As they gathered in a hotel room to discuss the fiasco, the partners doubted the story's legitimacy, threatening to kill people until the truth came out, and even obtained a samurai sword for purposes of intimidation. When they accepted the fact that no one had ripped them off, they sent out boats with scuba divers to try to recover the hash. By this time sacks of drugs were escaping out of the broken, sunken hull and floating to shore. A fishing boat had inadvertently snagged the *Falcon* in its nets, too, and alerted the Coast Guard. The deal was falling apart, and Riley decided he wasn't sticking around. As Wasserman and other partners stewed about the thirty thousand pounds of lost hash and began plotting their next move, Riley shocked them all.

"Well," he said, "I'm going fishing in Australia."

Such a swift departure did not endear Riley to the men gathering on Edisto Island, South Carolina, on November 1, 1981, to receive the ten thousand pounds of hashish aboard the *Anonymous of Rorc*. Those expecting him thought he had abandoned them. Still, the sailboat was coming in, and the show must go on.

Nearly a dozen men were scattered throughout Skip Sanders's grandmother's Edisto Island plantation, West Bank, waiting for the sailboat to appear. The men had been arriving since the day before, coming from Florida, Georgia, Minnesota, and New York. Byers arrived by private jet at the small airport in Walterboro, forty miles away. Traveling with him were two goons—men whom he called, perhaps half-jokingly, "Moose" and "Vinny." Byers wore an expensive suit and Italian shoes, in which he seemed to tiptoe. He wore shades, too, giving him "the look," according to Sanders.

Such fancy attire surely had struck Byers as impractical when his car turned into West Bank Plantation on Halloween, driving down a dirt road, past two hundred acres of bean fields and through forest and a covered clearing before finally reaching the water. The roadside oaks, arched overhead and trailing Spanish moss, made it seem like Byers was traveling through tunnels.

From West Bank's bluff, Byers could see old, dilapidated dock pilings and a creek that led to the North Edisto River. There, the kingpin was introduced to Sanders.

"Just what is it I'm buying here?" he asked.

"Not much of anything," Sanders replied, coolly.

Byers, nearly ten years older and with an entourage in tow, was intimidating. But Sanders had become something of an old hand in the smuggling underworld of South Carolina, too, used to dealing with such men who fancied themselves as kingpins.

In the last two years, he'd been paid for at least sixteen deals on his grandmother's remote property. Granny provided the perfect cover for Sanders, as no less than a retired DEA agent would later describe her as a "ninety-something-year-old pillar of the Edisto community." The matriarch lived in a small cottage on the property—a home the visiting smugglers referred to as "Granny's place."

Deceiving the sweet old woman wasn't ideal, says Sanders, but he couldn't pass up the lifestyle her plantation helped him afford. Plus she had been shocked enough when another grandson, Sanders's brother Johnny, had a month earlier been arrested and charged with driving under the influence. It was better, he decided, to keep her in the dark.

Staring back at Byers, Sanders continued his short sales pitch.

"Not much of anything," he said. "When a guy is doing something illegal, he wants nothing much else to be around."

Byers laughed, sold on the land and its seclusion. At this point, he had little choice but to land the load here, given the disappearance of Riley, the arrests of Campbell and his crew just south in Savannah, and the *Falcon's* sinking up north off New York. The *Anonymous of Rorc* was offshore and ready to come in, forcing Byers to make a fast deal with Sanders, a man whose land he'd never happened to use.

"Hey, kid . . . I like you," Byers said. "What's your name?"

"My friends call me Skip," said Sanders.

"So your friends call ya Skip, huh?" said Byers. "Did you hear that, Moose?"

Moose and Vinny started laughing, anticipating a punch line, perhaps one they'd heard before. Byers took his time, adjusting his collar, allowing for a dramatic pause.

"Well what the fuck should I call ya? Eh?"

Moose and Vinny were now rolling. Even Sanders cracked a smile and laughed at the wiseguy routine. He was about to collect handsomely. He could afford a joke at his expense.

The next evening, while Sanders kept an ear to the airwaves, men milled about in a clearing close to the bluff. Four vans were parked there, some packed with expensive groceries, including champagne, beer, soda, and steaks. The food would be welcome fare for the sailboat crew. The men had been sailing since leaving the coast of Lebanon more than two months before. The other vans had been unloaded, emptied of Zodiac inflatable boats, rope, an anchor, and an outboard motor. For purposes of stealth, the men covered the vans' brake lights and taillights with pads of masking tape.

Sanders had distributed handheld radios and nightscopes to the men that afternoon before using his Jeep to tow away a portable trailer from the bluff. He planned to keep a watch on things from his grandmother's house, removed from the action. Sanders was happy to take a cut for providing access to smugglers, but he wouldn't lend a hand lifting bales. Before dying, his grandfather had left Sanders with some advice he found useful as a so-called spot salesman: "If you own the plantation, don't work the plantation."

At his grandmother's home he turned on extensive surveillance equipment, though Sanders admits the "radars and all that were mostly for show . . . as if to portray the illusion I was on top of things."

More helpful than radars and radios, according to Sanders, was the black community living on Edisto Island.

"Island blacks have the uncanny ability to instantly receive updates on local activity. I don't know how they do it. They can't seem to peg it either," he wrote in a letter. "But if a dark blue Crown Vic would turn down my avenue? I would hear about it twenty minutes later when going into the Edistonian to pick up laundry from a very cool island queen named Annie Mae."

Critical to this underground island network was the island swing bridge tender, Brickman. Watching from the bridge's observation tower, Brickman could tell the weight of every vehicle that came onto the island. He also had a pretty good idea of where it might be going.

"Somehow, when any police car hit the island, Brickman would get the word to someone quickly," Sanders recalled. "And I would know, within minutes. Didn't matter if I was playing golf or boating, whatever. I've had greenskeepers tell me stuff, crabbers, oyster guys, you name it. It would be short and sweet, 'Hey, the Brick say must tell you police to ride to yo place shree deep.' And that would be it."

As darkness fell, Sanders felt at ease. He'd yet to have a problem at West Bank, and there was no reason to suspect that tonight would be different. A twenty-four-foot skiff sat in the water below the bluff, ready to meet the sailboat in the North Edisto and receive the hash. The tide had turned just after eleven o'clock, beginning its six-foot drop. If the sailboat didn't come soon, the off-loaders would be unable to bring the loaded skiff alongside the bluff.

The men drank beer and soda as they waited. Sometime after two in the morning, the smugglers got a message from the sailboat. They were ready to meet in the North Edisto River. The skiff cranked its engine and puttered away from the pilings.

The smugglers weren't the only ones out late in the South Carolina marshes that night. U.S. Customs Patrol officers Mike Bell and Louis Jefferson sat in a cramped trailer, listening to radio transmissions and keeping an eye on the North Edisto River. They probably could have stolen a few winks without consequence. There wasn't much to see. There had been a new moon five days earlier, and the slight crescent in the sky cast a faint light on the river and its offshoots. Passing clouds blocked what little moonlight shone. The officers had parked their trailer near a creek on Wadmalaw Island, about a mile from where the North Edisto met the Atlantic Ocean.

The kindest adjective with which Jefferson could describe the trailer was *ratty*. It was a utility trailer, meant to hold tools and machinery. Tonight it held the two men and shelves crammed with radio equipment. Jefferson's colleague, Bill Southern, had already volunteered for the first patrol shift that night, preferring to sit on a boat than hunker down in a sardine can. He left Jefferson and Bell behind, floating near the banks of Seabrook Island in his patrol boat, right at the mouth of the river. Behind him, inland, on each side of the river, were Wadmalaw and Edisto Islands.

At least it wasn't too cold, especially for the second day of November. A night in the stakeout trailer was even more miserable when the temperature dropped, forcing its occupants to light propane heaters, never mind the dangers posed by the trailer's poor ventilation. Jefferson, Bell, and Southern could be encouraged by the fact that tonight wasn't a total stab in the dark. Customs agent Claude McDonald told Bell that he had spied a suspicious trailer on Edisto Island while conducting aerial surveillance earlier in the week. It was parked on a bluff on West Bank plantation, which lay just across the river from the stakeout position. Tonight it was eerily quiet. No shrimpers or crabbers could be heard plying the waters. Jefferson and Bell knew the near–pitch-black darkness was pregnant with possibilities.

"It's a good night for smuggling," Jefferson told Bell, thinking out loud.

The waiting heightened the tension, allowing the officers ample opportunity to imagine what desperate men might do to avoid arrest and defend their multimillion dollar cargoes. Jefferson was all too aware that, besides guns, just about anything aboard a boat could be used to kill, from filet knives to fiberglass antennas. When Jefferson boarded a smuggling boat, he did so swiftly and fiercely.

"I took them all as a threat," he says of his outlaw quarry. "Normal people don't [smuggle drugs]. You have to have something twisted in your psyche."

Jefferson had survived two tours of duty in Vietnam, fighting as a member of the Army's mechanized infantry. Returning stateside to a job with U.S. Customs, he found it impossible to turn off the killer instincts that had kept him alive overseas. He considered his job an extension of his service in Vietnam.

"When we worked for Customs, it was a *war* on drugs. That's what it was called," Jefferson says. "Instead of dealing with gooks I was dealing with smugglers."

He pushed himself hard and pushed his colleagues hard, too, sometimes crossing the line. He'd been reprimanded for use of excessive force against suspects more than a couple times. He had been trained to eliminate threats, not reduce them. If you reduce a threat, he reasoned, it still exists. Nighttime raids in the marshes of South Carolina didn't help Jefferson shake his demons from Vietnam.

"I had the same mentality—you or me—every day."

Bell had seen his Customs colleague in action, and was glad to have such a hardened veteran as a partner, especially when things got hairy.

"Louis don't mess around," says Bell.

Sitting in the trailer, the men used their radio equipment to monitor the airwaves, listening for signs of smuggling. The officers had a VHF transmitter and receiver as well as what they called a DF, or directional finder. Since Southern was on the water with a radio, too, they could pinpoint the location of any other transmissions using triangulation. But the airwaves stayed silent. The only excitement of the night had come hours earlier, at about nine o'clock, when Southern heard an outboard motor. The trio of Customs officers waited in darkness, anticipating a break.

"It was like waiting for a storm," says Jefferson. "Everyone knows it is coming."

The clock was creeping toward two o'clock when the radio came alive. It was Southern: He had spied a green running light offshore. Bell and Jefferson snapped to attention.

A half-hour later, Southern called in again. A boat was heading their way, he said, entering the North Edisto River. A half-hour later he updated the men again, reporting that a large double-masted sailboat had passed him, still heading up the river. Bell and Jefferson scrambled out of the trailer, driving across Wadmalaw Island to reach an undercover patrol boat that the U.S. Customs Patrol kept docked behind the home of a friendly former government employee. By five minutes after three they were on the water, motoring quietly down the river. In the darkness they soon noticed the sailboat's weak running lights. With Bell at the helm, they approached the boat, passing slowly before turning and pulling in behind its stern. Bell activated the boat's bow-mounted, remote-controlled spotlight, suddenly throwing bright light across the water.

The shot of light illuminated not one boat, but two. Bell and Jefferson saw a twenty-four-foot skiff alongside the large sailboat. A man stood on the skiff's deck, reaching up to receive what looked like a bale. Stacked in the bow of the skiff were large white bundles. Bell noticed the sailboat was flying the Union Jack from the stern. He glanced at the transom, quickly reading "*Anonymous*" and a home port of "Jersey" before clicking off the spotlight and turning away toward sea.

There was no doubt in the officers' minds that they had witnessed smuggling. There was the late hour rendezvous, the suspicious bales, the foreign registry . . . it was obviously time to call in the cavalry. Floating a safe distance from the sailboat, the men turned their attention to the radios.

They reached Southern and asked him to rouse officers on the mainland. Wary of the smugglers listening to the airwaves, Bell used codes to reference Customs paperwork and his superior officer.

"Bill, we're going to have a forty-six twenty-one to fill out tonight. Go ahead and call one one oh one and let him know," said Bell.

Bell also called Sector Communications in Miami, an around-the-clock dispatch for Customs officers. He asked them to check any records for the *Anonymous*, unknowingly truncating the name of the boat. Miami responded that they had nothing, missing a potential record on the boat possibly filed under its full name.

Soon the airwaves were crowded with the voices of law enforcement officers across Charleston. As Bell later explained, you called everyone that could respond—"local cops, troopers, wildlife [officers]." He couldn't get a word in edgewise. Finally there was a break in the chatter. He was still worried he might tip off the smugglers, so Bell broadcast a mysterious message to the early risers, hoping Customs special agent McDonald would understand his reference to West Bank plantation and the trailer spotted on the bluff a few days earlier.

"Claude, you told me about somewhere interesting on the island. Send everyone over there."

Waiting for backup, he and Jefferson kept watch on the sailboat, peering through a nightscope.

The spotlight had only shined for a few seconds, but it sent shock-waves across the river. The off-loaders near the bluff had seen the light and were wondering if the Coast Guard had intercepted the sail-boat. Byers ordered someone to fetch Sanders from Granny's house.

Sanders had seen a string of vehicles streaming toward the island with the radar he had mounted on the roof. Brickman had called from the bridge, advising Sanders that seven cruisers had "just hit the island lights out at eighty plus." They were "dark blue and coming deep."

Sanders radioed the off-loaders and urged them to flee, but he was ignored or unheard, as some of the radios were broken. Against the advice of his grandfather, Sanders left the house to join those working his plantation. He conferred with Byers, who dismissed his suggestions to cut and run. "The Boss" was intent on finishing the deal. Other smugglers said Sanders was paranoid and spurned his recommendation to "hop on the speedboat and haul ass."

Soon the men heard an outboard motor. The skiff returned piled high with sacks of hash. Its operator, Mike Martin, wore a ski mask over his face, hoping to keep his identity a secret among the other smugglers. Martin had already finished a few trips in the skiff, ferry-ing back more than eight thousand pounds. He began poling the skiff as close to shore as possible in the extremely shallow water, the boat's outboard motor now turned off and raised to avoid scraping bottom.

Aboard the *Anonymous of Rorc*, Steele turned the boat out toward sea, cruising slowly. Brown was below deck, throwing hash sacks upward through the hatch. Buckland and Thompson grabbed the bales and tossed them overboard, reasoning that, should they be arrested, the less hash on board, the better. They considered jumping into the water, but given their distance from shore, their heavy clothing, and the cold temperature, such a move might be suicidal.

"There was no way I was going to jump in that river," says Buckland. "I would sink."

The Customs officers saw the sailboat pass them in darkness, about one hundred feet away. Bell told Jefferson they must stop the sailboat now, before it reached the open sea, where boarding would be more difficult; not that it would be a piece of cake on the river. Bell had hoped backup would have arrived before having to board, or that daybreak would come, or that at least officer Southern was there to help. Instead, it was just the two of them in the dark.

The preferred method of boarding a ship for Customs officers was to approach a vessel slowly, announcing "U.S. Customs" with their bullhorn as they surveyed the scene. "How many men are on board?" they'd ask with the bullhorn. "Do you have any weapons?" And so on.

After that, the patrol boat would pull alongside, asking for cooperation as they tied off to the other boat and secured fenders. Two Customs agents could board while a third Customs officer kept at the wheel of the law enforcement vessel.

Tonight Bell and Jefferson couldn't count on cooperation. In light of the sailboat heading to sea, the boarding could not be a protracted, by-the-book affair. The only choice was to "ram 'n' board" the sailboat, they decided, with Jefferson as the sole boarding officer.

Jefferson readied for a full-assault boarding, weapon drawn. He held a Smith & Wesson .357 revolver—a veritable cannon capable of instantly dropping a man. It was one of the few weapons the marine officer said he could count on not to be corroded by salt. Strapped to his body were speedloaders and at least five pairs of handcuffs.

Bell flipped on the spotlight again and gunned the motor. He turned on the boat's flashing blue lights, too, as he drove toward the *Anonymous of Rorc's* starboard stern. He knew that the spotlight cut both ways, illuminating both the smugglers and Jefferson. As the Customs boat pulled alongside, the sailboat turned hard, seemingly attempting to pull away and thwart the boarding. Jefferson, adrenaline flowing, vaulted from the Customs boat's bow onto the sailboat. The *Anonymous of Rorc's* teak deck sat much higher than the patrol boat, and such a maneuver was, said Bell, "like trying to get up on a horse."

Bell, yelling "U.S. Customs! U.S. Customs!" tried to stay alongside the veering sailboat. He could have benefited from some help, or at least a few more arms. He turned the wheel to keep the two boats close while also directing the spotlight via the remote control on the console. He left the helm to try tying up to the long sailboat. At the same time, Jefferson stormed the cockpit, the menacing Vietnam veteran confronting the men on deck.

"Don't shoot us, don't shoot us," the crew yelled.

"Anybody down below," Jefferson yelled inside the cabin "get your ass on the deck!"

Brown slowly emerged from the cabin and laid facedown on the deck. Brown said Jefferson shook as he pointed the gun at him, making him nervous and eager to explain he was unarmed. Jefferson straightened the wheel as Bell came aboard. Gathering the crew around the cockpit, Bell stood watch while Jefferson searched below deck, finding bales. The officers handcuffed the four sailors and continued their preliminary search, finding an automatic Chinese-made Mauser machine pistol and an AK-47 assault rifle, one tucked under a seat cushion and the other wrapped in a towel. The men had used the weapons for target practice at sea.

At West Bank, instructions crackled over the CB radio: "Drive the vans from the clearing to the bluff." As the vans pulled up, men moved frantically in the marsh to move the hash off the skiff and up to the vans on high ground. It was wet, dirty work.

"There was about six or seven people running around crazy," Dennis York, a driver from Atlanta, later recalled. "One guy backed me in, gave me directions where to go and everything; lights out and everything. And before I know it, they're just throwing the stuff in."

The vans were loaded within a half-hour, finished just as the sun was beginning to rise. The men then noticed flashing blue lights moving down the nearby roads. They panicked. York drove his red van away from the bluff and became lost on the plantation's dirt roads. In his haste he drove into a ditch. The van was stuck. He left the disabled vehicle and walked back to get help pulling it out.

Instead, he found the police.

"Some vehicle started coming down with a light and told me not to move," recalled York. "I moved."

Everyone, in fact, was moving. The off-loaders fled every which way as law enforcement of all stripes descended on West Bank plantation. Federal, state, and local police were arriving en masse. The masked man in the skiff took off by water. Others ran through the woods, including Ray Zeman and Jay Hoffman, both men dripping wet from wading in the water an hour earlier and unloading the skiff. At daybreak the pair ran back to the white vans in the clearing and changed into dry clothes. They returned to the woods and soon met with friends Mike Abell and Bob Roche. Roche decided to try to make it on his own, splitting from the group.

Law enforcement officers started gathering around the red van stuck in the ditch. The men milled about casually when Clark Settles, the Customs Patrol chief for the Carolinas, arrived on the scene. Moments before, an officer unleashing bloodhounds had asked the men to stick close to the van, or else risk erasing the fleeing smugglers' scent trails. Nonetheless, Settles was not pleased to see them standing around like sitting ducks.

His mind flashed back to a bust he worked years ago in the Florida Keys. There he and other officers relaxed around an abandoned van, oblivious to a smuggler with a shotgun sitting twenty-five feet away in tall grass. Fortunately the man did not blast away. Settles had always been thankful to walk away from that scene with his life.

"We can't do this," Settles told the men. "I've been through this before. We need to secure the area."

As the men scattered to look for suspects, Settles racked his shotgun.

"There are two sounds any man understands," Settles later explained. "One of them's a rattlesnake . . . the other's a pump shotgun being racked. Both of them will stand the hairs on your head up."

The shotgun was part of a barrage of sounds assaulting the smugglers' ears, making their hearts beat faster. The on-the-run smugglers could hear the crunching of leaves and twigs under police boots, barking hounds, chopping helicopter rotors, and the drone of an air-plane. Ace pilot Sonny Huggins of the State Law Enforcement Division had been called in to help with his eyes in the sky. Officers joked that Huggins was afraid of heights, because he never seemed to fly above one hundred feet.

Soon Huggins was on the radio, telling officers on the ground he had spotted a man in a bean field, lying close to the red van. Officers combed the rows of three-foot-tall plants until one policeman stumbled over a prostrate York.

Officers also arrested Roche when hounds picked up his trail. Martin, the man in the ski mask who sped off in the skiff, was arrested after he crashed his boat on a sandbar. And Customs officer Dean Patterson arrested a man leaving West Bank in a brown Pontiac. The man said he was from Miami and struggled to tell Patterson exactly why he was in South Carolina bean fields at seven o'clock in the morning. Patterson found a handgun on the passenger seat and crack cocaine in the man's pocket—the first time he had seen the drug.

Officers had also found the deserted white vans parked in the clearing. They took photographs of the hashish and groceries packed inside. McDonald arrived on the scene, itching to visit the cottage a half-mile away and see who might be around. Police cruisers soon were parked all over Granny's yard.

The officers found three men in the house: Skip Sanders; his brother, Johnny; and a man named David Evans from Miami. The officers, invited into the kitchen, had a barrage of questions for Sanders.

"Where were you all last night?"

"Did you notice anything unusual?"

"Why are you wet?"

"Why is there an antenna on your roof?"

"Are you aware you fit the profile of a smuggler?"

"Would you mind taking a ride with us through the farm?"

Sanders played dumb and answered their questions while trying not to incriminate himself. His grandmother vouched that the men spent the night in the house. She was puzzled why her grandsons were receiving so much attention and was clueless to the massive manhunt occurring on the other end of her large property. The officers didn't believe her or her grandson, but knew they had too little evidence to make arrests. As they continued to question the men, Granny interrupted, asking if they'd like any waffles. The officers declined.

Bustling about the crowded kitchen, confused, she and Sanders briefly bumped together. She leaned in close to whisper in his ear.

"Skipper, I tell ya one thing, that these people mean business about this DUI stuff," said Granny.

Sanders roared with laughter.

The officers were less than amused and soon left the house.

It wasn't long before they did loosen up, though. They had just made one of the largest hash seizures in the nation's history and arrested eight men. As they filled out reports at the U.S. Customs House in downtown Charleston, they made use of some of the smugglers' groceries found in the vans. While newspaper headlines announced the officers' success over the next few days, the escaped off-loaders cautiously emerged from the woods, hitching rides to Charleston and Atlanta.

As if things could not get any worse, a majority of the hash from the *Sea Scout* was still at sea, transferred to a scallop boat that was cruising up the East Coast from Virginia, its crew getting more nervous by the day. Every time they were told to bring it in, something went wrong. About twenty-five thousand pounds from the *Sea Scout* had gotten in successfully through the Chesapeake Bay, but another eighteen thousand pounds had been busted in Virginia. Now this scallop boat had thirty-seven thousand pounds, and no one was coming to get it. After ten days of sailing up the coast with it and no one able to claim it, the scallop boat crew dumped the hash overboard somewhere near Massachusetts.

So the massive hashish flotilla ended in disaster, with two boats busted, one boat at the bottom of the ocean, and more than one hundred thousand pounds, or $50 million, lost. Hash was washing ashore on New Jersey beaches, initiating a DEA investigation. South Carolina authorities were quizzing all the men they rounded up on Edisto Island. People were unhappy and looking for their money, from the

First National Bank of Chicago to those who had invested in the hash. The product that did make it in was of poor quality, derided as "camel shit." Hertzan, the owner of the *Sea Scout* and the inspiration for John Belushi's proposed *Kingpin* movie, was eventually shot dead by an unknown assailant on February 3, 1982, plugged execution-style as he entered his East Village apartment in New York. Riley was fishing, and the rest of the gentlemen smugglers were taking a breather, too, unused to failure, and unsure about their next move.

PART II:
OPERATION JACKPOT

Chapter Eight

On January 20, 1981, nine months before the bust at West Bank plantation, Ronald Reagan greeted Americans as the fortieth president of the United States. In his inaugural address from the U.S. Capitol, the former Hollywood actor and two-term California governor expressed optimism that America was on the brink of a rebirth, ready to reclaim a glory that had faded in recent decades. He declared that the country's stifling malaise, which former President Jimmy Carter had detailed eighteen months earlier in an unexpected televised address, could be overcome, and he challenged his constituency to help America regain its footing.

That same day, fifty-two American hostages were released in Iran after being held for 444 days. The Iranian hostage crisis had damaged the reputation of Carter's leadership, contributing to his defeat. Reagan also capitalized on Carter's alleged mishandling of fuel crises and a slumping economy. Americans were ready for a change, with Reagan winning the electoral votes in forty-four states. Carter, a Georgia native, fared best in the South. Although Carter lost South Carolina, Reagan's margin of victory there was less than twelve thousand votes out of nearly nine hundred thousand cast—a difference of just 1.3 percent.

The new president's folksy appeal and cowboy swagger appealed to many South Carolinians. Years later, when speaking at a fundraising luncheon for South Carolina gubernatorial candidate Carroll Campbell, he had an easy way with the crowd, boasting of his good fortune to visit South Carolina twice in two months. Then he told a joke about a Southerner outwitting a Yankee before praising the state and its people some more. Coming from the mouth of a less-talented politician, the remarks might have seemed blatantly patronizing:

> *Now, I've come to Columbia on serious business, but first I want you to know that these last couple of days we've been doing the kind of thing that I like best: getting away from Washington and*

getting out among the American people. As [White House Chief of Staff] Don Regan said to me when we got on the plane yesterday, he said, "Leaving the beltway; now we're going out where the real people are." Well, yesterday it was Texas and Florida, and Senator Paula Hawkins there. And today, it's a land of mountains and plains and broad, sandy beaches; of people who look to the future with confidence and to the past with pride. Texas and Florida were just grand, and yet nothing could be finer than to be in Carolina. And I know I shouldn't say this, but I ain't whistlin' Dixie.

Typical of their indifference to public affairs, the gentlemen smugglers seemed to pay little attention to the change in presidency. The same month Reagan entered office, Warren "Willie Frank" Steele sailed Bob "The Boss" Byers's luxury sailboat *La Cautiva* to Hilton Head and unloaded hashish at the Sawmill Creek oyster factory. If the gentlemen smugglers had ever taken a break from tossing bales and paid closer attention to Reagan's rhetoric, they might have found some of it alarming. While campaigning for the White House, Reagan appealed to conservative voters in part by demonizing drugs, especially marijuana. Reagan had put fellow Republicans on notice: We need to toughen anti-drug law enforcement in the Unites States.

Seizing on that crime-fighting momentum, U.S. Senator Strom Thurmond nominated thirty-three-year-old Henry Dargan McMaster to become South Carolina's U.S. attorney just days after Reagan's inauguration. The Columbia lawyer had worked for the senator as a legislative aide for nearly a year after graduating from the University of South Carolina School of Law in 1973. After that stint in Washington, McMaster moved back to South Carolina, working alongside his father in the law firm of Tompkins and McMaster. Upon his nomination, McMaster echoed Reagan and wasted little time in outlining a change in direction for the office, declaring his intention to curb drug smuggling into South Carolina.

"The drug problem is an insidious one that causes problems in the schools and destroys families," said McMaster. "It's a terrible thing and I'm going to do everything I can to solve that problem."

Since Thurmond was chairman of the U.S. Senate's Judiciary Committee, there was little doubt McMaster would be confirmed by the Senate. The selection of McMaster found local support, too, from the editorial board of Columbia's the *State* newspaper, which praised the choice of the "tall, personable" and "bright and hard-working young lawyer" with strong familial and professional ties to the state of South Carolina.

"Mr. McMaster has the credentials and the potential to be a first-rate and, we trust, nonpartisan chief federal prosecutor for South Carolina," said the *State*. "Although Mr. McMaster has limited criminal law experience, we are confident that he will carry forward the forceful tradition of some of his able predecessors."

McMaster was to replace forty-nine-year-old Thomas E. Lydon Jr., an energetic prosecutor appointed by Carter who prioritized the prosecution of white-collar crimes and political corruption during his tenure as South Carolina's U.S. attorney. Lydon pledged to help McMaster make a smooth transition into the U.S. attorney's office, but suddenly collapsed and died of an apparent heart attack on February 21, 1981, while vacationing on the island of St. Martin. As McMaster waited to be confirmed, an assistant prosecutor served as interim U.S. attorney. Meanwhile, he gave interviews, including one with reporter Holly Gatling of the *State* where he spoke of his conviction that local drug smuggling could be curtailed. He also revealed a softer side, speaking with Gatling, a fellow animal lover, about a dog his family owned and how striking animals' intelligence can be. The conversation endeared the reporter to McMaster, and he soon asked for her assistance. He needed help coining a name for a drug sting he was planning. Gatling, drawing on recent headline-writing experience, suggested "Jackpot."

"Jack for money, pot for drugs," she explained.

McMaster liked it. Gatling wrapped up the interview and wrote an article about the young politician, describing how, in his office, McMaster "stretched his long, well-jogged legs and cast a thoughtful, brown-eyed glance at the ceiling." McMaster, she added, has "an accent blending the most genteel of Southern tongues," and his "South Carolina roots run as deep as the Pee Dee River."

Some found the article a bit fawning. Soon after its publication, Gatling's mother, who held a doctorate in comparative literature, called to tell her daughter that she bet "Mrs. McMaster was very pleased with that article."

If McMaster's brown eyes, curly locks, trim build, easy smile, and thick Southern accent endeared him to a certain population, his tough talk on crime appealed to those unmoved by his youthful looks and personality. His attitude toward criminals was straightforward: "If you break the law, you ought to be punished." His public comments made clear he intended to vigorously prosecute anyone who dared cross Uncle Sam.

"Violent crime offends me more than white-collar crime, but I wouldn't lessen the effort being spent on white-collar crime. White-collar criminals ought to be in jail along with bank robbers and murderers," said McMaster. "When I hear somebody say, 'Please don't send him to prison—it's such a terrible place,' I turn a deaf ear. The idea of somebody stealing something makes me furious."

Drugs, in particular, riled the lawyer. For McMaster, drugs were at the root of nearly all major crimes, as he painstakingly explained in an interview for the July 1985 issue of the *Carolana Magazine*.

Some people don't think we, as a society, really have a drug problem. They say that if a grown man wants to ruin his health with drugs, that's his problem, not ours. But that is wrong, and here's why: If you've ever known a lady who has been knocked down and had her pocketbook yanked off her arm in a grocery store parking lot, then we've got a drug problem. Why? Because that thief was probably looking for money to buy drugs with. If you know someone who returned home to find their house ransacked—the television gone, silverware gone, stereo gone, jewelry gone—then we've got a drug problem. Why? Because the thief was probably stealing something to sell so he could get money to support his drug habit.

For the same reason, if you know someone who has had their car window bashed in and things stolen out of the car, we've got a drug problem. If you know a child who all of a sudden in school seems to have drifted away, who is not interested in the usual things anymore, who has lost his or her natural curiosity and energy, then we've got a drug problem. Why? Because that child has probably been talked into taking some sort of drug by his friends. And finally, if you know someone who has been raped, beaten or murdered, usually by one or more strong, young men, then we've got a drug problem. Why? Because if you follow those stories in the news long enough, you will usually learn that the attackers almost always were on some sort of drug. It might be cocaine, heroin, or marijuana and corn liquor, but it's always something. Those are the plain facts that any lawman in the state will tell you.

On May 21, 1981, the Senate confirmed McMaster as the U.S. attorney for the District of South Carolina, making him Reagan's first appointee as U.S. attorney. On June 5, 1981, McMaster stood with his blond and beautiful wife, Peggy, and father, John Gregg McMaster Jr., as he was sworn in at the federal courthouse in Columbia. More than six hundred people listened to Thurmond speak of his nominee, calling him a compassionate man capable of fearlessly prosecuting the guilty. Moreover, he does not "fail to see the forest," said Thurmond. "He is not obstructed by the trees."

For his part McMaster said he felt everyone has a civic duty, and that as the state's top federal prosecutor he could significantly do a lot of good for South Carolina.

"Some people may think that's corny," he said, "but that's how I really feel."

Whether he realized it or not, McMaster's pledge to combat drug smuggling in the state would pit him against some familiar faces. At the University of South Carolina School of Law, he graduated with Tom "Rolex" Rhoad. As an undergraduate history student and Kappa Alpha fraternity brother at the University of South Carolina, McMaster's peers in the Greek system included Lee Harvey and Les Riley, who were both members of Sigma Alpha Epsilon. Riley, in fact, had known McMaster since he was a kid growing up in Columbia, seeing him at a country club or around town, almost always hanging out with the same two buddies. Riley's father, the furniture-chain executive, spoke well of McMaster's father, too. Riley's acquaintance with McMaster and their mutual friends would have little bearing, however, on McMaster's upcoming assault on drug smuggling in South Carolina and his plans to enlist the help of a number of the twenty-two lawyers and fifty-five staff members under his control in the U.S. attorney's office.

The same year McMaster became U.S. attorney, a veteran IRS investigator from Los Angeles named Brian T. Wellesley became chief of criminal investigations for the IRS in North Carolina and South Carolina. Knowing the new U.S. attorney's desire to nab drug kingpins, Wellesley mentioned to McMaster how federal authorities in Southern California recently used an innovative approach to capture elusive drug criminals, creating task forces composed of investigators from a variety of federal agencies, each bringing unique expertise to the team. Just as important, Wellesley told McMaster, were financial investigations by the task forces that identified suspects through the discovery of large unexplained incomes and the purchase of expensive assets. Tax evasion cases had been used to nab well-known but slippery organized crime figures before, most famously against the Prohibition-era gangster Al Capone. But in this new strategy, the financial investigation was as critical to finding faceless suspects as it was to collaring them. One of the most successful cases made through this approach was the conviction of California heroin kingpin Jaime Araujo.

Authorities in California first got wind of possible impropriety regarding Araujo in October 1977, when a customs agent working in a currency analysis unit in Washington noticed a small bank in San Ysidro, California, reporting regular deposits of more than $300,000 to a customer's account. Scrutinizing the bank's records, the agent discovered that nearly $1.5 million had been deposited into the account in two months. Further investigation revealed the customer was said to be a Mexican architect in nearby Tijuana named Pedro De La Cruz-Alvarez. In the sixteen months the architect had the account, investigators discovered more than $13 million had been deposited, each chunk delivered to the bank via an associate of the architect, the cash packed into cardboard boxes. Yet, upon searching, Customs agents could not find any architect in Mexico or the United States by the customer's name.

Investigators determined that before being deposited, the money was being picked up at a home in Bonita, California, outside San Diego. For the next year a team of Customs and DEA agents followed the comings and goings from the house, identifying a group of suspects who transferred money and drugs, mostly cocaine and heroin, between Southern California residences. Agents placed a surveillance camera in a doghouse on property neighboring the Bonita home, obtained wiretaps, and eventually identified Araujo as the mysterious architect. But while the government had evidence that tied Araujo to narcotics trafficking and the massive currency transactions, it was weak and indirect. Araujo went to great lengths to insulate himself from the drugs and money. After a year's worth of work, the investigation lost steam and was in danger of being abandoned as agents focused on more promising leads.

Salvation came in the form of IRS agents. A year into the sputtering investigation, more than twenty agents began interviewing witnesses and served more than three hundred grand jury subpoenas to banks, car dealers, real estate agents, travel agencies, and others as they ferreted out information on Araujo, detailing his purchases of automobiles and real estate in recent years. Investigators also obtained Araujo's bank records from Mexico and established that money being deposited in the San Ysidro bank was often transferred to a Mexican bank before being sent back to the United States for real estate purchases. With this money laundering evidence and the other financial information, the government was able to strengthen their case against Araujo and his criminal network, indicting the kingpin for drug and income tax evasion charges. Araujo pleaded guilty and was sentenced in November 1979 to thirty-five years in prison and ordered to pay a $1.2 million fine—the largest income tax evasion fine in U.S. history.

Wellesley suggested to McMaster that a similar multi-agency financial investigation might be successful in South Carolina and the perfect way to catch elusive drug smugglers. McMaster latched onto the idea immediately and convened a meeting between himself and the U.S. attorneys in North Carolina, inviting experts to explain the mechanics of a financial investigation. He advised his North Carolina counterparts that it was a technique he would try.

McMaster soon planned another meeting, inviting the assorted local supervisors of federal law enforcement agencies. He asked them to send a representative to Columbia for a conference about investigating drug trafficking in the state.

Wellesley appreciated McMaster's earnest initiative, but he cautioned his new friend that his audience would likely be reluctant to participate, unwilling to cede control of manpower to a prosecutor's office and unwilling to share informants and information with other agencies. Additionally there was the issue of sharing credit for any successes. Wellesley advised McMaster to emphasize that with a big case, every agency could reap rewards. For example, uncovering a drug smuggling conspiracy might yield income tax evasion charges for the IRS, racketeering charges for the FBI, drug seizures for the DEA, *and* large currency violations for U.S. Customs.

The South Carolina supervisors accepted McMaster's invitation, either showing up themselves at the U.S. attorney's office in Columbia or sending a subordinate in their place. Driving up from Charleston came Special Agent Claude McDonald, representing U.S. Customs. From the IRS came Special Agent David Forbes. Along with representatives from the DEA and other federal offices, they gathered in the U.S. attorney's downtown office in an old federal courthouse on Laurel Street, wondering exactly what the newly appointed McMaster wanted them to do. Little did McDonald and Forbes know they would be given an assignment that would last the next four years.

It was no accident that Forbes and McDonald were chosen to attend the meeting. After Wellesley had introduced the financial task force concept to McMaster, he began perusing his personnel records, working late in his office in Greensboro, North Carolina, trying to identify candidates among his eighty or so staff members who could lead this type of investigation. Few names jumped to the top of the list. Many IRS investigators, Wellesley says, were content to make routine tax cases. Only a handful possessed enough ambition to tackle more complicated cases in which tax evasion would be among the least offensive of a suspect's crimes.

To sniff out sophisticated criminals and their hidden fortunes, "You have to have a very special agent," says Wellesley. "The agent has to be very, very creative."

Frustrated with the shortage of intrepid investigators, his mind turned to Forbes, whom someone had mentioned to him as an agent with an impressive record and experience in drug-related cases. Wellesley arranged to meet with Forbes in South Carolina and explained the task force concept to him in a bar. Wellesley says Forbes was initially noncommitted, but did mention McDonald as an agent in U.S. Customs who he worked well with. Wellesley said he could direct Forbes's supervisor to shift his caseload to other agents if he participated in the task force.

At the meeting in the U.S. attorney's office, McMaster addressed the men assembled before him. It was no secret that illegal drugs were coming into South Carolina. Everyone at the table knew that, as was the case in most of the country, law enforcement was only intercepting a small percentage of the marijuana, cocaine, and heroin being smuggled into the Palmetto State. When a bust was made, they knew, too, it was only the small fish being caught. McMaster said he wanted to change that. He wanted to nab kingpins.

To do this he pointed to the new law enforcement model recently debuted in California and how agents could conduct a financial investigation of suspected drug kingpins. Instead of sitting in marshes at midnight with a nightscope trying to catch smugglers red-handed, investigators would sift through public records and build a financial case against the men. Ideally any financial crimes, such as income tax evasion, would be just the tip of the iceberg and could be used as leverage to produce additional drug-related charges and construct a history of drug-related misdeeds. The first step, in any case, would be finding out who these kingpins were.

Forbes and McDonald left the meeting scratching their heads. The proposal was certainly novel, but there were so many uncertainties surrounding its premise. First, the conventional wisdom was that the country's major drug kingpins operated out of coastal metropolises like Los Angeles, New York, and Miami, not the backwaters of South Carolina. Second, who knew if Forbes's and McDonald's bosses, as well as supervisors in the South Carolina offices of the FBI, DEA, and Customs Patrol, would even play ball with McMaster's idea? When it came to drug enforcement, each of those agencies was notorious for its competitiveness and lack of cooperation. Finally, and most perplexing to Forbes and McDonald, was the question of how to begin to find kingpins you don't even know exist.

Nonetheless, Forbes and McDonald shared McMaster's suspicion that there were homegrown crooks to find in South Carolina, even if many of their colleagues believed the smugglers they occasionally snared were part of syndicates based outside of South Carolina.

Yet the pair of agents had received enough cryptic tips over the years regarding smuggling to believe locals were sneaking tons of drugs into the state, right under their noses. But these were only suspicions, and the men lacked hard proof of local smuggling networks. Driving together soon after the meeting, Forbes and McDonald turned to each other in the car and voiced their mutual concerns: What in the world are we going to do?

"We had nothing, absolutely nothing to work on except for our memories," says McDonald. "Remembering some of the things that had been going on."

If McMaster's idea to identify and pursue drug smugglers seemed comparable to finding a needle in a haystack, it was a feat McDonald had accomplished before. He had come to Charleston to work for the Naval Investigative Service in 1967, anticipating performing background checks for the Navy and Marine Corps. Instead, McDonald's superiors noticed his aptitude for problem solving and assigned him some criminal cases to investigate. He resolved them all. His superiors were particularly impressed with his handling of a case involving the USS *Tattnall* and two other destroyers, which were docked at the Charleston Navy Base. Shortly before their planned deployment to the Mediterranean, someone called a duty officer and reported sabotage aboard one of the destroyers, prompting searches of the boats from top to bottom. No sabotage was found, but the Navy was eager to catch the hoaxster, dumping the case in the hands of McDonald and another junior agent.

McDonald's only lead was that the call was made from a Charleston pay phone. He and his partner traveled to the phone and began questioning residents in the immediate area about whom they had seen at the time the call was made. Eventually, they got a tip that a man using the phone had been picked up by a taxi. Whether or not that man was the prankster was anyone's guess.

McDonald next went to the various cab companies in Charleston and began questioning drivers. Eventually he met a cabbie who remembered picking up a man at that pay phone who looked like he was in the military and was acting strangely. Eager to make an identification, McDonald showed the cabbie the cruise books from the destroyers, which featured pictures of the crew and were similar to a high school yearbook. Out of the hundreds of sailors' photos, the cabbie picked out his passenger. McDonald interrogated the suspect, who admitted to the prank call as a way to delay his deployment so he could see his girlfriend. For his persistence McDonald received a commendation from the director of the Naval Investigative Service and was asked to continue conducting criminal investigations.

Despite his knack for detective work, McDonald's entry into law enforcement was a result of happenstance. After growing up in the small town of Portland, Tennessee, close to the Kentucky border, he attended East Tennessee State on a football scholarship, playing fullback and safety. His playing career was short-lived. During spring practice his freshman year, he tackled the second-string fullback, crashing into the fullback's knee with such force it broke McDonald's helmet apart. The collision knocked McDonald unconscious, and, after being revived with smelling salts and sitting out the rest of practice, he fainted again at dinner, prompting a visit to the hospital and a diagnosis of a bad concussion. The severity of the injury made McDonald reconsider the direction of his life. He decided to quit the team and leave school, soon getting married and working as a shipping clerk in Nashville.

By this time it was 1958, and the military draft loomed. Seeking to forge his own destiny, he enlisted in the Army before his likely draft date and was sent to basic training camp in Fort Jackson, South Carolina, and then to Fort Gordon, Georgia, for military police training. His first posting as an MP was at the Sandia Base nuclear installation outside Albuquerque. There he finished his service, earned a degree from the University of New Mexico, and became a physical education teacher. He enjoyed teaching, though the pay was paltry, forcing him to give driving lessons after hours to help support his family, which now included a baby boy. One night when he returned home, a friendly neighbor hassled him, asking him if he was going to work himself silly the rest of his life or get smart. The neighbor, an agent for the Naval Investigative Service, urged him to submit an application with his office, though he warned him he'd likely have to leave New Mexico. McDonald did, was hired, and sent to Charleston in 1967, where he made a splash investigating the supposed sabotage. He transferred to U.S. Customs in 1971 when the Naval Investigative Service proposed sending young agents onto aircraft carriers to help police the ship, taking the investigators away from their families for months at a time.

If anyone had stopped to think about it, it might have seemed odd that the two lead agents in a potentially major drug investigation were Forbes, a former CPA, and McDonald, the accidental cop who entered and excelled in law enforcement only after the intervention of a serious brain injury, the draft, a nosy neighbor, and an unsophisticated saboteur. Yet conventional law enforcement officers had failed to catch, let alone identify, South Carolina's most prominent smugglers and the worldwide drug operations they managed. Perhaps, as McMaster suggested, it would require a different approach to apprehend these elusive kingpins, whoever they were, and Forbes's and McDonald's unique backgrounds could produce the results the prosecutor demanded.

Following the meeting with McMaster, Forbes and McDonald continued to work their normal caseloads, squeezing in time to try to start the fresh smuggling case. Embracing the financial investigation approach suggested by Wellesley and McMaster, the agents began following the money, figuring that real estate agents would be the most promising interviews. Visiting a slew of coastal realty offices, they asked the same question: Have you closed any unusually large cash transactions lately?

Their questioning was a stab in the dark, though, and yielded few results. The agents were glad to keep their usual responsibilities: If they worked on looking for drug kingpins day in and day out, McDonald says, they'd be sitting around scratching their heads with nothing to do. In addition to questioning real estate agents, they reviewed old cases and tips, trying to familiarize themselves with men who had previously been partial to the excitement of pot smuggling.

The investigation gained momentum. A man named Barry Foy, one coastal developer told them, had recently paid him $90,000 in cash for some land through a corporation named Agora, Ltd. Foy's name jogged McDonald's memory. He seemed to remember a tip years ago about Foy smuggling Jamaican pot into the country.

At the same time, Forbes and McDonald followed up on two Beaufort County phone numbers that had been found inside a sunken sailboat suspected of being scuttled after a drug deal. The sailboat, the *Seacomber,* was found in July 1981 when a shrimper noticed a mast sticking out of the Edisto River. Had the smugglers been more competent, they would have scuttled the boat in deep water, not in a shallow section of the river—especially not in the middle of the waterway, and especially not when eight-foot tides might reveal the mast, which had been cut but was still connected to the boat by its shrouds. When the boat was pulled out of the water, investigators scoured it for clues, finding a waterlogged piece of paper in which two phone numbers were barely legible.

As Forbes and McDonald discovered, one of those numbers belonged to a young woman who suspected her roommate's boyfriend had written it down when he was potentially aboard the sailboat. Fearful of being questioned by the investigators, she asked for her father, a dock builder, to be present when they arrived. During the conversation the woman's father mentioned to Forbes and McDonald that if they were looking for smugglers, they might want to examine an exceptionally large dock built on the back side of Hilton Head in the Sea Pines neighborhood. A corporation called Bahamas Leeward, Ltd. had offered to pay him cash, he said, in exchange for building it quickly and without following the proper permitting and building code requirements. He declined the job, he said, because something about the request smelled fishy.

The dock builder checked his records and contacted the investigators. A man named Les Riley, he said, had asked him to build the dock. Forbes recalled the tip he received years ago regarding Riley and two Mercedes automobiles: "He's living high on the hog down here and doesn't seem to have a job."

Excited to have received these leads, Forbes and McDonald started pulling deeds and tax records at coastal courthouses for property in the name of Bahamas Leeward, Ltd. and Agora, Ltd. They discovered a number of properties, and a pattern: A majority of the records listed real estate agent Wally Butler and lawyer Andy Pracht. They confronted Pracht, but he was evasive and nervous, refusing to cooperate with the investigators. Nonetheless, Forbes and McDonald knew they had made a breakthrough. They drove to Columbia and met again with McMaster, updating him on their progress. We need help, they told him.

Encouraged by Forbes and McDonald's progress, McMaster persuaded agencies to help establish a formal task force in the spring of 1982. An office was cleared for the agents on the third floor of the U.S. Custom House in downtown Charleston, and the IRS and U.S.

Customs agreed to allow Forbes and McDonald to work on the drug investigation full-time. McMaster also secured the help of three other full-time agents: Mark Goodwin of the FBI, Dewey Greager of the DEA, and Mike Lemnah of U.S. Customs Patrol. An assistant U.S. attorney, it was decided, would coordinate the task force.

There was little fanfare regarding the start of the investigation, and no press releases; those would come later. Within the DEA, FBI, and other agencies, information regarding Operation Jackpot was on a need-to-know basis. The task force agents, however, were not shy about introducing themselves to potential suspects and their associates, knocking on doors, asking them questions, and, if necessary, advising them to get a lawyer. The tactics flew in the face of conventional drug enforcement techniques, which relied heavily on stakeouts, undercover agents, and electronic surveillance.

"We threw out the damn book and decided to be innovative. We weren't covert at all," says Forbes. "We flashed our badges in their faces and said, 'Here we are.'"

Among the first to cooperate with the government was fireman Hank Strickland, who acted as a caretaker of Riley's property, supplied Riley with local law enforcement radio codes, and operated communications equipment during drug off-loads. After hearing that the investigators were making inquiries about the Rileys, Strickland's ex-wife, who had babysat for the couple, shared information with Forbes regarding her ex-husband's participation, including the fact that he kept radio equipment in a locker behind a couch. In the locker, she said, she'd also seen $10,000 cash and a brick of hashish. Forbes and his colleagues paid Strickland a visit at his home, intimating that they knew all about his misdeeds and it was time to 'fess up.

"Before we left his house, I said, 'By the way, Hank, those radios in that footlocker are evidence,'" says Forbes. "He was white as a sheet. He didn't know what to do."

Soon thereafter, an attorney hired by Strickland negotiated a deal: information in exchange for lenient punishment. The government cut a similar deal with suspect Wayne McDonald, a friend of Riley who worked for the kingpin as a money courier and caretaker. Suddenly, with these men's and others' cooperation, the agents were given a glimpse into a world they only guessed had existed. The amount of money and drugs discussed by Strickland, McDonald, and others was staggering. Furthermore, given the limited role Strickland and McDonald had in the smuggling organizations, the agents knew they were only scratching the surface.

After talking with Strickland, the task force had enough information to obtain a search warrant for the law office of Pracht, the man whose name appeared on records for both Riley and Foy and their offshore corporations. As investigators raided his office, Pracht cooperated, helping agents map out his clients' property holdings.

Forbes began working longer hours, trying to organize the flood of information the task force was receiving. He and the other agents started creating files for each person they interviewed. It was an archive that would soon be hundreds of folders thick. Forbes took on a coordinating role among the agents, and some of his colleagues and a few assistant U.S. attorneys nicknamed him "Captain America" for his devotion to sorting out the leads and assembling a case. Forbes considered the case a puzzle, and it could be exasperating trying to piece it all together.

"I had a tiger by the tail," says Forbes, "and I said, uh, I ain't turning this thing loose. I got something here. I ain't too sure what, but I got it."

Despite the investigation's fast start and McMaster's success in obtaining five full-time agents for the task force, obstacles regularly threatened to derail Operation Jackpot, or at least significantly stall it. One of the biggest hurdles the task force faced was achieving cooperation among its own members. Despite each man's personal commitment to teamwork, the task force was routinely hampered by protocol differences between the various federal law enforcement agencies and the tendencies of each agency to hoard information rather than share it. The investigators were often torn between loyalties to the task force and their home agency.

Historically there had been little sharing of information between the FBI and DEA, and each was used to being in charge of investigations. When it came to the IRS, past tax investigations by the agency had been politicized. When these scandals came to light, the IRS was restricted from sharing much information with other law enforcement agencies in an effort to reduce abuse of the agency's deep-reaching powers.

Lemnah, the task force agent assigned from the U.S. Customs Patrol, remembers having frustrating discussions about the case with Goodwin, the investigator assigned from the FBI.

"I can't believe you're telling me this," Goodwin told his colleagues, "because I can't tell you anything."

"Then you can't be part of the task force, because we share," was Lemnah's and the others' consistent reply.

Eventually each of the men conceded that the walls between the agencies were hindering the investigation. Their jobs protected, to some extent, by the autonomous structure of the task force, they began pooling information and sharing old tips and files collected by their home agencies, even if it didn't sit well with superiors. Lemnah was happy to see Goodwin embrace the task force wholeheartedly.

"Mark was kind of a new breed and a refreshing breed," says Lemnah. "I'm sure he took some flak over it, but he still did it."

Another annoyance was the issue of paperwork. Proper documentation of debriefings and interviews was critical to the investigation. Initially this paperwork was essential to understanding the scope of the smuggling networks. Ultimately the agents knew the documentation of their investigation would be important in the courtroom as evidence. Among the five agencies represented on the task force, there were a handful of different forms used to make reports, and, of course, each agent was partial to the one he was accustomed to using. The solution, Lemnah says, was to type up reports on sheets of blank white paper. That idea, he says, took six months to initiate.

"It sounds simple but it was a big thing back then," says Lemnah. "I think every agency had heartburn over that one."

Overseeing the effort was Wells Dickson, an assistant U.S. attorney who considered himself the secretary for the task force, keeping the paperwork straight and the agents engaged. He'd receive calls all day from agents in the field, hearing reports of whom they talked to and what they said.

"You'd get a call. We talked to somebody in Beaufort, we talked to somebody in Myrtle Beach, we talked to somebody in Greenville," says Dickson. "It was that kind of a situation."

⌒〜∧〜⌒

Outside of the office the agents were dismayed to be occasionally stonewalled by potential witnesses and suspects. Despite its promise the investigation was fragile, and the top suspects, Foy and Riley, were nowhere to be found. In fact, people the government interviewed had not seen them for months, if not years.

In September 1982 Forbes, McDonald, and one other agent visited the half-finished home of Jimmy MacNeal, a carpenter who had participated in a number of smuggling ventures in South Carolina. MacNeal was helping his neighbor move furniture when the agents arrived. They asked MacNeal to step into his own yard for a minute, then tried to get him to come in to Charleston's Custom House and make a formal statement to the government. They had talked to his old girlfriends, they told him, and it would be a good idea for him to cooperate. They weren't after the little guys, the agents said, but instead the kingpins, including Foy and Riley. MacNeal wasn't biting.

Walking around the house, one agent then remarked, "Gee, this is a big house. How many feet is it?"

MacNeal told him: eighteen hundred square feet.

Looks bigger, the agent said. How much money you got in it, the agent asked. Is that dock on deepwater?

MacNeal said he wasn't sure what the agent was implying, and that he would not be interviewed in his backyard. The agents left, but not before offering more advice.

"Get a lawyer," they told MacNeal, "but don't go see Andy Pracht."

Another time, Forbes recalls looking over the flight records of Harvey Hop, owner of charter jet service Hop-A-Jet, and seeing landings in Savannah, Georgia, but no passenger lists. When asked about the passengers traveling to and from Savannah, Hop, who was not required to keep passenger records, would not disclose his clients' names. This upset Forbes and the other agents.

"He knew, but he wouldn't tell us," says Forbes. "Asshole."

Subsequently, Forbes put Hop on a list of suspicious people. It was a lawful maneuver, he says, and one guaranteed to cause extra scrutiny of Hop's comings and goings.

A young Barry Foy in the Florida Keys, just as his smuggling career is taking off in the early 1970s. *Courtesy of Barry Foy*

Les Riley in his hippie days. *Courtesy of Les Riley*

Smugglers and friends relaxing at the docks, including Ashley Brunson, center, Les Riley, far right, and Jesse the black lab. *Courtesy of Les Riley*

Smuggler Ken Smith. *Courtesy of Ken Smith*

Les Riley and Barry Foy compete in a South Carolina fishing tournament. Foy is holding a baggie.

Barry Foy, Les Riley, and Wally Butler with a day's worth of king mackerel. *Courtesy of Les Riley*

Bob "The Boss" Byers's luxury sail-boat, *La Cautiva*, moored off Antigua.

Barry Foy's girlfriend and eventual wife, Jan Liafsha, in Ocho Rios, Jamaica. *Courtesy of Barry Foy*

Les Riley with his daughter, Leah. *Courtesy of Les Riley*

Les Riley, daughter Leah, and friends enjoying a "hat party" on the beach of Hilton Head Island, South Carolina. *Courtesy of Les Riley*

Ashley Brunson, Bruce MacDougall, and Les Riley celebrate Brunson catching an 1,100-pound black marlin off Australia's Great Barrier Reef in October 1980. *Courtesy of Les Riley*

Bruce MacDougall and Les Riley enjoying a day on the water. *Courtesy of Les Riley*

Barry Foy on St. Barts, walking on the beach along St. Jean Bay. *Courtesy of Barry Foy*

Barry Foy, far left, and Tom Rhoad, third from right, standing on a tarmac after traveling by private plane to Nantucket, Massachusetts. *Courtesy of Barry Foy*

The Operation Jackpot task force in front of the U.S. attorney's office in Columbia, South Carolina. From left to right, Dewey Greager (DEA), Mark Goodwin (FBI), U.S. Attorney Henry Dargan McMaster, Mike Lemnah (U.S. Customs Patrol), Brian Tim Wellesley (IRS), Claude McDonald (U.S. Customs), and David Forbes (IRS).

IRS special agents Edward Skowyz and David Forbes listen to Assistant U.S. Attorney Bart Daniel in the U.S. Custom House in Charleston, South Carolina. *Courtesy of* The Citadel Alumni News

U.S. District Court Judge Falcon B. Hawkins Jr. *Courtesy of* The Citadel Alumni News

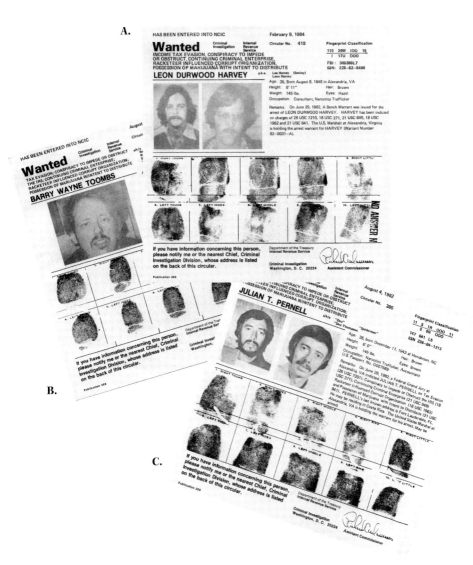

A. Wanted poster of Lee Harvey, a.k.a. "Smiley."
B. Wanted poster of Barry Toombs, a.k.a. "Ice Cream."
C. Wanted poster of Julian T. Pernell, a.k.a. "Doc."

"We probably made his life miserable," says Forbes. "You want to fuck with us? Fine. You're on a hit list."

Other men tried to casually dismiss the investigator's inquiries. In a letter to Forbes, Butler said he was overwhelmed by recent events in life, including Forbes's questioning, an imperiled engagement to be married, and separate legal matters.

"The pressure is frankly a little too much and too rushed and all at one time," Butler wrote. " . . . Becca and I are going to take a trip (maybe Honeymoon) and when I get back I'll be happy to answer any additional questions you or anybody else have."

Despite these difficulties, the task force was slowly building a massive case, requiring close cooperation with a growing number of assistant U.S. attorneys in Columbia and Charleston. These deputy prosecutors helped give direction to the case and assigned work to appropriate task force agents. The investigators kept returning with more and more leads.

"We all had different skills, and they just blended to make dynamite," says Forbes. "I knew the financial end of things, and how to follow the paper trails that don't lie. Claude remembered everything he ever knew, and every name he ever heard. He was able to make links that didn't occur to the rest of us.

"Dewey had a lot of experience in DEA putting together evidence on conspiracies, and he knew how to tie up all those loose ends. [Mark] was our best interviewer. He had a knack of making people think he already knew, so they might as well just tell us their side, when the truth was, we were making a lot of good guesses and fitting together a lot of pieces of information like a jigsaw puzzle.

"Lemnah was the one who pursued the civil forfeitures. He'd spend hours at a time tracing one car or one piece of property."

It was this action, the seizure of property suspected of being purchased with drug proceeds, that brought the task force to the attention of the public and helped spook a host of smugglers who had been lying low since catching wind of the investigation. For example, on October 4, 1982, federal agents seized property in downtown Charleston that was home to the fashionable restaurant 82 Queen. Assistant U.S. Attorney Bart Daniel described this seizure "as the shot heard round the world in our line of work," and the press paid attention. After the seizure of 82 Queen, the Charleston newspapers wrote some of their first stories on the mysterious drug investigation, noting that besides the restaurant, the government had previously seized a home from Riley, more than $344,000 of his money held in an escrow account, and two lots on Hilton Head owned by Butler. The value of these properties and cash was estimated to be more than $750,000. Prosecutors, including McMaster, declined to comment extensively on the seizures, though the paper reported some details of Riley's alleged smuggling that it found in court filings.

Since 1970 the government had the power to seize property like 82 Queen if it was suspected of being bought with drug proceeds, but only after a suspect was convicted as a drug kingpin. In 1978, however, a new law amended the government's civil forfeiture provision, allowing for property to be seized from drug suspects before, or even without, their criminal conviction. If a defendant wanted to challenge the government and reclaim the property, he would have to respond to government questioning, submit tax records, and reveal other sensitive and potentially incriminating information.

Because the facts were rarely on their side, and because drug suspects were fearful of goading the government and risking potential arrest should there be a related ongoing criminal investigation, the civil forfeitures were rarely challenged. Despite its power, though, the new law was not well-known among federal prosecutors and was used sparingly in the first three years since its passage. In South Carolina federal prosecutors had little, if any, experience with civil forfeitures. These types of seizures were so rarely made, in fact, that when Forbes and McDonald suggested this law be used as part of their investigation, Daniel initially dismissed the idea and turned them away.

"I wish it could be written that I enthusiastically endorsed their cause. Such was not the case," says Daniel. "However, their persistence paid off. I soon realized that the only hope for an end to their daily procession to my office would be to learn as much as possible about these civil forfeitures and convince them of the obvious: It could not be done. Surprisingly, I learned that such proceedings were possible but not commonplace."

It did not take long for Daniel and his fellow prosecutors to embrace the tactic, working with investigators to identify the best assets to try to seize. For their part, the agents on the task force were eager to launch a first assault against the suspects, especially the ones who were nowhere to be found. Ideally the seizure of homes, cash, and vehicles would hamper the smugglers, as well as strip them of illegally gained assets.

"The whole concept was not only to put them in jail," says Lemnah, the agent specializing in the seizures, "but to put them in jail broke."

After the initial wave of civil forfeitures, more followed. Two weeks after taking 82 Queen, the government seized land from Riley on Hilton Head, as well as a classic 1960 Mercedes 220SE automobile. After that the government seized cash belonging to Rhoad and two lots outside Charleston on the Intracoastal Waterway owned by the wife of Roy Riley. By the end of 1982, the government possessed a $160,000 certificate of deposit belonging to the Riley brothers from a safe deposit box in the Bahamas.

Daniel describes the office as moving faster than the speed of light during the end of 1982, seizing property right and left. By mid-December the drug investigation was identified in Charleston's *News & Courier* for the first time as "Operation Jack Pot." Later newspaper accounts would discard that spelling in favor of one word, Jackpot. Strangely, these news accounts reported, despite seizures of more than $2 million in cash, coastal land, and a fancy car, no criminal charges had been filed. What's more, the owners of all this property could not be found, not by reporters or, apparently, by the federal government. For the moment that didn't matter. Operation Jackpot was turning heads. As *Miami Herald* reporter Carl Hiaasen would later write, "The U.S. government is snatching up prime property in a campaign to bankrupt smugglers by taking their real estate—lock, stock and mortgage.

"Perhaps no single investigation has prospered so handsomely from real estate forfeiture," Hiaasen wrote, "as Operation Jackpot."

Chapter Nine

Virginia, the slogan goes, is for lovers.

To the dismay of federal agents, Old Dominion was also quite the place for marijuana smugglers, as proved by the regularity of drug busts around the Chesapeake Bay and on rural Virginia airstrips. DEA agent Jim Mittica was convinced Barry "Ice Cream" Toombs was behind a good portion of the smuggling, but lacked proof. He and others began an investigation in 1980 into Toombs, working out of a basement in Old Town Alexandria. For months Mittica pieced together clues regarding Toombs and other suspected marijuana smugglers, combing through phone records and collecting information found on scraps of paper left behind in an abandoned sailboat, aboard a pot-laden plane, and tossed from the cab of a marijuana-crammed camper truck.

To Mittica's satisfaction the notes all contained phone numbers belonging to Julian "Doc" Pernell, who had had been arrested with Toombs and Lee Harvey in Georgia in 1978. Other clues looped in Toombs. Mittica brought his findings to Assistant U.S. Attorney Karen Tandy, who, like her peer Bart Daniel in South Carolina, was initially underwhelmed.

"It was the hardest kind of [drug] case," said Tandy. "We had no undercover agent [inside the suspected ring], no informer, no one close to the group who could confirm our intelligence. It took [Mittica] three to six months to get me moving on the case, the outlook was so bleak."

Nevertheless Mittica and other police persisted. In the summer of 1980, Pernell and an associate of Harvey were seen, separately, leaving Washington, D.C. in chartered jets bound for the Bahamas. They carried a lot of luggage, but planned to return the same day. Agents suspected the men were leaving the country with bundles of cash, and they soon recruited IRS criminal investigator Patrick Lance Lydon to join their investigation. With Lydon's help investigator's zeroed in on Harvey, Pernell, and Toombs and discovered that drug proceeds were being laundered through the Caribbean and being returned to the United States for investment in legitimate businesses. By this point Tandy was interested, and Mittica and Lydon credit her with working tirelessly to lead the case, often staying in her office into the wee hours of the night. Although not even thirty years old, Tandy had a reputation for being tough. Colleagues said it was not unusual to see the tall Texan dress down an agent or subordinate if she was not pleased with his performance. She was also renowned for trying to use innovative legal strategies to the government's advantage, including the use of forfeiture law.

"She wasn't afraid to do anything," says Lydon. "She came up with an idea to do something . . . [and her logic was] nobody's ever done it before, so how will they know if we made a mistake?"

Tandy's aggressive tactics energized Lydon, Mittica, and the other young investigators working the case. Lydon says Tandy's intelligence and fearlessness contributed to a camaraderie in the office that was hard to beat. Most of the people working the case, he says, were in their late twenties or early thirties and "liked to win." They were convinced their savvy targets could be defeated.

"It was cowboys and Indians," says Lydon. "Bad guys versus good guys."

As innovative as Tandy and her cowboys were, they still had to present their cases to a grand jury, the groups of sixteen to twenty-three people who could review evidence for each case and listen to testimony subpoenaed by prosecutors before deciding if there was sufficient cause to charge suspects through an indictment. Judges, defense lawyers, and the general public are not privy to grand jury proceedings, which usually take place in a courthouse, behind closed doors. Presided over by prosecutors, grand juries do not render a verdict, but rather decide whether or not to grant approval for prosecutors to bring federal felony charges against a suspect. Unlike a trial, witnesses who appear before a grand jury are not protected by the Fifth Amendment and cannot refuse to testify without running the risk of punishment.

By February 1981, the government felt it had enough evidence to convene a grand jury in Alexandria, and began to introduce evidence of drug and tax crimes allegedly committed by Lee Harvey and his brother Michael. Not long afterward the government presented a separate set of evidence, again implicating the Harvey brothers, along with Toombs, Pernell, and others.

When presenting evidence to the grand jury in Alexandria, the government's challenge in proving the Harvey brothers' wrongdoing was considerable. From the start of the grand jury, prosecutors encountered resistance and endured obstinate witnesses. Outside the grand jury room, they fended off legal challenges from lawyers hired by the Harveys, including attempts to prevent the testimony of their mother and Lee's new wife, Havens Anthony, whom Lee had married weeks earlier. The government suspected the marriage was prompted by a subpoena for Anthony to testify in front of the grand jury, and that she would attempt to invoke a privilege in which she did not have to testify against a spouse. The government was quick to note that this privilege only shielded a spouse from disclosing communications that occurred during marriage, not beforehand.

In any case, this technicality didn't really matter. Lee's wife was not going to cooperate, no matter the subpoena. She came to the grand jury room "dressed to the nines," says Lydon, but didn't say much of anything. The Harvey boys' mother, he adds, was "really just a nice old lady" and was unaware of the details of her sons' criminal actions. At some point the potential yield from these two witnesses was judged not to be worth the trouble of protracting their testimony.

To complicate matters further, two other witnesses, including Kenny O'Day, refused to testify altogether, despite being offered immunity from prosecutors. A judge jailed O'Day for contempt in October 1981. Additionally, investigators had little faith there was any single witness who could relate a detailed account of Lee's criminal acts. Lee was extremely careful to divide jobs among accomplices so that few would understand the big picture. Even among his brothers, Lydon says, Lee could be mysterious. He didn't seem to trust anybody.

While investigating Lee's finances, Lydon learned firsthand how the alleged kingpin safeguarded his money, discovering an array of offshore corporations that held titles to his properties. He also found bank accounts in the Bahamas, Cayman Islands, Liechtenstein, Netherlands Antilles, and Switzerland. On Harvey's most recent tax return, however, none of these assets were reflected. Instead, just a small income was reported, allegedly earned at the family gas station.

"We really had to work hard to scrape up some good stuff on Lee in terms of net worth and expenditures . . . he was a very slick guy," says Lydon. "I would bet that he had a shitload more assets and investments than we ever found."

One valuable asset the government did find—and seized—in November 1981, almost a year before the Operation Jackpot seizures, was Lee's old farmhouse and ten acres of hilltop property on Burgundy Road in Alexandria. Lee had built a swimming pool near the house, and, during one winter, he had a dome inflated around the pool and heated the inside. From nearby Interstate 95, Lydon says, one could look up the hillside and see the glowing dome, which resembled a football cut in half.

More valuable, however, was a collection of Louis Comfort Tiffany lamps and glassware owned by Toombs that the government found in a New Jersey warehouse. Believed to be the largest collection of Tiffany glassware in the world, Toombs had purchased the art in 1977 for $550,000 from an elderly Armenian immigrant in New York City. During interviews with suspected smugglers, government agents had frequently heard mention of Toombs's extensive lamp collection and his self-taught antiques expertise, but no one seemed to know where the lamps were or how Toombs had acquired them.

Frustrated by the missing glassware, Lydon finally sent two agents to visit antiques shops in midtown Manhattan, approaching dealers with a picture of Toombs and asking if they'd sold him any lamps. After dozens of shop visits, they finally got a break and found the previous owner of the lamps, Mardiros Krikorian, who confirmed the sale. Krikorian told agents he had known Tiffany, the son of jeweler Charles Lewis Tiffany, personally in the early 1900s and would buy a piece or two at a time with earnings made from his job as a theater projectionist for Thomas Edison. Giddy with this information, and fearful that the fragile Krikorian's health could deteriorate quickly, IRS investigators soon picked Krikorian up at his apartment in New York and chauffeured him to Alexandria to testify in front of the grand jury.

Despite the few recalcitrant witnesses, on June 29, 1982, the grand jury in Alexandria indicted Lee Harvey, Michael Harvey, Pernell, Toombs, and sixteen others for participation in a smuggling ring that allegedly operated for more than nine years and netted more than $30 million in profits. All of the South Carolina kingpins, including Lee Harvey's partner, Les Riley, were spared from indictment, though some of these men were listed as unindicted coconspirators. In other words, the Virginia investigators were not unaware of the collaboration between the Virginia-based smugglers and many of the men in South Carolina, but their information against those in the Palmetto State was either not as strong or their crimes were concentrated outside of eastern Virginia. Additionally, the inclusion of too many far-flung suspects had the potential to overwhelm jurors, as well as investigators, who would be forever chasing a sprawling network of shadowy smugglers that seemed to have no end. When investigating the Harveys, Pernell, and Toombs, Lydon says he was wise to recall the advice of a veteran IRS investigator who cautioned him against chasing too many leads at the expense of resolution.

"At some point," says Lydon, repeating that advice, "you have to draw a circle around it."

Upon release of the indictment, the alleged kingpins were nowhere to be found. Despite their absence, the government persevered, seizing a number of the drug smuggling suspects' assets, including a 1949 Rolls-Royce automobile and property in Virginia and Florida. The government also subpoenaed two of the Harveys' lawyers to appear before the grand jury to testify about the fees they earned. Though a court ultimately disallowed this maneuver, it was the latest in a series of contentious exchanges between Tandy and the alleged smugglers' defense counsel. For their part, the Harvey family's lawyers had previously accused Tandy of prosecutorial misconduct in a complaint to the U.S. Department of Justice. Defense lawyers also complained that Tandy improperly shared information from the grand jury with federal agents to further their continuing investigation of Harvey. Tandy denied wrongdoing and dismissed the complaints as a "fishing expedition" by defense lawyers that aimed to "impede the grand jury investigation through the back door." An internal investigation by the Justice Department cleared her of wrongdoing, though an appeals court decision forbid her to sub-poena the defense lawyers.

Tandy's actions, of course, did not endear her to the opposing lawyers associated with the case. On being subpoenaed to testify, lawyer Bill Moffitt carefully says, "Those were not pleasant days." A colleague of Moffitt, John Zwerling, says Tandy was slick and not to be trusted. She acted like a crusader, he says, and made the cases personal. Tandy's colleagues, including Lydon and Mittica, regarded her differently.

"Karen was one of the most professional, honest, and appropri-ately aggressive prosecutors I ever worked with," says Mittica. "I never knew her to have any personal animosity against any defendants; she viewed them as violators of the laws of the United States and her job, as a representative of the United States government, required her to bring them to justice, as they say, 'without passion or prejudice.'"

One smuggler recalls very unpleasant experiences with Tandy after his arrest in which she routinely pressured him to give sensitive infor-mation. Much of her questioning, he says, revolved around Harvey.

"Her main goal in life was to get Lee," this smuggler says. "He was a phantom, and he was in her turf."

This smuggler and others would mention Tandy to Harvey when they saw him, expressing the passion that seemed to consume the prosecutor when it came to his case and his fugitive status. Harvey couldn't care less.

"Aw, fuck her," Harvey would say. "She's not ever gonna get me."

"She's got your number, Lee. She's gonna nail you to the cross."

"Fuck her. Who the hell does she think she is?"

When Toombs became aware that federal agents were closing in on him and his associates, he asked a college professor acquaintance which country he'd recommend hiding in if he needed to dodge the law. The professor's answer: Costa Rica.

The small, lush Central American country had earned a repu-tation as a safe haven for criminals, partially owing that legacy to its history of granting political asylum to the persecuted. American fugitives, in particular, were well protected because of a 1923 extradition treaty that was regarded as useless. During the first fifty-nine years of the treaty's existence, only a single American was extradited to the United States. One of the more famous Americans to escape to Costa Rica was fugitive financier Robert Vesco, who lived there from 1973 to 1978 before leaving for the Caribbean. In 1982 the U.S. Embassy in Costa Rica estimated that sixty U.S. fugitives had fled to Costa Rica in the previous two years.

Among those sixty fugitives were Toombs, Pernell, and at least four other drug smuggling associates from Virginia and Maryland. After fleeing the United States in December 1981, Toombs and Pernell moved into homes outside San Jose and invested in orange grove plantations. They ingratiated themselves into local society, authorities said, and obtained official status as retired pensioners through the help of a Costa Rican lawyer. Once settled into their own private colony, Tandy said, they began calling potential witnesses and drug smuggling suspects in Virginia, offering to fly them down to Costa Rica on private planes for a stay "until all this blows over."

Pernell even called Tandy in May 1982, trying to negotiate a deal. On one end of the line was Tandy, with agents Mittica and Lydon just feet away, hearing only her half of the conversation. On the other end was Pernell, with Toombs in the same room, hearing only his half of the discussion. Although there is some disagreement about the exact wording Pernell used, those present in Alexandria and Costa Rica said Pernell told Tandy he wanted to trade "their assets for their asses." Tandy responded that the U.S. government had already seized more than $3 million of his assets, to which Pernell said, "That's chicken feed." No deal was struck.

Investigators then thought of tricking Pernell and Toombs, having a smuggling associate offer to fly them to a Caribbean island to discuss a potential deal. What Pernell and Toombs would not know, Lydon explains, is that the associate was an informant, and that the plane they boarded in Costa Rica would be a DEA airplane flying to American territory at U.S. Naval Base Guantanamo Bay, where they could be arrested. Unfortunately, Toombs and Pernell wouldn't bite.

Finally the U.S. government submitted an extradition request to the Costa Rican government. Despite previous difficulties obtaining cooperation with Costa Rican authorities, prosecutors were hopeful that they could extradite the defendants by way of an international narcotics treaty that both the United States and Costa Rica signed in 1961. Additionally, the Reagan administration had been dangling economic incentives for Central American and Caribbean nations as part of the Caribbean Basin Initiative, creating a friendlier political climate in the Western Hemisphere.

In July 1982 Tandy and Mittica traveled to Costa Rica, lugging a suitcase full of copies of eighty-page indictments and supporting documentation of Pernell's and Toombs's alleged drug activity, all of it in triplicate. Before leaving, a colleague in the State Department advised them to dress up the documents to create an impression of authenticity and urgency. Mittica did so.

"I remember going out to an office supply store and purchasing red ribbon and gold seals. We punched holes in the margin of the documents, ran the red ribbon through the holes, and tied it in small bows; we affixed the gold seals on the cover sheets of all the documents and used a generic sealer to emboss the gold seal. There was really nothing legally special or official about all of this," he says. "But the packages sure looked good."

A week or so later, on August 5, 1982, Costa Rican special forces, some of whom Toombs alleges were hired guns, raided the homes of Toombs, Pernell, and their fellow fugitives. Toombs hid under a staircase until he believed the coast was clear, and then made a run for it, only to be arrested. Pernell credits media coverage of the raid for delaying an outright kidnapping of the fugitives.

"They had plans to kidnap us that morning, but they couldn't get my brothers out of the houses," Pernell later testified. "They got the [television] cameras and newspapers there. So then, by the time they got my brothers out of the houses, they realized they couldn't kidnap us, so we were locked up and held by the immigration authority in Costa Rica.

"We stayed there six months. We went to court three times. And the last time, we won by their supreme court. We would be getting out the next morning at eleven—

"The next morning, eight o'clock, U.S. agents with machine guns came in the jail, took us out to the airport, [put us] on a plane, nine hours later, I was in Washington, D.C."

Despite the displeasure of getting arrested, Toombs credits his time in Costa Rican jail as "the best thing to ever happen to me." Finally, he said, he received a break from alcohol, cocaine, and smuggling-related anxiety. For about six months he was able to rest.

Once returned to the United States, Pernell and Toombs each negotiated plea deals with the government and were sentenced to ten and fifteen years in prison, respectively. The deal required them to forfeit most of their assets, though they were able to retain interests in their orange groves in Costa Rica. Among the assets Toombs agreed to turn over was jewelry and cash held by his wife in Costa Rica. So nearly a year after their arrests, agent Mittica traveled back to San Jose, Costa Rica, and collected a Rolex watch, a six-carat Thai ruby, a check for more than $200,000, and more from Toombs's wife. As he prepared to go home, Mittica noticed that his passport had expired, though his visa was still valid. This triggered some fretting about what laws he might be violating by leaving Costa Rica without declaring such valuable items. He explained his predicament to a DEA agent stationed in San Jose, and the fellow agent promised to escort him through customs and security, but warned him not to pack any of the valuables in his checked luggage, which would be inspected.

"When I left the country," Mittica says, "I was wearing the Rolex, had the ruby hidden in my sock and the check and the rest of the jewelry in various pockets on my person and in a small carry-on bag. I was nervous; felt like a smuggler."

President Ronald Reagan once remarked that "a hippie is someone who looks like Tarzan, walks like Jane, and smells like Cheetah." Comments like this made plain his distaste for the liberal counterculture that thrived in the 1960s and 1970s. When it came to drugs, he was similarly repulsed. "Let us not forget who we are," said Reagan. "Drug abuse is a repudiation of everything America is."

Not only was it un-American, Reagan said, but crime and drugs were inextricably linked. In its 1982 attempt to dramatically decrease the supply of illegal drugs, the Reagan administration deployed Organized Crime Drug Enforcement Task Forces nationwide, including one in South Florida overseen by Vice President George H. W. Bush. Among the men chosen to draft guidelines for this strategy was Brian Tim Wellesley, the former IRS criminal chief of the Carolinas who had helped spark Operation Jackpot when he approached U.S. Attorney Henry McMaster and IRS special agent David Forbes. Just months earlier Wellesley had been promoted to director of investigations for the IRS, supervising more than forty-two hundred special agents and staff from his Washington, D.C. office.

While on the committee drafting rules for the national drug enforcement task forces, Wellesley submitted his and his colleagues' work to Associate Attorney General Rudy Giuliani. The task forces were modeled, Wellesley says, on the successful investigations in Los Angeles and South Carolina. Despite just forming, the South Carolina task force was achieving remarkable progress, a testament to its unique composition of investigators from different agencies committed to a financial investigation and the seizure of property through civil forfeiture actions. The other task forces to be created throughout the country would be similarly designed, creating an approach that a successor to Giuliani characterized as a "scorched earth policy" in which suspected drug kingpins had criminal charges lodged against them as their wealth and property were taken.

In December 1982, eight months after the start of Operation Jackpot, the U.S. Congress committed $127.5 million to Reagan's crime-fighting efforts, enabling the formation of drug task forces across the country and the hiring of 1,260 more government investigators and 200 federal prosecutors. That same month, Reagan gathered more than 20 federal agency heads and military leaders in the White House and told them, "We're rejecting the helpless attitude that drug use is so rampant that we're defenseless to do anything about it . . . We can fight the drug problem, and we can win." A month later he delivered the State of the Union, briefly mentioning the problem of drugs and his determination to stamp out its negative influence. "It is high time that we make our cities safe again. This administration hereby declares an all-out war on big-time organized crime and the drug racketeers who are poisoning our young people."

The escalation of the War on Drugs marked a major shift in the attitudes of the nation and its leaders toward illegal drugs, especially marijuana, which had a history of continually passing in and out of public favor in the United States. With Reagan's crime-fighting initiatives and strong support from the so-called moral majority, the pendulum had swung back toward prohibition of pot and narcotics, a sentiment shared a decade earlier during the administration of President Richard Nixon, who initiated his own War on Drugs and declared drugs "Public Enemy Number 1." During the Nixon administration, spending on drug-related law enforcement ballooned, police were given broader search powers, and, in 1973, a handful of federal agencies were combined to form the Drug Enforcement Administration. Nixon proclaimed that drugs were "a growing menace to the general welfare of the United States."

But as Nixon ramped up the rhetoric, conservatives and liberals alike saw little point in punishing moderate marijuana users. In 1973 a Nixon-appointed presidential commission urged the decriminalization of possession of small amounts of marijuana. This recommendation was supported by numerous national medical, legal, religious, and civic organizations, including the American Medical Association, American Bar Association, and National Council of Churches. Conservatives and libertarians were not overly concerned with people getting high, but rather with restrictions on personal freedoms and the growing amount of resources the government steered toward drug enforcement. As conservative columnist James Kilpatrick wrote, "I don't give a hoot about marijuana, but I care about freedom."

In 1977 President Jimmy Carter asked Congress to revamp the nation's drug laws, stating, "penalties against possession of a drug should not be more damaging than the use of the drug itself; and where they are, they should be changed. Nowhere is this more clear than in the laws against possession of marihuana in private for personal use." Congress ignored Carter's pleas.

Despite asking for more lenient drug-related punishments, Carter did not reduce the budgets for drug enforcement efforts. In fact these budgets had grown from $43 million in 1970 to $855 million in 1981, when Carter left office. Reagan inherited these bloated budgets, then pushed for more money in the War on Drugs and created the task forces. Reagan would also direct the military and CIA to help curtail trafficking by assisting civilian authorities, while, through a national campaign, First Lady Nancy Reagan urged American schoolchildren to "Just Say No" to drugs. In 1983 the First Lady made guest appearances on the soap opera *Dynasty* and sitcom *Diff'rent Strokes* to promote her anti-drug message. That same year, Drug Abuse Resistance Education (D.A.R.E.) classes premiered in Los Angeles classrooms.

For Operation Jackpot, Reagan's support resulted in increased staffing. By 1983 the task force included seventeen agents. New to the task force were investigators from the Bureau of Alcohol, Tobacco, and Firearms and members of South Carolina's state police force. But removed from the task force was Wells Dickson, the assistant U.S. attorney who had been coordinating the investigators. McMaster, Dickson says, was not happy with the amount of time it was taking to prepare indictments. After a falling out between the men, McMaster shifted Dickson to another job within the office.

Meanwhile, tensions were rising between McMaster and Lionel Lofton, an assistant U.S. attorney who had worked for twelve years in the Charleston office under at least three other U.S. attorneys, often prosecuting drug smuggling cases. Lofton had been a candidate for U.S. attorney, and, when he was passed over for McMaster, he stayed at his post. The hundred or so miles between the U.S. attorney offices in Columbia and Charleston did little to reduce friction between Lofton and his new boss.

"He didn't know diddly-squat about what he was doing," says Lofton, who bristled at McMaster's habit of courting publicity.

He also balked at the amount of memos McMaster issued and what Lofton characterized as "micromanaging." A majority of the memos, says Lofton, were for trivial reasons. One that particularly rankled Lofton and Dickson was a memo requesting the assistant U.S. attorneys in the office to attach personalized license plates on their automobiles that reflected their job, such as AUSA12 or AUSA13. Lofton and Dickson didn't do it, and they weren't the only ones.

"Why would I want a bull's-eye on my back?" says Lofton.

Then came another memo from McMaster, says Dickson, which read: "The people that have assistant U.S. attorney license plates should not let their wives drive the vehicles with their hair in curlers and children eating ice cream and throwing paper out the windows and stuff like that."

"That's paraphrased," Dickson says, "but that's the substance of the memo."

One day, Lofton had enough and called McMaster.

"Henry, you know, you're just as crazy an SOB as I thought you were," said Lofton. "I quit, as of Friday. If you want to send somebody down to review my files, I'm happy to do it, but Friday I'm out of here."

Dickson stayed in the office only a few weeks longer before he, too, quit.

Lofton and Dickson were not unique in their observance of McMaster's maneuvers for attention and publicity. In the early 1980s, the White House was in regular receipt of letters and news clippings from the young Reagan appointee meant to express support for the president and keep him abreast of reported progress in the War on Drugs. Among the first of these letters was a note dated April 13, 1982, in which McMaster sent Reagan an editorial from Columbia's the *State* newspaper applauding the president's recent visit to the islands of Jamaica and Barbados—the first such visits by a sitting president of the United States. McMaster felt similarly to the *State*'s editorial writer: "In my opinion, and in the opinion of everyone I know, you are doing everything just right," wrote McMaster. "Pour it on!"

On October 25, 1982, McMaster wrote the White House to thank Reagan for his response to the drug problem in America. "I deeply appreciate the excellent job you are doing on this and the host of other issues facing our country. Thank you, thank you, thank you." On December 17, 1982, McMaster sent Reagan five articles regarding drug task-force work in South Carolina. Six days later McMaster wrote the President to inform him of the seizure of 955 pounds of cocaine in Sumter, South Carolina, and included news clippings featuring photos of McMaster and U.S. Senator Strom Thurmond holding a bundle of cocaine.

On January 3, 1983, he sent another press clipping mentioning the new drug task forces across the country and thanking the President for all his "splendid help." Reagan responded to these letters with a note of his own, thanking McMaster for his dedication and promising support to those "fighting it out on the front lines in the war against crime." Despite Reagan's kind words, the letters seemed to tire the White House staff. On January 10, 1983, presidential writer Chuck Donovan sent a White House colleague McMaster's latest letter along with a scribbled note: "Here he is again. Hope he has time to fight crime."

Perhaps it was inevitable that the hard-charging McMaster would bruise some egos when he took the helm of the U.S. attorney's office and set his own agenda for prosecuting cases. He took personal offense to those who broke the law, and he sought innovative ways not only to catch crooks, but also to embarrass them. He regarded the press as an ally and would eagerly present his cases to television and newspaper reporters. Always, he viewed the world in black-and-white.

In May 1982, for example, McMaster's office filed 173 lawsuits against individuals who defaulted on their student loans. His office also provided a list of these people to newspapers, some of which printed the names, embarrassing the debtors. McMaster said he found this shaming tactic effective and later filed another wave of lawsuits.

"Of course, we had been filing a number of these cases each week all along, but that never got anybody's attention," said McMaster. "These mass filings did."

If some of his employees saw him as ostentatious, others were glad to work under a prosecutor as emboldened as the criminals the office sought to convict. The members of Operation Jackpot, in particular, were grateful for McMaster's support.

"If it wasn't for Henry, the task force would have never gotten off the floor," says Mike Lemnah, the agent detailed to Operation Jackpot from U.S. Customs Patrol. "I really liked the guy. He supported us 100 percent."

Claude McDonald and David Forbes, too, were thankful for McMaster's backing and his promise to secure any resources they needed. They also appreciated the way he removed obstacles. Forbes recalls one problematic agent in the DEA protesting the free rein enjoyed by Forbes and McDonald. His departure was swift.

"The supervisor here at the time called us all a bunch of cowboys, didn't know what the hell we were doing," says Forbes. "His ass got shipped to Washington, D.C. and put on a marijuana desk because he wouldn't get with the program. By Henry McMaster, I guess, and Strom Thurmond."

In Thurmond, McMaster had a powerful supporter with significant influence in South Carolina and Washington. By 1983 the former Dixiecrat had served as South Carolina's governor and worked as a U.S. senator for more than twenty-five years. During much of the Reagan administration, Thurmond served as president pro tempore of the Senate and chairman of the Judiciary Committee. His constituent service was legendary, as was his penchant for fitness and his romantic prowess. On his sixty-fifth birthday he impressed reporters by performing one hundred push-ups in his office. He was married twice, the first time to a secretary in his governor's office, Jean Crouch, who was twenty-four years his junior. After she died thirteen years later, he eventually married a former Miss South Carolina, Nancy Moore, who was forty-four years his junior. Thurmond's obvious vigor enchanted South Carolina voters, who would ultimately elect him to eight Senate terms.

McMaster made it a point to update Thurmond on the progress of Operation Jackpot and visited with the senator when he came to Washington. During his trips to the nation's capital, McMaster often stayed with Wellesley, who was still interested in Operation Jackpot's progress. Wellesley would then tag along with McMaster and meet Thurmond at ceremonies and receptions. Outside the senator's presence Wellesley remembers occasionally voicing concerns about another politician interfering with the investigation or a bureaucrat initiating a turf war. McMaster would dismiss the worrying, smiling and responding in his thick Southern accent that "Strom wouldn't put up with that."

With such forceful backing McMaster frequently challenged bureaucrats to get his own way. One of his deputy prosecutors, Daniel, recalls participating in a conference call in which McMaster butted heads with a high-ranking IRS official while they waited for Associate Attorney General Giuliani to join their phone conversation. Traditionally, says Daniel, the IRS decided when to prosecute suspects for tax offenses, and potential case reviews could take up to two years. Such a process, McMaster believed, was incompatible with the quick pace of Operation Jackpot, especially when South Carolina prosecutors had secured plea agreements with many of the accused, those men agreeing to plead guilty to tax offenses and forgo trial.

These cases were essentially closed, McMaster believed, so there was no need for the lengthy IRS reviews. The IRS official disagreed, insisting they follow protocol.

"It will not happen," said the IRS official.

Soon, Giuliani came on the line, and McMaster repeated his request to forgo the reviews, which sounded reasonable enough to the senior justice department official.

"That's not going to be any problem, is it?" asked Giuliani.

"No, sir," said the IRS official. "We'll get right on it."

McMaster resisted Washington's yoke when it came to the disbursement of seized assets as well, devising legal maneuvers to benefit local law enforcement agencies, including the South Carolina state police, at the expense of the U.S. Treasury. For example, when South Carolina smuggler Jack Burg negotiated a plea deal with the government, he accompanied federal investigators to the Caribbean twice in order to withdraw about $600,000. By voluntarily giving up the cash to the U.S. Attorney's office, as opposed to relinquishing it through a formal seizure by the government, McMaster explained, he was able to sidestep a requirement that it be forwarded entirely to Washington. He split the spoils in half and eight months later awarded the South Carolina State Law Enforcement Division $290,000 at a press conference, announcing the money would be used to buy a surveillance plane for drug investigations. Thurmond was on hand for the event, wide-eyed and marveling at the twenty-nine stacks of $10,000 placed on a table before television cameras.

"That's the most money I've ever seen in my life," said Thurmond.

Most alleged smugglers, however, were not willing to make similar donations, so government investigators continued to seize assets suspected of being purchased with drug proceeds. Roy Riley was a frequent target, with investigators taking BMW, Jeep, and Volvo automobiles. The seizures infuriated Riley. When his lawyer later warned him investigators were set to seize a Mercedes wagon he owned, he rushed to an auto dealership in Columbia, South Carolina, and traded it in for a Volvo. This tactic did not stave off investigators for long. Lemnah and other agents soon pulled Riley over and took the new Volvo, blocking his car and drawing their guns on Riley to prevent him from driving away.

"He was so pissed he couldn't see straight," says Lemnah.

Other seizures were less dramatic but well publicized, such as the home and two lots on Nantucket, Massachusetts, forfeited to the government in January 1983. Owned by offshore corporations controlled by Tom "Rolex" Rhoad, the twenty-five acres of island property were valued at more than $1 million.

These successes contributed to good morale among the task force members, and they sometimes gathered after hours at a Charleston-area riverside cottage rented by Forbes, Lemnah, and two other federal agents. On Friday nights they'd relax by catching shrimp and drinking beer. When McDonald came, his colleagues ribbed him for nursing a single beer all night long. Such teasing contributed to the camaraderie enjoyed by the investigators.

"[It was] a lot of work, a lot of hours, but it was worth it," says Lemnah. "No one complained."

At times the investigation served as an escape from turmoil at home. Both Forbes and McDonald were divorced while working on the task force, and both had children at home. Marital problems, however, were seldom discussed at the office. U.S. Customs Special Agent in Charge Clark Settles, who supervised McDonald, and later Forbes, says federal agents weren't particularly "touchy-feely."

"I expected the guys to do their damn jobs and take care of personal things in their own time," says Settles.

At this stage of the investigation—nearly a year after the start of Operation Jackpot—a critical part of the agents' jobs was to convince suspects it was in their best interest to cooperate with the government. Through lengthy debriefings with cooperating suspects, the agents could further their understanding of smuggling rings and help prosecutors prepare charges. By the spring of 1983, the prosecutors had also convened a federal grand jury in Columbia to present evidence of drug smuggling, hoping to secure indictments.

As they had done with certain residents of Hilton Head who worked for alleged kingpins Les Riley and Barry Foy, the agents tried to impress upon suspects that all was lost, their guilt a foregone conclusion. Each confrontation involved an artful mix of bluffing and intimidation. Forbes says he presented the facts plainly during these interactions and made it clear to suspects that the government was willing to negotiate prison time in exchange for cooperation, but that their assets would be taken no matter what. He held true to his word on that last point, helping coordinate the seizure of cars, land, and homes before charges were even filed.

"We got your ass," Forbes told suspects. "How long you wanna do?"

To some the act was heavy-handed and transparent. One smuggler recalls being brought to the top floor of the federal courthouse in Columbia to undergo a polygraph test about his recent debriefing. The ceiling in the room was low and the federal agents none too pleasant. One of their favorite tactics, the smuggler says, was for the agents to suddenly snatch a piece of paper off the polygraph machine, crumble it, throw it in a corner of the room, and scream that he was a lying son of a bitch.

Other suspects who cooperated with the government reported similar treatment. One man who was minimally involved with the smuggling rings said the investigators often played the good cop/ bad cop routine, with one investigator being exceedingly rude and the other very polite. As the bad cop raved and screamed that the suspect was a liar, the good cop would plead for cooperation to make his partner calm down.

"Listen, man, you've got to watch this guy, he hasn't had his cigarettes," the good cop would say.

With or without intimidation from government agents, the prospect of prison, humiliation, and loss of professional standing loomed large for anyone associated with the drug runners. Dickson, the prosecutor originally assigned to supervise the task force, recalls receiving a phone call from his colleague Lofton when Hilton Head lawyer Andy Pracht was brought in for questioning.

"Look, Wells, we just gotta back off. This guy's in here crying in the conference room," said Lofton. "We gotta cap it at like five years or something like that. This is just terrible. All he did was help them off-load boats. I mean, he wasn't a mover or shaker or anything, but he's willing to tell who's involved."

Pracht did share information with the government and pleaded guilty to tax evasion and currency violations. As word got around about his cooperation, he found himself reviled by men he formerly counted as friends. His former smuggling colleagues coined a new, rhyming nickname for the lawyer: "Pracht the Rat." He wasn't the only one to earn that harsh moniker.

Telling on your friends was unforgivable. At least that's how most people felt. Among the smugglers, contempt for rats was so intense that many professed they wouldn't piss on the loose-lipped men should they catch fire. What particularly rankled some smugglers, too, was the impression that a number of the government's initial cooperating witnesses spilled their guts when they had relatively little exposure to serious charges. They were minor players with big mouths who were unwilling to accept responsibility for their criminal actions. To many minds they served the case to the government on a silver platter, sparing themselves at the expense of their friends. It didn't help when at least one federal agent approached a drug runner and told him his former friend and fellow smuggler was the first person in the history of the DEA they had to beat with a hose to make him *stop* talking.

Or perhaps it was all just bitterness talking. Some who cooperated with investigators would argue they took a more practical approach when cornered by the government. If they didn't cut a deal and talk, someone else would when put in their place. And whereas some smugglers might wax romantic about the good old days, others felt little loyalty to kingpins who offered them pittances for illegal work and often didn't deliver on their promises, whether it was larger sums of money or legal representation. For some smugglers, too, debriefings with investigators were cathartic. For too long their lives had been moving too fast. They wanted to straighten out, stop drinking and drugging, and tell no more lies.

Horseshit, others say. They're nothing but rats.

One man who wouldn't talk was O'Day, the Virginian who sailed aboard the hash boat *Second Life* at the invitation of Toombs and Pernell. After refusing to testify about his smuggling ventures in front of a federal grand jury in October 1981, O'Day was indicted in June 1982. While considering whether or not he should contest the charges against him, he was surprised to learn that so many of his former smuggling colleagues, including Toombs and Pernell, provided information to Virginia investigators and agreed to serve as witnesses against him.

"I was a little disappointed with that, Barry [Toombs] being about the worst one, and other people I thought were my friends," says O'Day, who pleaded guilty without cutting a deal. "I just expected a little bit more loyalty from people, but didn't have it coming, I guess."

To federal investigators there was little surprise that so many smugglers could be flipped and made to tell on their friends. They'd seen it happen before, over and over again.

"When you've got them by the balls," says Forbes, "the hearts and minds will follow."

Chapter Ten

With his family life in turmoil, his smuggling partnership in ruins, and feeling seriously out of sorts, Les Riley gathered his longtime girlfriend and their kids and headed to the Caribbean. Although he was aware of a criminal investigation into smuggling in South Carolina, Riley says what really bothered him were his friends and acquaintances who seemed to swarm him wherever he went, bringing their problems with them. His girlfriend, Suzanne, was suffering from the extreme stress of living their undercover lives, and she was the one "who overlooked a lot of shit, particularly when I was running around," say Riley. He wanted desperately to right the ship. He later wrote in a letter to a judge:

> *I saw that there was no way the family structure could, or should, survive the social environment surrounding myself. The use of harder drugs, such as cocaine, which I now deplore, was becoming more prevalent. So was greed and dishonesty. Consciously and subconsciously I wrestled with the demons of hedonism and despair. My dreams of a decent and good life were ebbing away. I really didn't know a way out. Ensnared as I was in a morass partly of my own making and in a major way, beyond my control. I knew deep inside of me that I had to change. I needed guidance and counsel but had no one to turn to. I needed desperately to free myself from the maddening world of drugs and to put all of this behind me.*

After a year in the Caribbean, and as the Operation Jackpot task force began seizing property in South Carolina, the Rileys decided to move again, leaving St. Barts to travel through South America, Europe, and Asia before arriving in Australia. Riley spent his time fishing, and by December 1982, the family had moved into a home on lush and ritzy Whale Beach, north of Sydney. Each morning they'd send their children off to school in their uniforms of khaki shorts and checkered shirts. For now, they thought, they had found peace.

"Surely, we reasoned, no one would bother to seek us out on the other side of the world, but we were wrong again," Riley wrote. "This was absolutely too much for Suzanne and she was admitted to a hospital suffering a nervous breakdown due to stress from our ordeal and the fact that our past was apparently inescapable from former associates."

Among their visitors were Wally Butler and his fiancée, Rebecca. After leaving the United States, the couple moved in with the Rileys at their Whale Beach home. A few weeks later, when the quarters got too cramped, the Butlers moved down the street. Both families thought of Australia as a temporary home, a pleasant place to stay before moving on. Before he had left the Western Hemisphere with his family, Riley had talked about heading to French Polynesia with Bob "The Boss" Byers, who was also fond of the Pacific, and leaving the fast life behind. The Ocean 71 sailboat Riley had used to smuggle his first load of hashish was docked nearby, ready to set sail whenever they were ready. They'd go soon, he thought. But he never got the chance.

On May 5, 1983, Riley left his home overlooking Whale Beach for the local corner store, bounding out the door dressed in shorts and a T-shirt. Australian Federal Police officers were watching him, and had been for weeks, even staking out his house the night before. American authorities claimed their suspect was a prominent marijuana and hashish kingpin who was at ease operating in war-torn Lebanon and the jungles of South America. According to the kingpin's brother Roy, who had been interrogated by American agents, Les was a man who valued his freedom above all things and would rather die than go to prison.

Riley walked down the driveway to the road and sidewalk that paralleled the beach. He headed north, but did not make it far before a car drove toward him at high speed and stopped a short distance away. A man seemed to be propelled from the car, heading down a hill toward the beach. Riley stared hard at the car as two other men exited from its doors and approached him.

"I want to talk to you," said Detective Senior Constable Stephen Emes as he placed his hand on Riley's arm.

Riley, alarmed and unaware the strangers were policemen, immediately threw his arms in the air, breaking contact. Spinning on his heels, he sprinted off in the other direction, running only five paces or so before he spotted another man heading for him. Riley changed course instantly, dashing down a steep embankment toward an oceanfront home, unsure who these men were and what they wanted with him. The policemen gave chase, yelling for him to stop. At the bottom of the hill, he was tackled by Emes, though Riley broke free and regained his footing immediately, making it to the home's front door and slipping inside, startling the family within, including a nine-year-old girl who attended school with Riley's kids. Australian Federal Police officers swarmed the house.

Riley ran through a kitchen, into a living room, and then passed into a bedroom, where Emes tackled and lost him again, Riley punching his way to freedom and exiting onto a veranda. He placed his hands on a railing and prepared to jump onto a nearby tree, which he could climb down to the ground below. Before he could leap, however, a police officer appeared in the yard below, leveled a shotgun at him, and yelled for Riley to stop. Emes and Detective Acting Sergeant Raymond Alan Tinker then stepped out onto the veranda, sealing any chance of escape. Surrounded, Riley threw his hands in the air and shouted, "I give up, I give up."

The police grabbed Riley and threw him down on the veranda, where they handcuffed and searched him. They knocked him on the head once, says Riley, drawing blood. He told the police they were free to search his home and that they'd find no guns. They obliged, placing him in the rear seat of a police car, handcuffed to another officer, and toting him back to his house. When the police arrived at Riley's rented house, they found his common-law wife, Suzanne. She was sobbing, huddling close with her two young children. As she regained her composure, the head detective informed her they had an arrest warrant for her husband for narcotic offenses in the United States.

"Are you from South Carolina?" asked the detective.

"I don't want to answer that. Why do you have to do this to us over here?" said Suzanne.

"Your husband has been arrested as a result of a request received from the American authorities under the provisions of an international treaty. Do you understand that?" said the detective.

"You don't have to honor that treaty, do you?"

"Yes."

"I want to see my psychiatrist," said Suzanne crying again.

Back outside Tinker read Les the lengthy warrant for his arrest. Riley's body shook. As law enforcement would say, the suspect appeared extremely agitated. Tinker inquired if he was okay.

"I'm worried about my wife and children," said Riley. "They're innocent of all this."

Tinker assured him they were in good hands. In fact the detectives had taken a keen interest in the children, asking them where they might find "Uncle Wally," hoping the kids might clue them in to his whereabouts. Detectives asked Riley about Butler, too, telling him they knew he lived just up the street. Riley replied that he had seen Butler earlier that morning, driving his white Volkswagen.

As detectives searched the Riley house with Suzanne, they found small amounts of hallucinogens and bags of cash, which were hidden under a sink, behind a mirror, in a closet, and in the drawers of bedside tables. Other police went to Butler's house, meeting his fiancée, and then Butler, who pulled into his driveway.

"Federal Police, step out of the vehicle, please," they yelled at Butler, who calmly complied. Before being arrested and handcuffed, he consented to a search of the house and inquired if his fiancée, Rebecca, was okay.

At noon, more than three hours after police first confronted Riley, he and Butler were driven separately to federal police headquarters. During the trip Riley spoke with the men who arrested him, telling them he was aware of the drug investigation in the United States, but it was not the reason he left the country.

"How did you find me," Riley asked. "Who told you?"

"You don't expect me to tell you that, do you Les?" replied the police detective.

Arriving at police headquarters, Riley was questioned, but he repeatedly asked for a lawyer. He refused to sign a record of the unsuccessful interview, or read it aloud, as the police requested. Meanwhile, police stayed at Butler's house, finding cash under a carpet and speaking with Rebecca. She told the police she really didn't understand what this was all about and that she and Butler left the United States to avoid this kind of treatment.

"We just got scared. Two federal officers came to the house one day and asked a lot of questions about laundering but they went away. He wasn't arrested or anything like that," she said. ". . . If they call buying a few properties for Les laundering then I guess they have a good case, but I don't understand it all. He did nothing wrong."

She, too, was curious about how police had found them, asking a police officer if their phone calls had been traced. The officer pleaded ignorance, explaining he wasn't part of the investigation, just the squad making the arrest.

"I guess you wouldn't tell me anyway," said Butler's fiancée. "One good thing though, I'll get to see my family again. I've missed them a lot."

Months of travel and exotic surroundings had not distracted them from near-constant anxiety. Each time the Butlers and Rileys hopped a plane, changed houses, or moved between islands, it was only to buy time, delay the inevitable, and lead themselves farther away from loved ones and anything familiar. Now Rebecca and Suzanne were alone in Australia, their lovers handcuffed and taken away, charged with significant crimes. In a matter of hours, life had turned severely unpleasant, though Butler's fiancée tried to see a silver lining.

"You know, I had this premonition that something was going to happen today, it worried me all last night. But in a way I'm glad you caught up with us," she told the Australian police officer, according to his report. "I'd always told Wal[ly] that it's no use trying to hide forever and he should go back and clear things up one way or another. You can't live a normal life looking over your shoulder all the time. It's awful and it's upsetting me terribly. It's effecting [sic] Suzanne too; that's why she is having sessions with a psychiatrist."

The arrests provided Riley his first opportunity to see exactly what South Carolina investigators had uncovered and for which crimes he might be found guilty. The enormity of the government's case revealed itself as the thirty-eight-year-old marijuana kingpin reviewed the litany of charges against him. It became apparent that he could spend the rest of his life in prison for smuggling pot. Just as shocking as the severity of the allegations was who was behind them.

"Henry McMaster? From Columbia?" Riley said to his lawyer. "I've known him since he was twelve."

Back home in South Carolina, McMaster and the rest of the Jackpot team rejoiced at having captured two suspected kingpins. The arrests sent law enforcement into high gear, and two prosecutors, Cam Currie and Robert Jendron, along with investigator David Forbes, immediately prepared for a trip to Australia. Although they couldn't argue before an Australian judge, they could meet with Australian authorities before a bond hearing and advise them of the importance of keeping Riley and Butler detained until the men could be extradited.

The sudden developments, while reason to celebrate, had actually caught the Jackpot task force off guard. Currie, who had briefly dated Lee Harvey at the University of South Carolina fifteen years earlier, didn't even have a passport. In the next thirty-nine hours she'd board six flights, stopping in Atlanta, Houston, Los Angeles, Fiji, Melbourne, and Sydney, picking up a passport and Australian visa along the way. After her last flight landed, she slept for a few hours before heading to an Australian courthouse. There she spied Riley and Butler in the center of a courtroom, standing in the dock reserved for the accused. Meanwhile, an Australian tabloid ran a front-page article about the arrests, alleging Riley to be "America's 'Most Wanted Man.'"

Following the arrests in Australia, as well as the guilty pleas of nine cooperating suspects to drug- or income tax–related charges, Operation Jackpot was ready to ask a grand jury to indict. On May 19, 1983, two weeks after the capture of Riley and Butler, a grand jury returned criminal indictments alleging the existence of two massive drug smuggling rings based in South Carolina. Four days later the indictments were unsealed and made available to the press and public. The charges were staggering. In the last ten years, the indictments alleged, thirty-nine men and one woman smuggled more than 347,000 pounds of marijuana and 130,000 pounds of hashish into the United States. The street value of such drugs was astounding, totaling $697,216,000, given prices of $60 per ounce of marijuana and $175 per ounce of hashish.

Suddenly South Carolina residents learned the identities of all the men and the one woman targeted by the mysterious Operation Jackpot and the government's recent streak of property seizures. Their nicknames—Flash, Rolex, Bob "the Boss," Willie the Hog, and Disco Don—read like a roster of mobsters. Their regular travel destinations for acquiring drugs and depositing money—the Bahamas, Colombia, Jamaica, and Lebanon—conjured contrasting images of exotic, white-sand resorts and rugged, war-torn coasts. Surprisingly, more than half of these alleged international criminals were natives of the Palmetto State.

The first set of charges, formally known as Criminal Number 83-165 and informally known as the Foy indictment, alleged that twenty-six men, including kingpins Barry "Flash" Foy and Tom "Rolex" Rhoad, smuggled 159,600 pounds of marijuana and 30,000 pounds of hashish into the United States. Even more prodigious, however, was a second ring of twenty-four people, allegedly headed by Riley and Butler, which brought in 187,500 pounds of marijuana and 130,000 pounds of hashish. The case against them was outlined in the Riley indictment, or Criminal Number 83-166, including kingpin charges against Riley, Butler, Harvey, and Willie Frank Steele. Ten men were accused of participating in both smuggling rings.

Speaking to reporters, U.S. Attorney Henry McMaster emphasized the uniqueness of Operation Jackpot, praising the teamwork of federal investigators from five separate agencies and their ability to make a substantial case using historical and financial clues. He claimed these were the first indictments made by one of President Ronald Reagan's drug task forces and that they targeted senior members of sophisticated smuggling rings. McMaster conceded that Operation Jackpot did not intercept any of the hundreds of thousands of pounds of pot or hashish, as "most of it got through, a lot of it's been smoked." However, said McMaster, the investigation would help put a significant dent in the availability of marijuana in the years to come.

"The defendants included in these indictments represent the top and middle levels of involvement," said McMaster. "The indictments reach the people behind the scenes who, we believe, have been organizing, financing and operating these smuggling ventures with impunity for years."

Criminals. Uncle Sam pointed his big finger at South Carolina's gentlemen smugglers, cutting through their considerable charm, sex appeal, and smooth ways. No matter how suave their explanations, how cunningly they covered their tracks, or how desperate their tactics to disarm the suspicious, the government zeroed in on their transgressions. Point by point, the allegations typed in those two indictments plainly stated the smugglers' extensive criminal culpability: Here is where you were, here is what you did, and here is the money you illegally made.

Yet to their peers these men had been—and still were—cult heroes and folk legends, on par with Robin Hood, daring to distribute forbidden goods. They were the embodiment of, and sometimes inspiration to, counterculture songs by rock musicians like Jimmy Buffett and the Eagles. They were men who casually walked away from commitments to college degrees, who counted sun, sex, sand, and sailboats as more worthwhile than starter homes and good standing in their communities.

To their families—before they were on the run—they were healthy, wealthy, and happy, whether or not they were vague about their sources of income. Many parents and siblings were glad to celebrate their drug running success, impressed by the new cars and gorgeous girlfriends. Siblings joined their older brothers' criminal networks, and many parents lived vicariously through their sons. Rhoad's father was said to watch his son and other smugglers unload marijuana and hashish on his rural riverside property, Turkey Pen, near Branchville, South Carolina, though he was never charged for any wrongdoing.

Skip Sanders's actions and lifestyle were approved by his father, too. "the message I continually got from older guys, including my own dad was . . . live it up. dip the cooter, get the cash," writes Sanders. "worry about tomorrow when tomorrow gets here."

Other parents refrained from asking about their children's line of work, preferring to stay in the dark, or at least avoid confirming an obvious, yet dreaded, truth. Parents who disapproved took comfort that no one was getting hurt and that pot was thought to be no worse than alcohol. Only a few dared lecture their adult children or siblings, and did it at the risk of alienating loved ones who were clearly incorrigible. These men and women stayed silent, asking themselves what'd be the point of causing conflict with someone so self-assured. If they weren't lawful, at least they didn't forget to call on birthdays and Mother's Day.

In the eyes of lovers, the already exceptionally handsome men became even more intoxicating with each revelation of their daredevil status. To date these men was to be transported instantly to paradise, showered with expensive gifts, stimulated by innumerable drugs, and given lodging and much sexual attention in beachfront homes and the cabins of luxury sailboats. If the constant cheating could be crushing, the men at least did not make much pretense about it. It turned out to be a frequently forgivable offense, and few women had the nerve to leave.

To themselves the smugglers were harmless renegades who, through lots of trial and error, had carved a comparatively hassle-free niche in an American society chock-full of rules and obligation. The men had been sidelined when following traditional paths. Whether through schooling or work, their talents and zest had been marginalized by conventionalism. Smuggling satisfied their entrepreneurial urges and afforded freedom. Above all else the gentlemen smugglers abhorred following any rules but their own.

But to the government investigators and prosecutors behind Operation Jackpot, the gentlemen smugglers were the most egregious violators of federal law in the state of South Carolina. What their crimes may have lacked in repugnance they compensated for in frequency and flagrancy. For McMaster, a number were former classmates at the University of South Carolina and its law school. More important, they were men whose disregard for America's drug laws knew few bounds. They were men he, as U.S. attorney, could not tolerate.

In some ways, however, the indictments mischaracterized the gentlemen smugglers. The two alleged smuggling "rings" were artificial and arbitrary law enforcement constructs perhaps more appropriate for the mafia or a gang than these drug runners. Indeed, the smugglers were fond of saying they were part of disorganized crime. There was no central kingpin, just a network of scammers always available for hire with allegiances that shifted with the flow of money. Many men on the South Carolina coast organized smuggling ventures. It just so happened that a few people, including Byers, Foy, Riley, and Harvey, were better at it than others.

In some areas of the indictment, too, the government overstated its claims. Butler, for example, was elevated to a senior level of influence. But he was no kingpin. Although he played a critical role in securing secluded off-load sites, the other smugglers often ignored him. "Weird Wally" spent most work nights nervously wandering the property he provided with a radio, fulfilling a minor lookout role. He was a valued friend to the smugglers, and an enjoyable fishing buddy, but in no one's estimation, save the government's, was he top dog. It would have been more accurate, of course, to describe Harvey as Riley's equal and partner.

Also overblown was the value of the drugs imported by the smugglers, though the quantity was an understatement. The government did not compile an exhaustive list of every smuggling venture accomplished by the accused, nor did they pretend to do so. The ventures they did outline in the indictments, however, assumed the shipments of drugs were composed of top-grade marijuana and hashish, free from moisture, rot, twigs, sticks, and stones. In reality, many shipments were subpar, requiring innovative remediation. One smuggler recalls spreading rotting marijuana across a tarp-lined field in the South Carolina midlands, drying it by spraying it with grain alcohol and exposing it to sunlight, before mixing in spices and other pot and repackaging it. Still, it could not be sold for top dollar. The smugglers also sold pot and hashish at wholesale prices, perhaps a quarter of what could be made selling it to users for "street value."

Julian "Doc" Pernell, who had already pleaded guilty with Barry "Ice Cream" Toombs to drug charges in Virginia, later commented on Uncle Sam's appraisal abilities.

"The government has a funny way of evaluating things. When they value pot, they value street value. When they evaluate [our] assets, they estimated at liquidation costs," said Pernell. "In other words, I had a $10 million project in Hilton Head, South Carolina, which they sold for $3.6 million. I had a $5 million industrial complex they value at $80,000. The government had a funny way of evaluating."

The Jackpot case fell into the judicial lap of the famously even-tempered and uniquely named Falcon Black Hawkins Jr., who had been appointed to the federal bench four years earlier following a nomination from his former law partner, U.S. Senator Fritz Hollings of South Carolina. Although his temperament and Democratic leanings boded well for the defendants, his background was vastly different from many of the men he'd soon judge. The gentlemen smugglers had muddled through an extended youth, smoking pot aboard luxury sailboats and making vast amounts of money. Hawkins had joined the military at age seventeen and served in World War II, sending paychecks home to his widowed mother and four younger siblings. When he returned home, he attended the Citadel while working nights in the Charleston Naval shipyard to support his own wife and family.

Born in 1927, he was the son of a millworker and housemaker in North Charleston, South Carolina, and described his childhood during the Great Depression as unremarkable. Known as FB for much of his youth, Hawkins enjoyed hunting excursions to Hellhole Swamp and Four Holes Swamp in nearby Berkeley County, becoming a crack shot. In 1944 he joined the Merchant Marines, then the Army, which paid for him to briefly attend the University of Mississippi before calling him into service as the war intensified. He sent his military paychecks home to supplement Social Security benefits his mother received following his father's premature death.

After the war Hawkins received one of the first electronics apprenticeships offered by the Navy, learning about radios, radar, and sonar at the Charleston Naval Shipyard. He worked at the shipyard for twelve years, earned his degree from the Citadel, married, and started his own family. He'd be forever grateful to the federal government for the opportunities and assistance it provided his family, making him a lifelong Democrat and supportive of social programs.

Hawkins was more than thirty years old when he began law school at the University of South Carolina, moving his wife and three children to Columbia. He took courses over the summers to finish six months early, graduating in 1963. He enjoyed his time at South Carolina's only law school, forging strong relationships with the faculty and fellow students while excelling academically. Not only did he love law, but he was "crazy about it, to tell you the truth."

Hawkins's passion was rewarded soon after graduation. Before he passed the South Carolina bar, he was asked by Hollings to join his Charleston firm. Hollings had just finished a term as governor and was smarting from a loss to Olin D. Johnston, whom he had challenged for the Democratic nomination for the U.S. Senate. Before offering a job to Hawkins, Hollings had consulted with the dean of the law school, seeking a candidate who made good grades, but who was not at the top of the class. Hollings wanted a workhorse, not someone bookish, and he was impressed at how Hawkins, a military veteran, had put himself through school while working to feed his siblings and own family.

"He was one of the smartest fellows, most realistic, long on common sense, good judgment," says Hollings, who ribbed his new hire about the way he appeared in law school pictures. "I saw his picture, and he looked like he needed a lawyer. He looked like someone the FBI wanted."

Despite the jab, and having to constantly endure Hollings's stubborn personality, Hawkins didn't forget who courted whom.

"I don't say this in any kind of bragging sort of way, but he sent for me," Hawkins once remarked. "I didn't send for him."

Hollings and Hawkins, operating from their office on Broad Street in downtown Charleston, were not shy about handling a variety of high-profile criminal, antitrust, and business cases. The men also took on lucrative work helping developers create some of Charleston's first subdivisions and representing South Carolina's Piggly Wiggly grocery chain. The men put in long hours and required the same of their longtime secretary, Patty Kasell, who ultimately followed Hawkins to the bench.

"[Hollings] kind of believed in working about sixteen hours a day, so that's about what we worked," said Hawkins. "That was a little bit of a shocker for my wife when I started practicing, that you aren't ever home, all you did was practice."

When Hollings won election to the U.S. Senate in 1966, Hawkins assumed more of the cases and slowly grew the firm. When an opening on the federal bench came along during Jimmy Carter's presidency, he pounced on it, knowing the support of Hollings was critical to secure the position. He quickly earned a reputation as the South Carolina judge with the best judicial temperament, topping legal surveys conducted each year. Hawkins said he preferred letting lawyers try their cases without his interference, and Kasell remembers him banging his gavel only once. Hawkins was not unaware of his unusually serene disposition. "I don't get upset or excited hardly over anything. Every now and then. But it's got to be something pretty bad to cause me to get off my even plane," he said. "My philosophy . . . is be as fair as you can with the circumstance, and hope for the best. That's about the way I've labored."

Hawkins, though, was as sensitive as he was composed. Those tried before him recall him gazing out courtroom windows during testimony, but with an ear cocked toward the stand, paying close attention. He approached the sentencing of convicted defendants with the greatest reluctance, but feeling bound to punish as a duty that he accepted by oath. Such decisions weighed heavily on the judge's heart.

"Usually, if it was a bad one, I'd say, 'Let's leave him alone for a few minutes,'" says Kasell. "He'd settle down."

Since Hawkins ascended to the bench at a time when marijuana smuggling was particularly popular and brazen in South Carolina, he handled a number of drug cases during his early years on the bench. In his comments during sentencing hearings, Hawkins repeatedly struggled to understand why so many educated men from seemingly upstanding families embarked on journeys explicitly designed to break the law. He expressed a certain amount of disbelief that fun and money would ever be sought, and repeatedly achieved, at the expense of abiding the laws of the United States.

There was a disconnect between Hawkins and the drug defendants who came before him, as the smugglers rebelled against the assorted institutions the judge revered. Hawkins worked nights to pay his way through college, while the smugglers, by and large, dropped out of school, forfeiting the tuition paid by doting parents. Hawkins served in World War II, a conflict the country entered with a strong moral and retaliatory imperative. Many smugglers avoided Vietnam, and those who did serve were shaken by the war. Its purposeless chaos and killing contributed to personal undoing and steered its discharged soldiers into danger and drugs back home. Government, politics, and the American legal system were similarly embraced and opposed. For Hawkins such things were at the core of his life. The smugglers wanted to be left alone by the rules and theater that saturated those institutions.

When it came to marijuana, its pleasures were no doubt alien to Hawkins, but its potential to pervert the American dream was plain, evidenced by the apologies, regret, and pleas for mercy he so often heard in his courtroom from convicted drug defendants. Marijuana did not spur hard work and create strong families and communities, but instead seemed to go hand in hand with the increasing amounts of self-absorption and lust for wealth that President Carter, a fellow southern Democrat, outlined in his speech pinpointing American malaise.

Eight months before being assigned the Jackpot cases, in October 1982, in the midst of the operation's initial wave of property seizures, Hawkins sentenced six men on drug smuggling charges, all of them from out of state and disassociated from South Carolina's gentlemen smugglers. Hawkins seemed fatigued having to handle another drug case, saying he'd lost track of how many defendants had come before him on similar charges.

"There's really nothing much to say. I ought to just go ahead and sentence you. But my nature won't let me do that in the hope that somebody out there hears about it and repeats it and prevents some other person from doing harm to their family, their country, what you fellas are doing . . . [I]f you bring drugs into this district and get caught, there will be a period of incarceration."

Chapter Eleven

Since the colonial era in Charleston, anyone with sense—and money—changed households come summertime. At the close of the eighteenth century, some wealthy South Carolinians left to tour Europe or moved from coastal plantation houses to grand downtown mansions when the temperature rose, leaving their slave labor behind for the season. In the city, planters and their families enjoyed summer breezes off the harbor and minimized their risk of catching malaria or yellow fever, which festered in the mosquito-filled marshes and swamps on their estates. But the breeze only helped so much. Downtown living was a hot and humid affair, with city streets and pedestrians alike baked by the sun. To step outside was to be bathed in sweat.

In the nineteenth century, Charleston's well-to-do dodged the heat by heading inland to the Blue Ridge Mountains in western North Carolina. There, rushing rivers, tall forests, and a higher elevation made for pleasant summers. Flat Rock, North Carolina, became so popular with the Low-Country elite that its seasonal residents knew it as the "Little Charleston of the Mountains." Christopher Memminger, a Charleston lawyer and politician who served as secretary of the treasury for the Confederacy, kept a summer home in Flat Rock. Wade Hampton III, a fabulously wealthy planter, Confederate officer, South Carolina governor, and U.S. senator, kept a hunting retreat and plantation in nearby Cashiers, North Carolina.

Many of the twentieth century's gentlemen smugglers had similar means to escape the summer heat, but in August 1983 ten men were obligated to stay in Charleston as defendants in the first Operation Jackpot trial, all alleged members of a smuggling ring headed by Barry "Flash" Foy and his sidekick, Tom "Rolex" Rhoad. On the first of the month, the defendants, their lawyers, and a slew of government agents, prosecutors, and witnesses reluctantly donned suits in the ninety-degree weather and headed to the tenth floor of the Summerall Building, which overlooked the Ashley River. Because the federal courthouse on Broad Street was being renovated, temporary courtrooms had been created on the top floor of the tall building, and space was tight. Among the defendants crammed into a courtroom were Skip Sanders, whose family owned West Bank plantation on Edisto Island; Kenny Gunn, friend and frequent sailing partner of Christy Campbell; and Kenny Thomas, the captain of the shrimp boat *Gulf Princess II*, which, three years earlier, had been stopped by the Coast Guard after an off-load and found with a mere seventeen grams of pot aboard—pot that the smuggler steadfastly maintains was planted by law enforcement agents after he and his crew had scrubbed the boat clean.

The first Jackpot trial was only the latest legal hassle for Thomas. Since his arrest on the shrimp boat, Thomas had been put behind bars twice. His first stint was a year in jail after refusing to testify in front of a grand jury regarding the *Gulf Princess II*, which had successfully unloaded eighteen thousand pounds of pot to Foy in August 1980. The second time was after being convicted for his role on that smuggling boat and receiving a ten-year sentence. Now he faced fresh non–*Gulf Princess* charges in the Jackpot trial. As before, he refused to plead guilty or cut a deal with the government.

Notably absent from the makeshift courtroom were Foy and Rhoad, the two alleged kingpins. Eleven other men were missing, as well, regarded by the government as fugitives. Defense lawyers wasted little time mentioning to the jury that half the men indicted by the government, including those with the most substantial charges, were on the loose. The government had gathered, they argued, a group of inconsequential, if not completely innocent, men. Beaufort lawyer Jim Moss marveled at how the government could accuse his two clients of participating in a nearly decade-long global conspiracy by allegedly helping to smuggle for one day. In the forty-one-page indictment, Moss said, some defendants were mentioned only in a single sentence or single paragraph. Orlando-based lawyer Meredith Cohen and other attorneys complained, too, about how their clients were being associated with those on the lam.

"I call this case the tip of the iceberg," said Cohen, who represented Beaufort resident Larry McCall. "These people that have not been caught are the rest of the iceberg."

The government disagreed.

"These aren't the little men," said Assistant U.S. Attorney Bart Daniel. "These are not just nickel-and-dime drug hustlers. Little men haven't made hundreds of thousands of dollars."

For Daniel and his fellow prosecutors, perhaps more trying than the shortage of high-profile defendants was the lack of physical evidence tying the defendants to their alleged crimes. The Operation Jackpot task force had excelled at making a case using financial data and informants' grand jury testimony, but that information was compelling only to a point. No drugs had been seized as part of Operation Jackpot, and no smugglers had been caught red-handed. Prosecutors were being forced to try a major drug case involving an alleged 160,000 pounds of marijuana and 30,000 pounds of hashish, but could present the jury with no drugs. As Cohen pointed out: "They don't have ten thousand pounds, they don't have a pound, they don't have one gram."

To compensate for these weaknesses in their case, the government called twenty-six witnesses, including Virginia kingpin Julian "Doc" Pernell. In significant detail Pernell told the jury how he and his partner, Barry "Ice Cream" Toombs, had successfully completed forty-five of fifty-two attempted smuggling ventures, unloading many marijuana shipments on the South Carolina coast. He explained how he considered himself the president of a corporation and how he had separate lieutenants in charge of purchasing boats, finding isolated off-load spots, and operating stash houses. He detailed how he laundered money, how he paid off a corrupt prosecutor in Key West, and how he fled to Costa Rica. Though he spoke often of his work with Foy, at no point did Pernell mention working with any of the defendants in the courtroom, nor could he identify them. Through cross-examination, defense lawyers made sure this was clear to the jury.

After Pernell, prosecutors called Toombs, who shared stories of a shrimp boat that sank in a storm off Florida with twenty-five thousand pounds of pot and how its crew was rescued by a passing oil tanker. He mentioned how German bank robbers piloted one pot-laden ship, and how he once sold a briefcase with a hidden compartment to Rhoad for $1,500. It could hide a kilo of cocaine, he said, or $100,000. Defense attorneys pounced on the issue of relevancy.

"Your Honor, I again note my objection," said Moss. "This hasn't anything to do with this case."

If Pernell and Toombs did not personally know the men on trial, it was no matter. They were damn good tour guides of America's marijuana underworld, the prosecutors' logic went, and their unfamiliarity with defendants could be seen as an indication of just how sprawling a network of smugglers existed and the severity of South Carolina's drug problem. In short order the jury was introduced to the brazen escapades, startling amounts of money, and utter disregard for law that were standard components of the drug smuggling trade. Surely, the prosecutors figured, such a world would be sufficiently shocking to the students, teachers, nurse, welfare worker, and others that comprised the twelve-person jury, two-thirds of which was female.

Following the testimony of Pernell and Toombs, prosecutors called witnesses from South Carolina, many of whom were targets of Operation Jackpot who had agreed to plead guilty to assorted charges and testify in exchange for lesser punishment. These eyewitnesses, who claimed to have worked side-by-side with many of the defendants, posed their own challenges for the prosecutors, and the defense attorneys sought to throw doubt on their testimony every way they could. Like Toombs and Pernell, these witnesses were self-admitted criminals, the defense attorneys said, with suspicious motivations and compromised credibility. They were willing to spout a government-friendly version of events, the defense lawyers added, in order to shave time off their sentences. Assistant U.S. Attorney Daniel could only shrug his shoulders and plead to the jury that "there weren't any nuns or preachers at those off-load sites late at night."

That the government's witnesses were mere pawns or puppets, eager to recite memories conducive to the government's case, as the defense claimed, was misleading. To the government's frustration, many of the witnesses in the first Jackpot trial were particularly unreliable, either unwilling or unable to identify their alleged coconspirators who sat in the courtroom. Some witnesses had been offered money not to make an identification. Others tried to walk a fine line when testifying, upholding their commitment to the government by taking the stand, but preserving loyalty to their fellow smugglers and friends by feigning an inability to recognize defendants. And some witnesses, no matter how earnest, could legitimately not identify a defendant, at least not with 100 percent certainty. Oftentimes they had met a defendant only briefly, among a group of strangers who gathered at night on marsh banks, their faces obscured by darkness. In the years since their meeting, the defendant could lose or gain weight, change his facial hair and hairstyle, age, and likely be dressed much differently.

For example, Steve Ravenel, a smuggler who had called on both Foy and Lee Harvey to salvage smuggling ventures gone awry, testified about traveling from Key West to the Bahamas in 1979 aboard a shrimp boat provided by Foy. In the Bahamas the boat picked up eight thousand pounds of marijuana from a tiny island, along with the three Colombians who had been guarding the drugs. The boat then left for McClellanville. Ravenel spent more than a week on the boat with the men, and recalled the captain of the boat was heavyset, had curly hair, and was named Kenny. Still, his memory of that trip four years ago was fuzzy, and he offered an explanation why.

"There was a captain and two crew members, none of which I had known prior and none of which I would know after, just three people that [Foy] probably drug off the streets at the last minute to put on there. It was no real big formal introduction. It was three o'clock in the morning and we just cranked it up and left," Ravenel said of boarding the shrimp boat in Key West.

"We had these three, plus three more Colombians on board," Ravenel continued. "I was really not interested in really getting to know these people, because I knew that would be the end of it as soon as we got off, and I just wanted to get it over with and get in."

The government hoped Ravenel would finger defendant Kenny Thomas as the "Kenny" referenced in his testimony, and a prosecutor asked Ravenel to stand and identify the captain of the shrimp boat. Looking around the courtroom, however, the witness faltered, perhaps out of loyalty to a friend.

"I don't know," Ravenel testified. "I don't see anybody that looks like him."

Other defendants had similar difficulty making identifications, and it was soon apparent to those attending the trial that witnesses' memories were not always accurate. On the second day of trial the government dropped charges against defendant Kenny Gunn after it was discovered that a witness had confused him with Kenny Thomas. The next day, charges against another defendant, Charles Wallace Martin, were dropped, too, for lack of evidence, leaving eight defendants.

Defense attorneys, meanwhile, argued that many of the government witnesses' memories were flawed because of drug and alcohol abuse. Government witness Jimmy MacNeal testified about various smuggling ventures in Beaufort, Edisto Island, and McClellanville before admitting, under cross-examination, to snorting cocaine less than twenty-four hours earlier. Another government witness's drug use was not quite as recent, but similarly extensive. Julian "Bunny" Morse Jr. owned up to a fast lifestyle when Charleston defense attorney Arthur Howe asked the McClellanville smuggler how he spent the hundreds of thousand dollars he made smuggling.

"Threw it away," Morse said. "Drugs, fast cars, just lived like a fool."

"Lived like a fool," Howe responded. "And you were coked up half the time, weren't you?"

"Maybe not half the time," Morse answered. "Sometimes all of the time."

After the close of the second day of trial, defense attorney Michael J. Cox asked Hawkins if they could work through the weekend and wrap the case up. The judge responded that the government anticipated having a few days of testimony ahead, prompting Cox to quip that "there must be some witnesses coming up who know something about this case."

Hawkins was not amused by the remark.

"I don't know what you mean by that, but anyway be here promptly with your clients, and I will remind the U.S. attorney, too, nine-thirty, ready to go."

The next day, Cox apologized to the court.

If the quip was inappropriate, it was not completely inaccurate, as the government was paying a heavy price for the witnesses they called to the stand. Their dubious choices culminated with the testimony of Maura Mooney, Rhoad's former girlfriend. Mooney, known as the "Space Cadet" and the "Sea Monkey" by some of the gentlemen smugglers, was a risky witness for the prosecution. On the one hand she was familiar with at least six of the remaining eight defendants through her relationship with Rhoad, and she could place them on the scene of various smuggling ventures. On the other hand she was easily confused about past events, had acknowledged a $500-a-week cocaine addiction, had admitted to being institutionalized and under psychiatric care, had pleaded guilty to embezzling from a Vermont ski resort, and had worked for the DEA as a paid informant and participated with federal agents in a failed setup against Rhoad.

During her testimony she recalled traveling with Rhoad to Hawaii and St. Barts for pleasure, and the Bahamas and the Channel Islands to deposit money. She was familiar with the major kingpins targeted by Operation Jackpot, including Foy, Harvey, and Les Riley, and even helped Rhoad sell pot, earning a commission from her lover. She also claimed to have cooked a meal for an unloading crew before a shipment of hashish arrived on Hilton Head. Despite her familiarity with many of the defendants, she couldn't keep them straight and confused defendants Mike McEachern and Glenn Cappleman, perhaps because the men purposefully switched shirts before she attempted the identification. She became agitated on the stand—"I can't stand this," she said at one point—and was unable to identify another defendant, "Disco Don" Powe. All this led to attacks by defense attorneys under cross-examination.

"You got a lot of names mixed up, didn't you," asked Moss.

"How do they pay you, like Mr. Rhoad in cash, or do they pay you by check? The government I'm talking about," said attorney Stephen Scaring.

When the defense attorneys were finished, Mooney stepped down from the stand and proceeded to cause an uproar. Among the many asides during her testimony, she said that she had suddenly seen the defendant Powe, and could in fact identify him. That comment, made when the jury was temporarily out of the courtroom, had gone either ignored or unheard by all but the court reporter. But now, while leaving the stand, Mooney bent down and leaned in close to Powe and whispered "Hey, Don." The defense attorneys went berserk.

"Judge . . . she went up to Mr. Powe and said something to him . . . it almost looked like she gave him a kiss," said Scaring. "The jury was looking at it, I don't know if counsel observed that. That was very improper of that witness to do that."

Hawkins was at a loss for how to remediate Mooney's bizarre action, and said such an interaction was not unusual, even recalling a woman who once hit Scaring's fellow attorney, Howe, in the head with a pocketbook after stepping down from the stand.

"What do you want me to do?" replied Hawkins. "To call back the jury in and tell them to please disregard the witness about the kissing."

Powe's lawyer moved for a mistrial, but Hawkins denied his motion. The judge pleased the defense attorneys, however, by forbidding the government from allowing their final witness, Customs agent Claude McDonald, to present the jury with a chart summarizing different smuggling ventures and which defendants were allegedly involved. Hawkins also dismissed ten charges against seven of the defendants, further reducing the government's case. After the government rested, only a few defense attorneys called witnesses, most opting to argue simply that the government had made an altogether unconvincing case riddled with inconsistencies.

"This Operation Jackpot is really 'Operation Crackpot,'" said Sanders's attorney, Ed Bell. "The case is falling apart. If you allow these defendants to be convicted on half truths than you're giving them half justice.

"The entire case," he added, "is people who are in the prosecutor's noose."

After more than thirteen hours of deliberation, the jury returned with verdicts, convicting five of the defendants and acquitting three. While Sanders was elated to be found not guilty of conspiracy charges, Thomas, the boat captain, was among the less fortunate, convicted of two separate smuggling ventures.

For as much publicity as Operation Jackpot attracted, critics considered the five convictions underwhelming, if not humiliating. The biggest crooks were still on the loose, they said, and the government fumbled its case against the men they did manage to get in the courtroom. The trial's chief prosecutor, Assistant U.S. Attorney Cam Littlejohn, concedes that things did not go smoothly. It was a nightmare, he says, considering the number of defendants who were dismissed and the fact that witnesses could not keep their memories straight. Littlejohn was assigned to the Jackpot case just three weeks before trial, introduced to an overwhelming amount of detail concerning nearly a decade's worth of smuggling.

"It was just a mess," Littlejohn says, "because no one had done a historical investigation."

U.S. Attorney Henry McMaster told reporters the trial was difficult, but dismissed criticism that the government netted no big fish.

"As far as the Operation Jackpot team is concerned, everybody who is involved in drug smuggling to any degree is a major criminal," said McMaster. "It's a matter of opinion as to which of these defendants was on a higher rung on the ladder."

Besides, he said, another trial was on the horizon.

"These convictions mark significant progress for Operation Jackpot," said McMaster, "but we still have a long way to go."

If prosecutors were smarting from the three acquittals, they quickly recovered from any disappointment. Four days after the end of the trial, on August 12, 1983, police arrested Willie Frank Steele, the boat captain of the *Anonymous of Rorc*, in Satellite Beach, Florida. Since being arrested nearly two years earlier on Edisto Island, South Carolina, with nearly ten thousand pounds of hashish, Steele had pleaded guilty to drug charges and was sentenced to prison. He skipped bond, however, and went on the run, living in Grenada and Florida while working with Bob "The Boss" Byers on more smuggling ventures. In lieu of full payment for these jobs, Steele agreed to captain three boats for Byers in exchange for a 50 percent ownership interest in *La Cautiva*, Byers's exquisite, eighty-five-foot steel-hulled sailboat. While he continued smuggling as a fugitive, Steele was indicted as part of Riley's smuggling ring and charged as a kingpin. Now he was in custody.

Prosecutors were ecstatic about the arrest, and even happier when they learned Steele was willing to cut a deal and talk. He pleaded guilty to a continuing criminal enterprise charge, becoming the first Jackpot defendant to be convicted of the so-called kingpin statute, or CCE. This law, similar to a racketeering charge but specific to drug trafficking, was passed in 1970 as part of the Drug Abuse Pre vention and Control Act. To convict a defendant of continuing criminal enterprise, a prosecutor must prove the suspect's involvement in drug felonies, demonstrate he made significant amounts of money in repeated operations, and establish that he supervised at least five different people during his illicit activities. The punishment for this offense was severe, requiring a prison term of at least ten years and up to life behind bars, without parole.

As investigators milked Steele for valuable information, ten defendants named in the Riley indictment prepared for trial. Among them was Gunn, who had charges against him dropped weeks earlier in the first Jackpot trial. Also preparing to stand trial was Gunn's friend and sailing partner, Christy Campbell, who had recently returned from the Bahamas to turn himself in.

During a pretrial hearing in October 1983 regarding the suppression of evidence, two Coast Guard officers were called to the stand to testify about their arrests of Campbell, Gunn, and Ashley Brunson aboard the *Love Affair* in 1978. First went Commander Thomas Braithewaite, the former commanding officer of the U.S. Coast Guard Cutter *Steadfast*. Then came Lieutenant Brian O'Keefe, who had boarded the sailboat and found it loaded with nearly eight thousand pounds of pot. Just before Hawkins recessed court for lunch, O'Keefe testified that prosecutors had shown him photographs of suspects that morning, but that he could not identify Gunn or Campbell, whom he had last seen five years earlier.

Returning to the courtroom an hour or so later, O'Keefe took the stand again and informed the court that while he ate lunch at the nearby Marriott hotel "a gentleman identifying himself as Mr. Chris Campbell came up and introduced himself, said hello, basically nice to see you again. Shortly thereafter, introduced Mr. Gunn."

O'Keefe said he was dining with Braithewaite, his former commanding officer. Campbell introduced himself to Braithewaite, too, before telling an acquaintance that the Coast Guard officers had been "real nice guys."

"He asked if any of the people who were on board the ship back then were still on board," said O'Keefe, "and he asked about another particular officer who had been on board at that time, who he had, I guess, a reasonable amount of conversation with."

After O'Keefe finished his testimony about the boarding, the court was stunned, with Hawkins exclaiming that "hardly ever do we get a reverse identification. Usually the agents identify the defendants. In this case, we have the defendants identifying the government agents. It's unusual."

Campbell's lawyer, Mark Kadish, asked Hawkins to go easy on him.

"I wish the court would stop throwing the darts into my body," said Kadish.

Next, the government called witnesses of events surrounding Campbell's and Gunn's arrests in Savannah, Georgia, after docking the *Caroline C.* in 1981. A dockhand testified that the men drunkenly celebrated their landfall at a marina, flashed a machine gun, and paid him generously to wash the boat. Next, a U.S. Customs Patrol agent described how he and others found the main salon of the *Caroline C* in shambles, with dirty dishes strewn about and damp clothing and blankets piled on the floor. The ship, he said, smelled of marijuana. Then U.S Customs agent Rachel Fischer took the stand and related her encounter at the Savannah airport with Gunn, Campbell, and their crewmate Peter Millikin. As she approached the men, she said, Gunn offered her a can of beer and gave her a kiss on the cheek. She answered his advances by displaying her badge.

Fischer identified Gunn in the courtroom, along with Campbell. Although it had been two years since the arrests, she said, she had no trouble remembering Gunn.

"Why's that?" asked a prosecutor.

"I never forget a man that kisses me," said Fischer.

For the second Jackpot trial, Gunn's fellow defendants included Riley's younger brother, Roy, and two of Harvey's younger brothers, Tom and Michael, along with seven other men. During a number of subsequent hearings held by Hawkins, the roster of defendants dwindled, both because Hawkins decided to sever the list of defendants, scheduling another trial, and because some defendants, including Steele and Campbell, struck plea agreements with the government.

Michael Harvey remembers meeting with some remaining code-fendants when his attorney, Larry Turner of Gainesville, Florida, came into the conference room, telling the men, "Guys, Christy Campbell just turned on y'all." The news was crushing. Not only had the government gained the cooperation of a charismatic witness with firsthand knowledge of numerous smuggling ventures, but those on trial were unsettled by a friend committing what they considered a betrayal. By this point there were only four men due to be tried. Each man—Gunn, Bruce MacDougall, Sanders, and Michael Harvey—had some kind of relationship with Campbell.

As the recent testimony of the Coast Guard officers and Customs agents attested to, Gunn had sailed often with Campbell throughout the Caribbean and twice to the Carolinas from Lebanon. Now Gunn's friend and former captain was potentially going to finger him in court. MacDougall helped off-load boats that Campbell sailed into Massachusetts and South Carolina. Sanders and Campbell grew up in the same South Carolina town of Beaufort. And Michael Harvey knew Campbell as one of his older brother Lee's most trusted and talented boat captains, someone he would turn to for the most daring trips. When Campbell met with some of the defendants to inform them personally of his decision, Harvey says he was not received warmly.

"I could wring your fucking neck if you don't get out of my sight," said MacDougall. "If I ever see you again, I'll kill you."

Besides paring down the number of defendants, Hawkins ordered the trial be held in Columbia, where there were more spacious courtrooms. Many of the people involved in the trial chose to stay just blocks from the courthouse in the new downtown Marriott hotel, including three of the defendants. There, the alleged smugglers were celebrities, and a sign hung in the lobby, pleading for the court to "Free the Marriott Four." Sanders, the lone defendant not to stay at the Marriott, had not met his codefendants before the trial, but says they were friendly to him and often asked him to "join the party" in their suites at the hotel.

"let me tell ya, their idea of a party scared me," writes Sanders. "They seemed to know they were toast and I suppose decided to blow it all out. Which they did.

"I went to their room with one of my preppie buddies one night, and [was] immediately approached by a couple hookers. real hookers. They were wide open. Strippers, I guess. Cause they stripped just for the hell of it. One of the hookers said she'd never been picked up by the fuzz. and just when I thought . . . well, that's good, at least a little bit careful about this . . . she said, 'but I have been slapped around by my tits a time or two.'

"that was a wild place, boy," writes Sanders. "not my cup of tea."

The hotel became even zanier when the defendants' lawyers arrived for lodging. The legal team included Bill Moffitt and John Zwerling, two prominent criminal defense attorneys from Alexandria, Virginia, representing MacDougall and Gunn, respectively. These men, and a few of their partners and colleagues in Virginia, were famous for their sympathetic attitudes toward marijuana, advocacy for changes in drug law, and representation of high-profile drug clients. Nicknamed the "Dope Bar" by Washington, D.C.'s law enforcement community, these lawyers would often be recommended in the pages of *High Times* magazine, says former Virginia-based DEA agent Jim Mittica, and were "notoriously anti-establishment, anti-government and pro-legalization." Some of these lawyers belonged to the National Organization for the Reform of Marijuana Laws (NORML), and many pledged through NORML not to represent defendants who agreed to cooperate with the government. Mittica says their defenses never lacked spirit or creativity, though the feisty lawyers sometimes wore a judge's patience thin. Says Mittica:

> They rarely had the merits of any case on their side so they tried to bury the government in a zillion motions. Most of the motions they filed were so esoteric that the judges almost invariably ruled in the government's favor—often before even hearing the government's motion. For some strange reason, however, they were particularly popular among the dopers in Northern Virginia. There's no doubt that they vigorously defended their clients but they rarely won their cases. If I were a drug defendant back then, facing potentially significant time, they would be the last attorneys I would choose.

It didn't help, Mittica says, that Zwerling sometimes wore bib overalls to court with marijuana pins stuck in the straps. Although there's no indication such attire was worn before Hawkins, Zwerling and the other defense lawyers had little problem gaining the attention of the mild-mannered judge, quickly putting him and the government on notice that, in contrast to the rather passive approach taken by the defense counsel in the first Jackpot trial, the out-of-town lawyers would fight the charges aggressively. At times their performance was off-putting to the prosecutors, and Cam Currie, the assistant U.S attorney credited for organizing much of the Jackpot investigation and trials, said she remembers being offended by some of the defense lawyers' "hardball" tactics, including accusations that the government encouraged its witnesses to lie on the stand.

Currie had missed most of the first Jackpot trial to attend extradition hearings in Australia for Riley and Wally Butler. Returning home, she worked with fellow prosecutors Cam Littlejohn, Bart Daniel, and Bob Jendron to prepare for the second trial. This time around the government would benefit from witnesses like Campbell and Steele, who could testify for hours on end, sharing their unique perspectives of South Carolina's empire of marijuana smuggling. Such testimony allowed the government to avoid calling the less reliable witnesses that had plagued their case in the first Jackpot trial.

Cognizant of the damning testimony men like Campbell, Steele, Pernell, Toombs, and others might give, the four defendants chose to argue they were victims of double jeopardy. Gunn, MacDougall, and Sanders had all been indicted as members of Foy's ring, but were not convicted in the first Jackpot trial. These new charges, their lawyers argued, were indistinguishable from the old, and the government had erred when it alleged separate conspiracies organized by Foy and Riley. Any drug offenses that took place, they said, were part of a single conspiracy in which men regularly participated.

In pleading this point to Hawkins, Moffitt used an argument devised by Zwerling, stating that the Foy and Riley rings were like two teams that conspired to play an illegal game of baseball each Sunday. Sometimes, he said, Team A would be short a few players and would borrow people from Team B. Other times, Moffitt said, Team B would borrow players from Team A, but the teams always conspired to play a single game of baseball each week.

Or, as Zwerling put it, the smugglers in the two indictments were like teeth in a zipper. Without one side, the other would be useless.

"The crossing over is constant," Zwerling said. "All the way up the line starting from 1975."

The government was quick to counter these analogies, arguing it was illogical to classify all smuggling offenses under the umbrella of a single conspiracy.

"We are not talking about two baseball teams, and only two baseball teams. We are talking about two separate drug organizations that are maybe two of fifty or a hundred that run up and down the East Coast. And they don't do business every Sunday or every day. They do business when they want to do business, and sometimes they use common means," said Jendron. "It's becoming apparent in the United States, and particularly in organized drug smuggling, that there is some floatation between the different distinct organizations . . . and what it's called is 'contracting.'"

In the case of Michael Harvey's double jeopardy defense, lawyer Larry Turner told the court how Harvey had been imprisoned after pleading guilty to drug charges in Virginia, only to be indicted in South Carolina eight days after being paroled. Turner complained his client was being punished twice for the same offense.

"Someone said to me just today that it's a little bit like young Johnny, when he hits the baseball through Miss Matilda's window and it breaks the window and it carries on through and it breaks her spinster sister's lamp," said Turner. "How many spankings does little Johnny get for that? Does he get two, or does he get one?"

Hawkins was ultimately unmoved, agreeing with the government in pretrial hearings that there existed separate and complete drug smuggling conspiracies. The defense lawyers were dismayed, but not surprised by the decision. Before the trial began, they appealed the case to the U.S. Court of Appeals for the Fourth Circuit, which issued a stay and soon ruled that it would indeed review an appeal on the grounds of double jeopardy, but could only do so if the appeal was made after a conviction, not before one. In other words, the defense lawyers may have to concede a conviction at trial in Columbia before having it potentially overturned by the appeals court in Richmond, Virginia. It was their best shot, they decided, though it wasn't worth conceding the men's guilt entirely to the jury, especially in instances where their client's alleged involvement did not overlap with activities alleged in the first Jackpot trial.

During the first two weeks of the trial, the government called dozens of witnesses to testify about scores of smuggling ventures. The defendants were placed on smuggling sailboats and at off-load sites, exchanging gemstones and driving trucks. They were at parties, on plantations, and aboard Learjets and the Concorde. Money and drugs, the witnesses said, motivated all those activities. The testimony was frequently interrupted by sharp exchanges between the prosecutors and defense lawyers. If the government was occasionally taken aback by the constant challenges from their counterparts, the defense was caught off guard, too. Among some of the defense lawyers there was a feeling, which was perhaps enhanced by South Carolina's reputation for good ol' boy politics, that all was not above board.

Zwerling remembers being in the courtroom lobby one day when he was introduced to Hawkins's son, who said he was clerking for South Carolina Supreme Court Justice Bruce Littlejohn. Zwerling was shocked, and minutes later he approached Sanders's lawyer, the South Carolinian Ed Bell, to confirm that the son of the trial judge was clerking for the father of the assistant U.S. attorney, Cam Littlejohn. Bell said yes, and, to Zwerling's disbelief, shrugged off the potential conflict of interest.

"Down there it was no big deal," says Zwerling. "Up here [in Virginia], it would have been a big deal."

For Moffitt, there was uneasiness about being a black lawyer trying a case in a federal building and U.S. courthouse named for former segregationist and current U.S. Senator Strom Thurmond. At one point in a heated debate, he says, he asked Littlejohn how he'd like to try a case in the Malcolm X Courthouse. That moment, Moffitt says, likely occurred about the same time the defense lawyers noticed an increased amount of security in the courtroom and prosecutors coming out of the judge's office. Curious as to what was happening, Zwerling and Moffitt made inquiries to Hawkins, only to be told it was something unrelated to the case. Zwerling could not understand how that was possible, and Moffitt became convinced the good ol' boy system was hard at work.

Eventually the defense lawyers learned Hawkins had been conferring with FBI agents and prosecutors because a Death Row inmate named Doyle Cecil Lucas had written letters to a juror. This was not the first time the convicted murderer's name had come up during the trial. Weeks earlier Bell disclosed that he and Sanders visited Lucas after the inmate contacted them from prison and said he wanted to talk about the Jackpot case. During the meeting Bell said Lucas asked if they wanted him to "fix the jury" and cause a mistrial—an offer Bell said he declined, cutting short their conversation. The episode was bewildering, Bell said, and he was astonished by the Death Row inmate's knowledge of the case and its participants.

Hawkins sympathized with Bell, perhaps because of his own peculiar relationship with convicted South Carolina serial killer Pee Wee Gaskins. Before becoming a judge, Hawkins told Bell and the other defense lawyers and prosecutors, he had once represented Gaskins and got him acquitted.

"He sent me lots of customers," said Hawkins. "I get a lot of letters about [how] Judge Hawkins can help you out."

Now, weeks after Bell and Sanders's meeting with Lucas, the government had become aware that the inmate had written to a juror and was concerned that the killer had contacted other jurors as well. After the defense lawyers' protests, Hawkins gathered lawyers from both sides in his chambers, along with a court reporter, to discuss the unusual communication and the potential effects on the jury. Hawkins was adamant that discussion of the letter be kept under wraps, and he excluded the media as he shared more details of the correspondence from Lucas.

"I'm not going to have any press. What I'm calling open court is right here. This is open," said Hawkins. "We'll even go further than that. And I've really got that gag order in effect—if you all don't think I'll put you in jail—really he wrote two letters."

For the defense lawyers, such interference was troubling. The possibility existed, they told Hawkins, that anyone who received letters from Lucas about acquitting the men on trial might go out of their way to convict the defendants just to "prove their virtue," as

Zwerling put it, and not do the killer's bidding. Hawkins proceeded to ask the juror about the letters she received, and, after initially denying anyone had contacted her, she admitted to receiving a single letter from Lucas, but said that she tore it up and spoke of it to no one. Hawkins excused her, and everyone present agreed the juror, who was thought to be related to Lucas through a common-law marriage, was not being completely candid. She would have to be replaced, they decided, and so might other jurors if they had been contacted. Hawkins started questioning the other jury members and uncovered even more problems.

A male juror from Orangeburg, South Carolina, told Hawkins that a pawnshop owner had recently asked him to visit his store, ostensibly to show him a guitar amplifier he had looked at days earlier. But when he arrived, the juror said, he learned the owner had a different agenda.

"He asked me, was I on jury duty. And I told him, 'Yes, sir,'" said the juror. "And he said he heard that fellow that was in trouble with this smuggling operation was going to try and get out of it by paying some sum of money, and he mentioned the name Les Riley."

The juror informed Hawkins he had mentioned this incident to another juror, which upset the judge and required him to question her next. Hawkins was not pleased at the turmoil that had been brewing within his jury. Moreover, the confusion was addled by a logistical problem: Court officials were running out of rooms trying to keep separate a growing assortment of groups, including the judge and lawyers, the media, questioned witnesses, and unquestioned witnesses. Hawkins worried about having to replace the entire panel of jurors.

"Things aren't working too well along through here, and I would say, if they get worse, like this case seems to have a habit of working itself, then, you know, I'm almost hesitant to even ask the next lady the question," said Hawkins. "Mr. Clerk, I need another room . . . I'm sure the press, by now, knows that something terrible is going on."

In the end Hawkins replaced the juror who had been contacted by Lucas with an alternate—an action the press reported, though the media did not know why the switch was made. After an interruption of several hours, the trial resumed. The prosecution continued to call their witnesses, while the defense lawyers tried to depict them as the most contemptible of men for cooperating with the government and testifying against friends in exchange for a reduction in charges.

"What they are bargaining with here is the lives of other people," said Moffitt. "And that is the worst kind of bargaining that you can make."

When former Hilton Head fireman Hank Strickland took the stand, Moffitt elicited an admission from him that he violated public trust by sharing law enforcement radio frequencies with smugglers. Moffitt also quizzed him about the light punishment he received after providing Jackpot agents with critical information early in the investigation.

"So you got a complete walk," said Moffitt. "You walked away from these events without ever having to go to court, without ever having to sit and hear your name come up in anything like this, didn't you?"

To the defense counsel's pleasure, not every witness the government called was cooperative. One alleged the police planted evidence. Another, Kenny O'Day, wore jeans and a bandana when testifying, an apparent protest against the suits other government witnesses wore. Although he grudgingly identified Gunn as a crewmate aboard the *Second Life,* a reporter described him as a "most reluctant government witness" and Hawkins even remarked about his hostility. While on the stand, O'Day explained why he had refused to testify in front of a Virginia grand jury, and how he regretted testifying now in South Carolina, though he felt compelled to do so in order to avoid serving any time beyond his current sentence for drug crimes in Virginia.

"It's been instilled in me since childhood, it's not the right thing to do to tell on somebody else," said O'Day. "Morally, I don't think it's right."

After the prosecution rested, the defense called very few of its own witnesses. The exception was Sanders's lawyer, who sought to establish an alibi for his client during the early morning hours when the *Anonymous of Rorc* was busted on Sanders's grandmother's property, with suspects fleeing into the woods. Among these witnesses was Granny herself, Ella M. Seabrook, a ninety-year-old woman who Bell said was famous for her waffles and breakfast.

"Oh yes," Seabrook replied to that compliment. "I'm an old girl at cooking."

Seabrook had little to say about the night police swarmed her property, except to say that her grandson didn't keep radios in the house and she didn't appreciate the police mulling around her yard and coming inside.

When it came time to cross-examine the sweet old woman, Currie gingerly stepped forward. The prosecutors were aware they had to tread carefully when questioning the senior citizen, that they could not abuse her, even if they suspected she was not being forthcoming. Currie, being the lone female prosecutor, was regarded as the best choice for the delicate task. Her colleagues nicknamed her "Mikey" for cross-examining difficult witnesses, referencing the popular Life cereal commercial in which a youngster named Mikey is given a bowl of cereal after his older brothers balk at eating a food "that's supposed to be good for you."

"Let's get Mikey," the brothers say in the famous commercial clip. "He won't eat it."

But Mikey does eat it, and he likes it.

In the trial, though, there was no place for such lighthearted humor, even with Granny taking the stand. The prosecution and defense lawyers became increasingly antagonistic as the witness lists were exhausted and the trial neared its conclusion. The opposing lawyers' passions contributed to sharpened tongues during closing arguments, with the defense launching a final attack on the credibility of the smugglers who testified for the government. Zwerling and Moffitt, in particular, expressed disgust with the methods used to compel witness testimony.

"No matter how reprehensible they feel it is, no matter how morally degrading they feel that what they're being made to do is," said Zwerling, "the government has found a way to scare them, threaten them, squeeze them or pay them off to do something—come here and tell what the government wanted."

Moffitt told the jury that the men who took the stand were no different than Soviets who informed on their own neighbors.

"Please understand that because you are our last resort; you are what separates us from the Iranians and the animals," said Moffitt. "Do not let testimony be bought and sold. Do not let lives be bought and sold. Protect us all from that because we need to be protected."

Rebutting Zwerling's charges, Littlejohn sniped back, belittling the defense's arguments as bluster intended to distract from the plain facts.

"When you have a case and you're defending it, and the case is not good, you attack the witnesses, when the case is even weaker, you attack the prosecution," said Littlejohn. "A cheap lawyer trick."

Responding to Moffitt's geopolitical comments, Littlejohn argued that the real menace to America was not the smugglers who confessed to their crimes, but rather the unrepentant criminals who denied wrongdoing.

"I don't know where Mr. Moffitt grew up, but where I grew up everybody was supposed to respect law and order, cooperate with law and order; if they knew a crime, they were to tell about it," said Littlejohn. "Mr. Moffitt goes on to talk about the moral outrage of bringing these people in to testify under oath. Ladies and gentlemen, the moral outrage in this case is the flood of drugs that is coming into this country every year . . . .

"He goes on to say, 'Protect us from the government . . . ,' I say, 'Protect us from drug smugglers like Bruce MacDougall.'"

When Littlejohn finished, defense lawyer Bell, who referred to government witnesses as worms in his own closing argument, complained to Hawkins about some of Littlejohn's comments. The griping triggered the usually elusive temper of Hawkins, who soon verbalized the frustrations he had so far endured in the two Jackpot trials. He was not spare in his criticism.

"I have never in the years I have been practicing ever heard attorneys address fellow attorneys or to accuse them of things I have heard in this argument," said Hawkins. "And the only thing that even comes close to it was the last trial we had, and, as you recall, I called some lawyers down for it.

"I can really understand why the public kind of holds lawyers in with the little bit of respect that they do, rather than the great respect that they would have, when they come here and sit and hear them accuse one another of matters such as I have heard during these arguments," said Hawkins. "If I had been the government attorneys, I suspect you would have had a lot more objections and grounds for mischarge, if . . . I had had the abuse heaped on me that was piled on them here last night and today."

Hawkins's diatribe, part cathartic, part scolding, weighed heavily on the defense counsel. The next day, the lawyers returned to court and apologized to Hawkins, informing him that they had also made peace with the prosecutors. Hawkins accepted their apology, but said he was concerned about a trend he had observed in his courtroom. More and more lawyers were embracing hardball tactics, he said, and their behavior often suffered from a lack of respect. Zwerling engaged him on this point and said some government prosecutors could be similarly heavy-handed, mentioning a client he represented in Virginia who was threatened with a barrage of charges and a prison term in a maximum-security facility if he did not cooperate with the government. Zwerling said he perceived this as an example of a distressing imbalance in the legal system, where the government can offer a defendant rewards for testimony, whether it be dropped charges, immunity from prosecution for other offenses, or furloughs to visit with spouses. Defense lawyers, Zwerling noted, could offer none of that.

Zwerling's observation was not without example. Earlier in the trial, fellow defense lawyer John Keats mentioned the difficulty he had in trying to subpoena testimony from smuggler Clark Swift.

"He told us, in no uncertain terms, that he didn't want to testify, that he was sorry he had ever talked to us in the first place. That he didn't care, of course, what happened to our client. As far as he was concerned, they could all do forty years apiece," said Keats. "And, more importantly, if we tried to put him on the witness stand he would take our case and—I'll use the term 'screw it up'; he used a little bit more infamous expletive than that—and warned us repeatedly, if we, in any way, attempted to secure his testimony on the record, in this case, he was going to do everything within his power to literally sink our ship."

Having Hawkins's ear, Zwerling continued to air his own grievances about the legal system. It was an inspired speech, but one made as an aside at the conclusion of a trial, outside the presence of the jury. As an anxious courtroom awaited the jury's return and word on the defendants' fates, Zwerling raged against the government's habit of enlisting, and rewarding, suspects in order to enable their investigations and bolster their cases against those who choose to exercise their Sixth Amendment right to a speedy and public trial by jury.

"There's been a change in the last two years, and people aren't allowed to just plead guilty and do their time; if subpoenaed, come in and testify to the truth," said Zwerling.

"There is tremendous pressure being put on people, not only to plead guilty and tell the truth if subpoenaed, but to come in and, for whatever they're going to get out of it, make a cooperating agreement and have to go through the debriefings and the polygraphs and all of this other thing.

"It's not, 'I did wrong. I want to do my time. And if I'm subpoenaed, I will tell the truth,'" said Zwerling. "That's no longer good enough."

With so much bargaining occurring between suspects and the government, Zwerling lamented, justice was traded away. Pity the last man standing, for he will have nothing to bargain with and everyone against him.

Chapter Twelve

Willie Frank Steele sat in a county jail in October 1983. He'd already decided to help the government, admitting his guilt as a drug kingpin and agreeing to serve as the lead witness in the second trial against his former smuggling colleagues, which was in progress a few miles away in downtown Columbia. The government didn't need him today, but still he wanted to talk. He placed a call to Jackpot investigator and DEA agent Dewey Greager.

When court finished for the day, David Forbes and Greager paid Steele a visit. The prisoner asked for a favor, and told his company it'd be worth their while. Bring me a copy of the latest yachting magazine, he said, I have something to show you. Forbes and Greager scoured local bookstores and newsstands and soon returned to the jail with the requested copy. Steele took the magazine in hand and flipped to the classified ads in back. He stuck his finger against a page, pointing to a particularly fine-looking sailboat listed for sale in Antigua. Although the advertisement didn't list the vessel's true name, Steele was certain it was Bob "The Boss" Byers's eighty-five-foot steel-hulled sailboat, *La Cautiva*.

"That's her," Steele said. "She's one of a kind."

The agents didn't doubt him. Steele was in love with the world-class sailboat and likely smarting over the fact that he'd never again take her helm. With lustful eyes Steele stared at the small magazine picture and gabbed to Forbes and Greager. Find the boat, he told the government agents, and you'll find Byers.

Steele's motivation for sharing this tip is unclear. Divulging the whereabouts of *La Cautiva* was not part of his plea agreement with the government. The disclosure wouldn't necessarily result in reduced prison time, either, though prosecutors could emphasize his exceedingly cooperative spirit to Judge Falcon Hawkins when it came time for Steele to be sentenced. Perhaps Steele wanted to clear his conscience, or maybe he just couldn't keep the magazine advertisement to himself. It's possible he was exacting revenge on Byers, his former friend, who was still on the lam. Before returning to Florida, where he was arrested two months earlier, Steele had been living in Grenada but was running out of cash. He asked Byers for money owed to him, but Byers said he'd have to come to the United States to collect. Now Steele found himself in a jail cell, and still without the money owed him. One smuggler speculates it was Steele's drug-addled brain that made him tell on friends without even wincing, recalling Steele telling him proudly that he "handed [the feds] Bob Byers on a plate."

"He was a druggie," says the smuggler, "and druggies do weird shit."

In any case, Steele was unabashed about his cooperation, and later trumpeted it throughout federal prison, which was bewildering to smuggler Ken Smith, who worked with Barry Foy and Les Riley on their early Jamaican ventures, and was an acquaintance of Steele.

"You don't talk about snitching people out when you're in the joint," says Smith. "As informal as we may have made it, it's still fucking federal prison, and you can die there very, very quickly."

Smith recalls running into Steele in prison, just before Smith was due to be released for drug offenses outside the scope of Operation Jackpot. As Smith passed by a cell holding Steele and six other men, Steele called out loudly to him.

"Dude, did you tell them everything?" asked Steele, approaching the bars that separated them and putting Smith instantly on guard.

"No, Frank, I didn't tell them everything. I hardly told them anything at all."

"Man, I did," said Steele.

Smith was incredulous. He leaned in closely and spoke very seriously to his friend.

"Frank, stop talking like this, man. You're not at the fucking Howard Johnson's."

"Oh, fuck these guys. I'm on my way to [federal prison in] Tallahassee."

"That's great. You need to get out of here," said Smith, preparing to walk away. "You need to shut your mouth."

Steele, however, still wanted to talk.

"Did you tell them about Europe?"

"No, Frank, I didn't tell them about Europe," said Smith, now frightened he might be given more time due to Steele's revelations. "What did you tell them about Europe, because you didn't have a fucking thing to do with me going to Europe?"

"Well I had to tell them when I went there for Les."

"And?"

"Well I had to tell them that you're the one that did it first and showed us it could be done."

If Steele was plagued by logorrhea, agents like Forbes and Greager weren't about to offer him any remedy. Upon hearing the information about Byers and his boat, they quickly hatched a plan, one that violated protocol. Since Byers was on the run, says Forbes, they should have turned their sailboat tip over to the U.S. Marshal Service, the agency charged with finding fugitives. The Jackpot task force feared Byers would not be considered a priority, however, so Greager and Forbes decided to take action themselves. They would travel to Antigua and pose as businessmen interested in purchasing a luxury sailboat, hopefully meeting Byers on board the boat or on the island. Using an undercover DEA phone line, Greager quickly called the boatyard listed in the ad, asking when *La Cautiva* could be seen. Not yet, said the broker, since the boat was in Grenada having her hull repainted. But he would call back, he promised, when she and her owner returned to Antigua.

Grenada, like other former British colonies in the Caribbean, had recently earned its independence. Five years after that, in 1979, the new government was overthrown by Marxists in the New JEWEL Movement, led by Maurice Bishop, a lawyer educated in London. Popular at home, his actions as prime minister alarmed other Western leaders. Under Bishop's leadership, Grenada suspended its constitution, created an army, outlawed opposition political parties, and welcomed assistance from Cuba. The United States and other Caribbean nations grew concerned about the militarization of the country, the absence of political freedom, and Cuba's influence on the island. Through Cuba's assistance, a new airport was being built, and the American government feared it could be used to support Soviet aircraft. U.S. President Ronald Reagan mentioned the airport in a March

1983 speech on national security that has since become known as the Star Wars speech, based on its emphasis on creating a network of ground- and outer space–based defenses to protect against nuclear missile attacks:

> *On the small island of Grenada, at the southern end of the Caribbean chain, the Cubans, with Soviet financing and backing, are in the process of building an airfield with a 10,000-foot runway. Grenada doesn't even have an air force. Who is it intended for? . . . The rapid buildup of Grenada's military potential is unrelated to any conceivable threat to this island country of under 110,000 people and totally at odds with the pattern of other eastern Caribbean States, most of which are unarmed. The Soviet-Cuban militarization of Grenada, in short, can only be seen as power projection into the region.*

Six months later, in October 1983, Grenada's government showed signs of severe stress, as relations between Bishop and other party leaders soured. It was about this time when Byers returned to the island to ready *La Cautiva* for sale. He had kept it docked in Grenada for a year and was keen on selling it to replenish his diminishing cash reserves. Although he was famously secretive, friends guessed he was selling off his assets in preparation for setting sail to Fiji and leaving the smuggling business behind. Among *La Cautiva*'s needs was a fresh coat of bottom paint. Byers had her hauled out of the water so workers could access the hull. There it sat on a lift, suspended in the air, when troubles began on the island. Byers later recounted:

> *There was quite a civil uprising there at the time. Maurice Bishop was in control of the island at the time, and he was having a tendency to swing away from communism, was the nearest I could tell, and they took him prisoner and they put him under house arrest. There was a lot of demonstration going on in the streets at the time, and I was there getting the boat ready to sail out of the country when the shooting started, and I was more or less—not a hostage—but . . . caught in the crossfire.*

While the military wanted Bishop held under arrest, the public wanted him freed. The protesting crowds succeeded in having him released on October 19, 1983, but soldiers captured him hours later. Along with other leaders, Bishop was stood against a wall before a firing squad as the fighting worsened. Byers said he witnessed some of the violence, seeing soldiers attack civilians. American students from St. George's University Medical School begged Byers to ferry them off the island when his boat was operable.

"The Grenadians started shooting up schoolchildren and people protesting," said Byers, "and they ended up eventually shooting the prime minister, Maurice Bishop."

Following Bishop's death, a general appointed himself ruler of the island and imposed a four-day curfew. Anyone who violated it, he said, day or night, could be shot on sight. Meanwhile, the execution of Bishop and associated fighting had unnerved the United States. A U.S. invasion of the island was feared, and Grenadian soldiers prepared themselves for more fighting. Byers said:

Radio Free Grenada was advising us that an invasion was imminent, and they were telling everybody to come and pick up guns. They were going to push the capitalist pigs back into the sea. Most of the boats that were capable of leaving left and most of the Americans that could leave left on boats. My boat was out of the water. It was high and dry on the synchrolift and the bottom was being painted. When the curfew was invoked, they shut off the electricity and the workers couldn't come to work because of the curfew.

On October 25, six days after Bishop was killed, a team of Navy SEALS and more than one thousand Marines and Army Rangers invaded the island. Soon after, paratroopers landed on Grenada, bringing the invading force to six thousand U.S soldiers and three hundred troops from other Caribbean nations. Over three days of fighting, eighteen Americans, sixteen Grenadians, and fourteen Cubans were killed as American forces took control of Grenada.

Although the island was stabilized, Byers's boat still could not be lowered into the water, and the medical students Byers had promised to evacuate were airlifted off of Grenada by the American military. *La Cautiva* was not completely useless though, as its vittles and sophisticated electronic equipment were attractive to American soldiers. According to Byers:

> *When the invasion was over and our troops started to infiltrate the particular part of town I was in, I did assist them in locating a downed helicopter, and they came to me and asked me to translate for them on various occasions. They said that even though those West Indians were speaking English, they had a hard time understanding them. I helped the United States SEAL team on several occasions with reconnaissance. They came to me and asked my opinion of what the attitude of the Grenadian people was in the city, and if I thought it was safe to enter the harbor and move their manpower into the city.*
>
> *I dealt with several colonels and a couple of captains, but I didn't take their names to any effect where I could remember who they were. They came by several times and had beers and drinks with me and I supplied them with what cigarettes I could get them. I bought cases of Coca-Cola and Sprite for them and gave them directions.*

No matter his patriotism, Byers was first and foremost a businessman, even when his country's military was serving as protector. In exchange for soft drinks, cigarettes, Heinekens, and advice, Byers was given a portable rocket launcher, ostensibly to repel potential pirate attacks in the Caribbean. The lightweight rocket launcher, known as a LAW, or light anti-tank weapon, fired a single sixty-six-millimeter rocket capable of penetrating an armored vehicle. Fired into a boat, it would easily blast a hole through the hull and likely scorch and fragment what, or who, was inside.

As life returned to some normalcy in Grenada and the shooting stopped, Byers finally had his boat lowered into the water and set sail for the nearby island of Bequia. On board with him were several Grenadians who feared for their lives and wished to flee the island, including two doctors, a family, and others. After reaching Bequia, he headed to Antigua, where he cleared customs and immigrations through the use of a fake passport in the name of William Dennis Wilcox. After his arrival he heard from the yacht broker. Someone was interested in looking at *La Cautiva.*

Back in South Carolina, closing arguments were made in the second Jackpot trial. At their conclusion, the jury was sent off to decide the fates of Kenny Gunn, Mike Harvey, Bruce MacDougall, and Skip Sanders, charged to determine the extent, if any, of their involvement in the alleged long-running marijuana and hashish smuggling conspiracies. After nearly twelve hours of deliberation, the jury returned to the court. The men were found guilty on each and every count.

The prosecution "just bowled us over with evidence," said jury foreman Leon Temples. In the case of Gunn and MacDougall, Temples said, they "didn't have a dog's chance" of escaping conviction. Following announcement of the verdict, Hawkins raised the men's bonds to amounts that all but Gunn were unable to immediately post, sending them to jail to await sentencing. Justice moved swiftly. As the men were led away and the courtroom cleared, defense lawyers said they expected such a verdict and vowed to appeal on grounds of double jeopardy. On the government side, U.S. Attorney Henry McMaster seized on the momentum, telling reporters the convictions sent "a message to all the millionaire smugglers and their jet-set henchmen.

"We've had twenty-four convictions or guilty pleas, seized more than $5 million in property, and have had only three acquittals. I guess the score now is twenty-four to three," said McMaster. "The key has been our personnel. We've got the best lawyers and the best agents in the country."

Next for the government was the trial of another five defendants, including Les Riley's younger brother, Roy. Months earlier, Roy had agreed to a plea deal with the government and participated in two days of debriefings before he and prosecutors reached an impasse. The government was dissatisfied with the information he shared, complaining his recollections were incomplete and lacked detail. They also took issue with his refusal to discuss his finances and assets—a deal breaker for the prosecution. Such lack of cooperation, the government argued, constituted a breach of his duties, and they moved to dissolve the agreement. In hearings prior to Roy's trial, Hawkins sympathized with the government, ordering Riley to stand trial. He pleaded not guilty to the alleged drug offenses.

As the second trial finished with the convictions of the Marriott Four and the government prepared for a new trial in Charleston, Greager received the phone call he had been waiting for. It was the yacht broker in Antigua, calling to tell him *La Cautiva* had returned and was moored in Antigua's English Harbour.

"I'm looking at her now," said the broker, who was, of course, unaware he was speaking with an undercover DEA agent.

Greager, portraying himself as the CEO of a fictional Colorado energy company, said he could fly down to Antigua the next day to see the boat. He'd like to bring the firm's comptroller, too, Greager said, in case he was interested in making an offer and discussing terms of a potential deal. The broker said he'd make an appointment with the owner to show the boat and that they would expect the businessmen soon.

Forbes and Greager were on a flight to Antigua the next day. They wore shorts and T-shirts, giving the impression they were businessmen kicking back in the tropics, glad to be away from cold weather. Although he had no undercover police experience, Forbes felt comfortable acting as a comptroller. Given his undergraduate accounting education, his brief work experience as a CPA and his extensive investigative work for the IRS, Forbes was a natural fit for the role. He also knew a little about sailing—or at least more than Greager.

Such expertise could prove crucial in convincing Byers that they were legitimate businessmen. Given Byers's fugitive status, he might be distrustful of strangers from the United States. It was more likely, however, that Forbes and Greager would blindside the alleged kingpin. What were the chances the classified ad would be brought to the government's attention and the pictured boat be revealed as *La Cautiva*?

Despite having the element of surprise on their side, the American agents faced numerous challenges in the upcoming meeting. They'd be meeting on Byers's boat in the middle of a harbor, away from any Antiguan police backup. As Americans federal agents, they had no power of arrest in Antiguan territorial waters. They also weren't permitted to carry concealed weapons. Such limitations required creative thinking about how to apprehend Byers should they indeed meet him on board his sailboat.

Forbes put forth an idea to ask Byers for a test cruise, and to have him sail *La Cautiva* away from Antigua into open seas. When the sailboat entered international waters, he suggested, a Coast Guard ship could intercept them and take Byers into custody. U.S. diplomats, however, frowned on that course of action, disappointing Forbes.

Another tactic was for Forbes and Greager to board the sailboat, inspect the vessel, and conduct negotiations for its purchase. They would make a visual identification of Byers and then return to shore, where they could inform Antiguan police they had confirmed Byers's presence in their country. From there, though, it became complicated. Should the Antiguans arrest Byers, he could fight extradition efforts, much like Riley and Wally Butler had now done for seven months in Australia. Not only would the United States have to be patient for his return, but the Antiguan government might be unwilling to fight an extended legal battle, as it would be expensive for the small island nation, requiring them to devote prosecutors to the case and jail the high-profile alleged drug kingpin for an indefinite amount of time.

Unwilling to endure the potentially long legal process, in which extradition was not guaranteed, the DEA instead insisted that the Antiguans deport Byers should Forbes and Greager identify him. Preferably, the deportation would be to a U.S. territory, where DEA agents could arrest Byers. Considering the difficulty the Operation Jackpot task force had in locating its top suspects, the DEA was eager to get its hands on alleged kingpins any way it could.

Forbes and Greager arrived in Antigua and quickly headed out to see *La Cautiva* in English Harbour. Stepping aboard the sailboat, they met a short, heavyset man with a beard and balding hair. He offered them Heinekens and regaled them with stories of escaping from Grenada, where he had witnessed intense fighting. Despite the bloodshed, the man said he enjoyed the intimate company of various women seeking to leave the island aboard his sailboat. He bragged that he had never gotten laid so much in his life. Without a doubt, the agents knew, this was Bob "The Boss" Byers.

During the ninety minutes or so Greager and Forbes spent with the smuggler, both sides refrained from asking about each other's professions and instead focused on the sailboat. Byers promised to take them on a sea trial the next day and also said he'd get them laid that evening if they'd like. Impressed with *La Cautiva*, they struck a potential deal for the sailboat. Byers insisted on receiving cash and agreed to an offer from Forbes of about half a million dollars up front and another half million or so in the next few months. Forbes and Greager then headed back to shore, leaving Byers convinced he had found a buyer.

Upon reaching land, the investigators met with Antiguan police, disclosing that they had identified Byers.

"Ain't no doubt that's him," said Forbes.

Enjoy the beach, the Antiguans responded, we'll take care of it from here. They promptly headed out into the harbor and arrested Byers, who initiated a scuffle with the Antiguans, unwilling to leave his sailboat without a fight. Once he was restrained, the Antiguan police told him he'd be deported for entering the country with a false passport. He pleaded not to be sent to a U.S. territory, admitting he was a wanted man, and tried bribing officials to send him elsewhere. The Antiguans would have none of it and booked him on a flight to the nearest city in an American territory—San Juan, Puerto Rico. He sat in the plane handcuffed to an Antiguan immigration officer, with a plainclothes DEA agent seated nearby as a precautionary measure. When the plane touched down in Puerto Rico, Byers was greeted by federal agents and placed under arrest.

"Bob," said the agents, "it just ain't your day."

On November 30, 1983, a few days after Byers was arraigned in South Carolina and held on a $7.5 million bond, the third Jackpot trial began in Charleston. Facing smuggling charges were Roy Riley; Oliver Mayfield; Kenny Pearce; and Kenny Floyd, the man who, two years earlier, had been arrested after leading South Carolina wildlife agents on a speedboat chase with John "Smokin' Sneakers" Jamison while their smuggling colleagues unloaded thirty thousand pounds of hashish. Days earlier Lee Harvey's brother Tom ducked out of the trial by pleading guilty to conspiring to import hashish.

Just as in the first two Jackpot trials, this one began with the government's lead witnesses taking the stand for hours and providing a primer on the intriguing marijuana smuggling underworld, but rarely, if ever, mentioning involvement with the defendants in the courtroom. During testimony from Steele, Julian "Doc" Pernell, and Barry "Ice Cream" Toombs, Les Riley's name came up often, and one of Roy Riley's defense lawyers, Bob Fierer of Atlanta, cautioned jurors against punishing the youngest Riley for the actions of his older brother, whom he said Roy idolized.

Additional witnesses implicated Roy in assorted smuggling ventures. They testified, too, about trips to the Bahamas with Roy, concealing large amounts of bundled cash under skirts and inside pants. His role was minor, they said, with Roy serving as a lookout, or bagman, or driver. One witness, Wayne McDonald, described Roy as a "go-fer," or errand boy, for his older brother. Another, Christy Campbell, said he didn't even bother asking Roy about the considerable amount of money he was owed by Les and Lee Harvey.

"He was bottom of the barrel," Campbell said. "He just wasn't powerful."

For the Riley family, the past year had been a tumultuous time. Government agents interrupted their Thanksgiving by seizing a car. In May 1983, Les and Roy were indicted and Les was arrested in Australia, where he still remained imprisoned six months later. For Roy's bond, his parents put up their home and other land to guarantee he'd show up for trial. There was at least some good news: Nine days before being indicted, Roy's wife gave birth to their second son.

Their sons' legal problems weighed heavily on the elder Rileys, as Roy told a reporter a few months before his trial.

"I'm very close to my parents," said Roy. "They are as upset as you might think. Whenever we get a notice that there's a hearing, they think somebody's going to come in and arrest us all."

He also told the reporter that the government had exaggerated his role, perhaps because of his family name.

"I don't know 90 percent of the people named in the indictments. Maybe if they showed me pictures, I could recognize some of them,"

Roy said. "The government makes it seem like a whole lot more than it is because you've got two brothers. You've got two brothers with the same last name."

During the trial, however, Roy was depicted as standing on his own often enough in smuggling ventures, and his involvement was more significant than that of the other defendants. Roy's case suffered from the testimony of close friends, one of whom taped their conversations for the government, and another who had chosen Roy as his best man at his wedding three years earlier. Nevertheless, his lawyers sought to downplay Roy's involvement. In response, the government used their familiar argument that "in the dope business, there were no little men."

Predictably the defense attorneys tried to poke holes in the prosecutors' case by attacking the government's witnesses. In one inspired argument, Floyd's lawyer, Jim Moss, was particularly inventive, making reference to nearby symbols of justice hanging in the courtroom.

"If that eagle on that great seal could have come off that seal and seen the vermin that testified in this courtroom," Moss said, "he would have taken them out and dumped them on the street."

In the end his argument fell short, as did the one made by Roy Riley's lawyers. Both Riley and Floyd were convicted of the majority of counts against them. Pearce was acquitted, though, and Mayfield had changed his plea in the middle of trial, admitting to conspiring to import marijuana. McMaster was ecstatic over the results and claimed Operation Jackpot had stemmed the flow of drugs being smuggled into the East Coast. The public, he said, stood behind him and his deputies in the war against drugs.

"We're confident," he said, "that South Carolina juries are sending a message to drug smugglers that they're fed up with the misery they've caused South Carolinians over the years, and they're simply not going to take it anymore."

The government's strong showing, as well as the recent capture of Byers, cemented Operation Jackpot's reputation as an effective crime-fighting investigation. In a December 4, 1983, editorial, the *State* newspaper praised the task force, saying, "Determined efforts like Operation Jackpot finally are showing concrete results where rhetoric once prevailed." The paper didn't know, however, that the Jackpot investigation was nowhere near finished.

For the Jackpot task force, the seizure of assets remained an important component of their investigation, even as trials were ongoing and manhunts were underway for the missing kingpins and other defendants. In August 1983, following the first Jackpot trial, investigators seized a 1979 Lincoln Continental from South Carolina Representative Thomas N. Rhoad. The elder, sixty-year-old Rhoad had been given the car by his son, Tom "Rolex" Rhoad III, after Rolex had won the car at a raffle on Hilton Head Island. The government reasoned that the younger Rhoad used drug money to purchase the raffle tickets, so the car was illegally obtained. Jackpot agents Mike Lemnah and Forbes seized the car from the state legislator, who was serving his first term.

"My son gave it to me," said Rhoad. "He won it in a raffle."

"We know that," said Lemnah. "We're still taking it."

Driving away, the agents left Rhoad fuming, though they allowed him to keep his statehouse license plate.

Months later, in March 1984, the government garnered headlines by debuting at Sotheby's in New York—the first time Uncle Sam disposed of seized assets through a high-end art auction house. Up for sale was smuggler Toombs's collection of Tiffany lamps and glassware, which Virginia investigators had seized two years earlier. Sotheby's described the art as the "finest collection of Tiffany glass and Art Nouveau objects to come on the market in several years."

Prior to the sale, Sotheby's Art Nouveau expert had claimed Toombs's collection was composed of high-quality counterfeits, confounding the government and DEA attorney Steve Zimmerman, who had pushed to sell the art through an auction house. The Sotheby's expert later changed her mind, however, and Sotheby's held an all-day event on March 24, offering 273 pieces, including lamps, vases, paperweights, mirrors, candlesticks, and more. Some floor lamps featured Tiffany's patented colorful Favrile glass in designs of poppies, peonies, and bamboo. Table lamps being auctioned featured water lilies, poinsettias, and lotus leaves. And "the most fanciful and fragile flower-form vases," said a writer for the New York Times, "are equally arresting but far less expensive. These delicate designs translate petals, stems and bulbs into a wonderland of satiny soft colors."

Interested bidders lined up outside Sotheby's more than an hour before the auction house opened. It was a motley crowd, at least compared to the more well-heeled art enthusiasts who regularly frequented Sotheby's auctions. Once the bidding started, the auction house was standing room only, and bidders also called in from Tokyo, Palm Beach, Florida, and California, with Hollywood director Steven Spielberg purchasing a table lamp.

The prices bid for the lamps and other auctions greatly exceeded Sotheby's estimates, with at least five lamps selling for more than $40,000. The highest bid received was a record $64,900 for a red, zig-zagged Tel El Amarna Tiffany vase made circa 1910. At the end of the day, the art was auctioned for nearly $1.8 million, or $700,000 more than Sotheby's best estimate. After deducting a commission and expenses, Sotheby's gave the government a check for $1,451,824.50, an astounding amount for Toombs's collection, the bulk of which he had acquired in a single purchase for $500,000.

"I think we've done our bit to reduce the [federal] deficit," said Robert Woolley, a Sotheby's vice president and the sale's auctioneer.

Some observers, however, thought the prices had been inflated by the hoopla surrounding the auction.

"When a sale has a lot of publicity—as this one did—people get auction fever," said Paul Nassau, an art dealer. "They see people are bidding them up and they feel what they are paying is worth it. Some of the prices seemed senseless to me."

The government could not have cared less if buyers overpaid. Their creative thinking regarding the art's disposition had reaped large rewards.

"Fantastic," said Zimmerman, the DEA attorney. "It was a risk which paid off and it's hard to take risks in the government."

After the conclusion of the first three Jackpot trials, Hawkins scheduled sentencing hearings for early 1984. He would decide appropriate punishment for the convicted and those who had pleaded guilty. For the Jackpot defendants, punishment was tricky. He judged the men to be gentlemen from the country's "finest stock" who, for reasons that baffled him, got caught up in too much adventure and fun. He didn't believe the majority of the men to be hardened criminals, but felt duty bound to punish the men as a deterrent to other would-be drug smugglers. During the sentencing hearing for Michael Harvey on February 22, 1984, Hawkins described his reasoning and the thoughts that troubled him:

> *I don't think there's any really big secret to how I feel about drug traffic, so there's no point in me repeating all of that. Mr. Harvey was a bad guy. As you say he's a nice fellow, he's a good fellow, but he made some mistakes. And his situation is even worse in that in Virginia he'd already, I guess, thought he was home free when all that was over, but it turned out that was not the case, and that's, of course, not been the case with, I guess, a lot of young fellows and older ones, too, involved in the Operation Jackpot. A lot of them thought they were home free. It's turned out to be, I guess, a real nightmare for them.*
>
> *And you know, I lay awake at night not counting sheep. It's worrying about whether I am doing what's right not only to the defendants and their families but to the public and to myself and to the people that practice in this court. Then I have to resolve all that and weigh it and make a decision, and I never like any of it. I can almost name you every one that I have ever made.*

Harvey, he said, would serve seven years in prison. Hawkins gave his codefendant, Gunn, eight years. The other two men on trial with them, Sanders and MacDougall, each were sentenced to ten years. From the first Jackpot trial, the stiffest sentence drawn was twelve years, by Larry McCall.

Those who cooperated with the government got much less severe sentences, either through the prosecution dropping charges or by Hawkins taking into account the help they provided government agents and prosecutors. When sentencing Steele and Campbell, the government said each man volunteered significant amounts of information and served as credible and authoritative witnesses. They noted how each man initially struggled with providing information harmful to their friends, but ultimately made a decision to cooperate fully. When the thirty-two-year-old Campbell went before Hawkins, he apologized for his actions, attributing them to immaturity.

"I would like to say that this was someone else's fault, and that maybe I was with the wrong group of people or something . . . but it's not really the case," said Campbell. "I got into this on my own. I shouldn't have. I apologize to everyone for it, but it's just taken a long time to grow up, and I think this might be the case of a lot of people involved in this group."

Steele and Campbell were among the most familiar of the gentlemen smugglers for Hawkins. For days, during two trials, he sat next to them as they testified. He observed their candor, humor, and matter-of-fact storytelling approach and found them to be attractive and agreeable men. He sentenced each of them to ten years in prison.

Such sentences could be considered surprisingly light given Steele's and Campbell's extensive involvement in the smuggling rings and the number of times they captained sailboats loaded with marijuana and hashish. Roy Riley, on the other hand, whom Campbell had described as "bottom of the barrel" and others had characterized as an errand boy for his older brother, was given the most severe punishment to date in Operation Jackpot: twenty-one years in prison. During Riley's sentencing hearing, Hawkins dwelled on the fact that Riley's wealth had become such a stumbling block in his case. Riley's refusal to discuss his assets, for fear of them being seized, had derailed his plea agreement with the government, Hawkins noted, and the judge was struck at how Riley's legal team hired an accountant in an effort to combat the government's claims of what assets were obtained with illegal proceeds. To Hawkins, these actions were an affront to the court, as the defendant and his legal team demonstrated that Riley's financial interests deserved their foremost consideration, not the criminal charges against him. Hawkins bristled at the audacity of conducting cost-benefit analyses in the halls of justice.

"He determined, rather than divulge his assets . . . that he would rather run the risk of the Court," said Hawkins. "It really brings to bear on my mind the real business nature of the matter. It all really boils down to dollars and cents again, I guess, and weighing the costs for the profits. And I'm sorry it's that way."

While the youngest Riley brother said he was flabbergasted by the sentence, it was considered appropriate by McMaster.

"We have no sympathy at all for these drug smugglers," McMaster told a reporter. "Drug smuggling is a serious crime and deserves a serious sentence."

A month later, in April 1984, Hawkins handed down an even stiffer sentence, sending Byers to prison for twenty-five years after the kingpin pleaded guilty without striking a deal with the government. At issue was Byers's refusal to forfeit, let alone discuss, his assets with prosecutors, including his sailboats *La Cautiva* and *Energy*. He didn't want to see those vessels go the way of the *Anonymous of Rorc,* which had been seized in November 1981 during the hashish bust on Edisto Island. That luxury sailboat, says one federal law enforcement source, was then used for a time by the CIA to sail through the Caribbean and spy on Cuba.

Undeterred by Byers's obstinacy, Assistant U.S. Attorney Cam Currie devised an innovative legal technique to have Byers disclose his assets through a judgment debtor examination. When Byers still refused to answer questions, Hawkins held him in contempt and jailed him, which delayed him from reporting to prison and beginning his twenty-five-year sentence.

Following this maneuver the government was bullish on its prospects of having Byers divulge details of his fortunes. McMaster wrote to Associate Attorney General D. Lowell Johnson in May 1984, "We think [Byers] will decide to talk before he finishes eighteen months 'dead time' in the Charleston County jail."

Despite the confidence expressed in the letter, McMaster and the Operation Jackpot task force were not willing to wait for Byers's cooperation when it came to persuading the Antiguan government to release *La Cautiva*. Since Byers's deportation, an Antiguan police officer had been living on the boat and acting as caretaker, and the Antiguan government suggested it would not be a problem to sail the boat to the United States when the Americans provided a crew, so long as they got a share of the money it brought at auction. After realizing the sailboat had an estimated value of nearly $1 million, however, some Antiguan officials began having second thoughts about parting with such an expensive vessel. Fearing the Jackpot task force might lose *La Cautiva*, McMaster urgently lobbied U.S. Attorney General William French Smith for assistance.

"Our problem is that the Antiguans refuse to give us the boat," McMaster wrote the attorney general in April 1984. "They want to keep it for themselves. We don't blame them; it's beautiful and valued at about $900,000.00."

McMaster then suggested that the justice department enlist the help of Secretary of State George P. Schultz, characterizing the sailboat as an important symbol in the War on Drugs. Perhaps, McMaster wrote, Schultz could send a note to Antiguan Prime Minister Vere Bird emphasizing the importance of the sailboat's return to the United States.

"We think it is important to go to these lengths in order to convince the drug smugglers that President Reagan is dead serious in his efforts to wipe them out," wrote McMaster. "This would send them a clear, unequivocal message."

Through memos among senior staff, the justice department would ultimately decide against enlisting Reagan's cabinet members to get the boat back, despite noting *La Cautiva* was one of the top ten sailboats in the world. The justice department's Office of International Affairs, however, did permit Assistant U.S. Attorney Bart Daniel and task force agent Forbes to travel to Antigua to negotiate with the foreign government, so long as they wouldn't spark an international incident. Upon their arrival, Forbes and Daniel were taken out into English Harbour to see *La Cautiva*—the second such trip for Forbes. Boarding the boat, the men scoured it for clues to Byers's financial holdings, examining papers and taking pictures, but finding little of significance. To their relief the boat was still in immaculate condition, save for a scrape against the hull from brushing against a buoy. The next day, Daniel and Forbes met with assorted ministers in the Antiguan government, who indicated they'd soon vote to give the boat to the United States. Forbes and Daniel promised to have a sailboat crew to Antigua within forty-eight hours of their decision.

While Daniel and Forbes met with staff members at the U.S. embassy, their agreement with the Antiguans hit a snag. A deputy attorney general who had attended the negotiations called over to say he could not support giving the boat to the Americans and that he'd recommend the Antiguan government return *La Cautiva* to Byers or his Antiguan attorney. The issue, he explained, was that the Antiguans could only seize property from suspects *they* arrested and charged with drug offenses. In his opinion, since Byers had been deported for passport violations, the Antiguan government could not legally seize the boat.

Alarmed by this report, Forbes and Daniel urged the Antiguan deputy attorney general to meet again at the U.S. embassy. There the men hammered away at the official, ultimately persuading him to soften his stance. Daniel later wrote to McMaster, summarizing their success: "After several hours of discussion, Mr. Henry agreed to dilute his original opinion that the vessel must be returned immediately to Byers. While he still felt the vessel had been illegally seized and that the Antiguan Government would subject itself to legal action by Byers, he tempered the opinion."

Ultimately *La Cautiva* was given to the U.S. government, though it was not a swift process, owing to hesitancy from the Antiguan government. According to Daniel and Forbes, it was seized and sailed by the U.S marshals, then sold, with the U.S. government keeping about 30 percent of the profits and the Antiguans taking the rest. As an extra legal precaution before seizing the sailboat, Forbes says, the Justice Department's Office of International Affairs asked him to have Byers sign an affidavit regarding *La Cautiva*. Considering Byers's exceptional lack of cooperation, Forbes couldn't believe the request, judging it hopeless. Nevertheless, he called an FBI agent and asked him to try to have Byers sign the affidavit, warning him "he's probably going to tell you to kiss his ass."

A few days later, the agent called back.

"Well, you got it?" asked Forbes.

"I got it, but it ain't signed," the agent replied. "He didn't say 'Kiss my ass.' He said, 'FUCK you.'"

As Operation Jackpot sought to seize more assets and obtain significant sentences for its convicted defendants, they were also making other arrests and preparing for a new indictment of thirty-four men and women accused of participating in a South Carolina–based smuggling ring operated by Joseph Allen Patterson IV of Beaufort and Rocky Bradford, whose plantation home outside Charleston was seized in August during the first Jackpot trial. In five years, the indictment alleged, the accused smuggled more than $100 million worth of marijuana into the United States, making more than $30 million in profit. Over the summer of 1984, four more men were added to this indictment, and a woman named Carol Amend was arrested in the Everglades in Florida, accused of working with Bradford and Patterson and charged as a drug kingpin.

Although these smugglers also used the South Carolina coast, they operated independently of the men charged in the indictments with Foy and Riley. Among the newest targets of Operation Jackpot were a handful of curious characters, including a Beaufort game warden nicknamed the "Masked Marvel" for his habit of wearing a ski mask when helping to serve as a lookout in South Carolina marshes. Indicted, too, was Freddy Fillingham, a small, scrappy smuggler and talented sailor who, along with Amend, his former girlfriend, made a daring escape from a jail on St. Martin in 1979 as hurricanes David and Frederic pounded the island. Fillingham went first, during Hurricane David, slipping his slender frame out a jail window and taking with him a chair to which he had been handcuffed. Later, when Hurricane Frederic came through, Amend used a bobby pin to open her cell door and sneak out, meeting her crew on a beach before getting off the island.

By August 1984, two months after the Patterson indictment was unsealed, twenty-nine of thirty-four defendants had pleaded guilty. One of the few willing to challenge the charges brought by Operation Jackpot was the forty-year-old Amend, an astute ocean enthusiast unique for her Cleopatra-style haircut and eclectic assets, which included emeralds, Arabian horses, an avocado grove, and *Dutch Treat,* a yacht valued at $450,000. The government moved to seize it all, and Amend pleaded not guilty.

Operation Jackpot announced yet another indictment as Amend prepared for trial in September 1984, charging ten people in an alleged marijuana-smuggling ring based out of Little River, South Carolina, just north of Myrtle Beach. This ring, the government alleged, had smuggled more than $40 million worth of marijuana into Little River in the last five years. Among those charged as kingpins were Murray Bowman Brown, sixty-four, and his son, twenty-five-year-old William Murray Brown.

Amend's trial began in October, and her Miami lawyer, whom she paid, in part, with ninety pounds of silver bars and coins, conceded to the jury that she was guilty of nearly every offense save the most severe one of being a drug kingpin. It was a flawed strategy, and a jury convicted Amend of every charge. Weeks later Judge Charles Simons sentenced her to thirty years in prison—the stiffest sentence yet given to a suspect in Operation Jackpot. To make matters worse for Amend, who had a two-year-old daughter, her husband would die three months later in a plane crash in South Florida.

During Amend's trial, McMaster visited Salt Lake City to tout the success of Operation Jackpot to a meeting of the International Association of Chiefs of Police, a group he told a reporter was "the premier law enforcement association in the world." It was the latest in a number of speeches he had given about the innovative techniques South Carolina agents and prosecutors were using to investigate suspected drug smugglers. McMaster relished the opportunity to share news of his office's success in convicting drug smuggling defendants. Two years into Operation Jackpot, his contempt for this class of criminals was as strong as ever. McMaster told a Charleston newspaper in January 1984:

Drug smugglers are like a high-altitude bomber who flies high overhead, drops his bombs and returns to base, never seeing the damage. These people smuggle drugs into the country, turn them over to distributors, and leave and go back to the peace and quiet of their beach houses or vacation retreats. They never hear the bombs explode and they don't think of themselves as dangerous criminals causing harm to other people.

But in fact they are inflicting terrible pain and suffering onto fellow citizens, and all for money. That's how we see them.

These drugs cause all sorts of problems in our society, related to all kinds of crimes. We know that people commit crimes while on drugs, they commit crimes to get drugs, and they commit crimes to get things to sell for money to buy drugs.

McMaster found receptive audiences at meetings of bar associations and law enforcement conferences from Baltimore to Boston, Denver, Chicago, Maine, and Washington. Drug use was on everyone's mind, seared into the public consciousness in the early 1980s thanks to First Lady Nancy Reagan's nationwide "Just Say No" campaign. But marijuana was often given second billing, with crack cocaine becoming known as an urban scourge and cocaine earning a dangerous reputation. *Time* magazine wrote cover stories on the narcotic in 1981, 1983, and 1984, and the major television networks each broadcast hour-long (or longer) news shows and documentaries on drugs in 1982, including NBC's "Pleasure Drugs: the Great American High" and ABC's "The Cocaine Cartel." In 1983, the film *Scarface*, with only slight exaggeration, showed the astonishing menace of South Florida's cocaine cowboys. As Al Pacino portrayed the fictional Cuban refugee Tony Montana, chainsawing and machine-gunning his way to become a Miami cocaine boss, true-life kingpin Pablo Escobar was equally as murderous in becoming one of the world's richest and most powerful men. In 1982, despite his notoriety, Escobar even managed to get elected to Colombia's congress.

It was within this national drug dialogue that McMaster submitted the story of Operation Jackpot. Occasionally listening to his speeches was his friend and colleague Tim Wellesley, the criminal investigations director at the IRS who helped spearhead Operation Jackpot. Wellesley says McMaster would take the stage and, in his deep drawl, tell jokes taken from Southern comedian Jerry Clower, substituting names and places to suit his audience. Eventually he'd segue into the mechanics of Operation Jackpot. His determination to decrease crime and his passion for promoting cooperation across law enforcement agencies, Wellesley says, made him popular with cops and prosecutors. In South Carolina McMaster was just as effective a speaker, wowing rotary clubs with stories of his investigation, including how smugglers forced a ceasefire in Lebanon so they could be loaded with hashish.

At times, however, McMaster's song and dance was sloppy. When describing the ceasefire to the Charleston Trident Chamber of Commerce in August 1984, he said the smugglers stopped fighting between the Palestinian Liberation Organization (PLO) and the

Jewish Defense League (JDL). The JDL, however, is an America-based organization. And while dedicated to fighting anti-Semitism, it has no domestic or overseas militias.

In that same speech McMaster told the crowd of 250 people the "amazing" aspect of Operation Jackpot was that "of the one hundred two people that have been charged, only one of them was ever suspected of any drug smuggling or any kind of illegal activity before." Only thanks to the task force's financial investigation, he said, were these inconspicuous citizens revealed as criminals. In fact many of the most prominent members of the alleged smuggling rings did have criminal records, including the government's recent star witnesses, Steele, arrested aboard the *Anonymous of Rorc,* and Campbell, arrested twice before Operation Jackpot for smuggling charges. Additionally, Harvey had been to federal prison twice for drug offenses; Foy was suspected of bribing his way out of a drug conviction in Columbia, South Carolina, and having charges dropped; and Amend had been convicted of drug charges in Mississippi before she jumped bail. Riley and Byers also had criminal records, though for minor offenses.

Regardless, minor misstatements and exaggerations did not take away from the sixty-two convictions secured by Operation Jackpot through August 1984. An editorial that month in Charleston's *Evening Post* recognized the work of the task force and praised its ability to combat men powerful enough to interrupt wars.

"Even if you discounted some segments as apocryphal—and we do not suggest they are—the Operation Jackpot story continues to come across as U.S. Attorney Henry D. McMaster describes it: '. . . the most amazing story going on in law enforcement in the United States today.' "

If McMaster was riding high in the fall of 1984, Byers was in the depths of despair. Nearly a year earlier, Bob "the Boss," kingpin extraordinaire, was aboard *La Cautiva* in English Harbour, Antigua, enjoying the Caribbean's temperate autumn weather and making plans to cash out and head for the Pacific. Now he sat in the Charleston County jail, being asked to agree to a deal with the least desirable of terms. Reveal your property and bank accounts, the government said, and we'll let you begin your twenty-five-year federal prison sentence.

Judge Hawkins had transferred Byers to the Charleston County jail after his lawyers complained their client was suffering from depression and would benefit from being closer to his psychologist. In Charleston, however, Byers's mood did not lighten, and his position on speaking to the government did not change. He made reading lists composed of novels that depicted the criminal underworlds he recently inhabited and sought to acquire a variety of thrillers, horror stories, and tales of espionage and intrigue. He jotted down thoughts on writing pads and scraps of paper, questioning the purpose of his imprisonment.

"I feel like the side of the battery that says negative," read one note.

"Human tide washed up on the shores of justice," read another.

"County jail = waiting room to hell," said one more.

Byers spent his time monitoring exchange rates and gold prices, too. He received love letters and notes from friends: correspondence that detailed trips to the beach, time on the water, and a trip to Costa Rica, all places he'd not be seeing for quite some time, if ever again. His friends and girlfriend asked if they could send photos and cookies.

Byers's mood likely soured further when he was moved from the jail's maximum-security wing, where he was kept with other inmates, to a solitary confinement cell. Agents had received information that Byers was contemplating trying to escape, prompting them to isolate him and limit his telephone and visitation privileges. Eleven days later, though, agents persuaded the Charleston County sheriff to release Byers back into the general population. He had indicated he'd be willing to cooperate with the government, and he would need access to a phone to pass on information and speak with his lawyers.

Byers's promise of cooperation was short-lived. During a shift change at 6:37 a.m. on September 22, 1984, jailer Albert Chubb called Byers's name and asked him to report to a doctor's appointment. Byers exited the cell he shared with a dozen other prisoners, then sprinted to the back of the jail, where an exterior door had been left unlocked. Chubb, who had unlocked the cell door, then allegedly spoke to another inmate: "Don't say anything and there will be something in it for you."

Exiting the jail, Byers found a white Chevy Malibu—an unmarked police car—parked outside. The keys, he found, were inside the car. Byers turned the ignition, put the car in gear, and drove away, the high-profile defendant leaving a Charleston jail much like "Gentleman Pirate" Stede Bonnet had more than two-and-a-half centuries earlier. For the next ten hours, Byers's absence went unnoticed. Two other jailers performed head counts that day, reporting all inmates accounted for. It was not until the dinnertime head count that jail officials realized the drug kingpin was gone.

As soon as the headlines screamed that Bob "the Boss" was missing, the finger pointing started between Charleston County Sheriff Charles F. Dawley and the Operation Jackpot task force. Dawley blamed federal agents, not his own jail staff, for Byers's departure, complaining that members of the Jackpot team received information from an informant two days before the jailbreak that a guard was performing favors for Byers and that something suspicious was happening. McMaster denied this charge, but Dawley immediately asked for South Carolina's state police force to investigate.

The federal agents on the task force were crushed. Byers was among the most prominent smugglers and kingpins netted by Operation Jackpot, and it took a considerable amount of investigation and luck, as well as a cunning undercover operation, to capture him. Beyond his arrest the government had secured a lengthy sentence for Byers without going to trial. Now, they grimaced. The savvy smuggler had fled without forfeiting his considerable assets, and it was more than likely he had sailboats and large bank accounts at his disposal in locales across the world. To make matters worse, they had no idea where he might be headed. Immediately following Byers's escape, there were no clues as to his whereabouts or that he had left in the unmarked police car.

"I got a call at night that he'd escaped," says Claude McDonald, U.S. Customs agent. "It just made me sick."

Assistant U.S. Attorney Daniel got a call, too, from a Jackpot agent who advised him to lock all his doors and windows and arm himself if he had a weapon. Byers disliked Daniel, and no one was sure what he might do while on the loose.

The agents and local police were amazed that Byers could escape, though it didn't take long for them to guess how it had occurred. Within three days the fifty-five-year-old jailer Chubb was suspended. Within two weeks Chubb was indicted for allegedly enabling Byers's escape.

"I never heard of anyone escaping from the Charleston County jail. It's very secure," says McDonald. "There's only one door in and one door out, that I know of. For someone to get out, they had to be let. And we knew that."

Chubb's arrest, however, did not stop the investigation by the state police. Moreover, Dawley wrote to U.S. Senators Fritz Hollings and Strom Thurmond, asking them to request the FBI investigate the Jackpot agents. Specifically, he urged the FBI to learn why federal agents urged Dawley to move Byers out of solitary confinement and why they withheld the informant's tip, which had allegedly been shared between a member of the state police, a U.S. Customs agent, and Daniel. Both senators forwarded Dawley's request to the director of the FBI, with Hollings writing that "the involvement of the Federal investigators demands review, and I would like your report as soon as possible." McMaster couldn't believe it.

Shortly after Byers's escape, a lieutenant in the state police came into McDonald's office and requested the Customs agent allow him to ask a few questions about Byers's escape. McDonald obliged him, but strangely, he says, the questions became accusatory. The lieutenant had some kind of theory that McDonald and Forbes had arranged Byers's escape so the kingpin could lead the Jackpot team to other suspects. McDonald became furious and screamed at the lieutenant, his words clearly audible to coworkers in the open office within the Custom House.

"Are you out of your damn mind?" McDonald asked the agent. "You sonofabitch, you can leave this office right now. Get up and get out of here."

Forbes, says McDonald, was similarly offended when he learned of the state police officer's theory, especially since Forbes had been one of the two agents to go undercover and board Byers's sailboat *La Cautiva*.

"It just rubbed David and [me] the wrong way to be even considered as a means for him to escape. That would have been the last thing we did," says McDonald. "It was a ridiculous thought. But I guess [the lieutenant's] theory was we were so innovative doing things that hadn't been done before, we might try anything, including letting someone out of jail to get other fugitives."

Though inmates said Chubb released Byers, he denied helping the fugitive. Prosecutors did not believe him. Among the incriminating evidence was a statement from an inmate in the Charleston County jail that he and Byers were smoking pot in the cell the evening before Byers left, when Byers turned to him and said, "I'll be leaving you tomorrow."

On Tuesday, three days after Byers had escaped, federal agents spent the day watching a large sailboat docked on the Ashley River alongside downtown Charleston. When the sailboat left the harbor and headed for open ocean, agents boarded a Coast Guard boat and chased after it. They boarded the craft, but found no sign of Byers. Agents also checked into the passengers on a Learjet that had landed in Charleston over the weekend to see if it's arrival was tied to Byers's escape.

The same day the sailboat was stopped in Charleston, police in Knoxville, Tennessee, called to tell the Charleston sheriff's office that they had found an unmarked Charleston police car in a downtown parking lot beside a fraternal lodge, its license plate smeared with mud. It had been sitting there for at least two days, they said, abandoned. The Charleston police, who still hadn't realized the car was missing, requested the FBI dust it for Byers's fingerprints. In short order they found a match, and they concentrated searches in eastern Tennessee.

Knoxville is "at the top of the list," said U.S. Marshal Mike Brown. "[But] there's any number of places he could have gone—we're running in all directions. He never divulged anything about where his finances were."

In fact Byers was long gone from the Volunteer State, having arranged for a friend to pick him up in Knoxville. "The Boss" faded away, and the U.S. Marshals Service eventually placed him on its list of the fifteen most wanted criminals. Because a rocket launcher was found aboard his sailboat in Antigua, authorities regarded Byers as "armed and dangerous."

Chapter Thirteen

News of Bob "The Boss" Byers escaping from the Charleston County jail reached Australia in two days. Upon its receipt, jailers kept a close watch on prisoner Les Riley. Byers was known to be a close associate of Riley, an Australian Federal Police report noted, and the fugitive had visited Australia before. His sailboat *Energy* had still not been found, and, as the same report noted, Riley had previously explored the possibility of escaping his Australian prison by sea, hoping to use a fake British passport to enter Goa, India.

Riley wasn't counting on Byers to cross the world, break him out of prison, and escape by slow-moving sailboat. He denied the escape plan allegations by the Australian Federal Police, and searches of his cell and his wife during prison visits turned up no incriminating contraband or material. When Riley heard about Byers's jailbreak, it was a rare bit of good news. Since being imprisoned in Australia sixteen months earlier and launching a legal fight against extradition, most of the reports passed on by his lawyers were gloomy. There had been four large indictments of fellow marijuana smugglers and three Operation Jackpot trials. Many of Riley's former friends ended up testifying for the government, and, during debriefings and grand jury proceedings, surrendered information about Riley's criminal activities. He couldn't believe so many men squealed on their friends. Also disheartening was his brother Roy's conviction and twenty-one-year prison sentence.

The Australian prison conditions for Riley and Wally Butler were severe. The facilities were dirty, overcrowded, and underfunded, said Riley's American defense attorney, Martin Bernholz. Riley lost weight and complained of being fed lousy food with poor nutritional value. Bernholz compared it to chum, and when he visited his client, he brought a piece of chicken in his suitcase for Riley to eat.

Prisoners were often put in lockdown, and Riley had infrequent access to fresh air. He participated in scrums when prisoners rioted against the guards, otherwise known as screws or hacks, demanding better treatment and more freedom to contact loved ones and receive visitors. Guards stood on gangways and fired rubber bullets into the rioting crowd.

In one prison, Riley counseled a despondent friend, only to find the man hanging dead in a self-made noose the next morning. He encountered another prisoner stuck dead with a shiv. He stepped over the corpse and kept walking. Gallows humor began to infect Riley. He was once imprisoned with a man accused of butchering his spouse to death, and when Riley saw one guard had brought in a freshly slaughtered cow to share with his colleagues, Riley commented on the box of meat and bones lying in plain view. The screws had become compassionate, he said, and were allowing the accused murderer a contact visit with his wife.

Riley's fellow prisoners loved the jest. The accused murderer wanted to chop up the American, too. Jokes could only lighten Riley's mood so much. He was dispirited by the chance of receiving a sentence of life imprisonment and the overwhelming amount of testimony against him, said Bernholz, though he kept a stiff upper lip and didn't complain when visitors came, not wanting to scare them off or spread any despair. In a letter, Riley described his Australian prison experience as a "nightmare" and said, "I have witnessed a way of life I never believe[d] existed among human beings."

When Riley and Butler were transported to court hearings, Australian authorities undertook extreme security precautions. One Australian prosecutor said Operation Jackpot was the biggest drug operation ever mentioned in an Australian court. Helicopters were put in the air, snipers were stationed on roofs, and metal detectors were placed in the courthouse. During the short commute from the prison to the courtroom, Riley and Butler were made to lay facedown on the floor of vans, their hands cuffed behind their backs. Australian police kept their feet on the suspects' backs to keep them from rolling about the car. During one trip shortly after their arrest, according to Riley, a policeman said he hoped no trucks backfired and startled him, otherwise he just might shoot Riley in the head.

"They treated Les like he was Al Capone," says Bernholz, who was himself searched thoroughly in Australia, while Interpol agents followed Butler's American lawyer through Asia.

Conditions were a bit more relaxed in the courtroom. Butler's wife, Rebecca, brought her husband hamburgers to eat. After Butler's arrest, she had gone home to Hilton Head for a while, but returned, saying she was "lost" apart from her husband.

"I get to the point when I say, for my own well-being maybe I should go back [to the United States]. I get into a depression, but it lasts about a day . . ." she told a newspaper reporter. "Wally's in Alcoholics Anonymous. He quotes me things out of that about accepting things."

Life was no easier for the Riley family, and the children were sent to live with Suzanne's relatives while she stayed in Australia.

The legal fortunes of Riley and Butler had seesawed. When one side was unhappy with a ruling, they appealed to a higher Australian court, and because the legal questions were novel, the higher court agreed to hear the case. The conflict in the case boiled down to whether Riley and Butler could be extradited to the United States and tried for Continuing Criminal Enterprise. Extradition treaties between nations require that suspects can only be returned to a country to be tried for crimes that exist in the other country. While Australia had drug offenses on its books, it did not have a law exactly like the American kingpin statute, and Riley's and Butler's lawyers argued they could not be tried in the United States on that charge, which was the most severe one of those leveled against them. Australian prosecutors, supported by the American government, believed other Australian drug laws were similar enough to allow extradition under the kingpin statute.

The case lingered in the courts, Riley and Butler staying in prison. The men hired American attorneys, who could not participate in Australian court, as well as Australian solicitors, barristers, and Queen's counsel, who were certified to participate in varying levels of the court system, and charged varying prices by the day. Among their attorneys were a former member of Parliament and the former Australian attorney general.

In Australia, says Bernholz, hearings could last for weeks. All arguments are made orally, as opposed to the American legal system where lawyers can submit written briefs. As Riley's legal saga dragged on, the cost of paying for high-priced lawyers on two continents became substantial. Riley wrote one check to his lawyers for more than $700,000.

As Riley and Butler approached a two-year anniversary in Australian prisons, there were indications there would be some resolution. The High Court of Australia, the equivalent to the U.S. Supreme Court, would rule on the case. A judge's most recent ruling against being extradited on the kingpin statute encouraged the prisoners and their lawyers. Another favorable ruling, and Australia might be prevented from extraditing them on the most serious drug charges.

By 1985, Operation Jackpot had been declared an unparalleled success over and over again, most often by the man who had initiated the investigation and its promotion, U.S. Attorney Henry McMaster. The prosecutor had coordinated indictments for 117 suspects in four marijuana smuggling rings, and 92 people had been convicted or pleaded guilty. McMaster found himself the target, however, of complaints from colleagues within the federal government, including the DEA, who griped that McMaster's marketing of Operation Jackpot overshadowed successful drug busts not associated with the investigation. The criticism was loud enough to attract the attention of the Department of Justice in Washington, who chided McMaster for not giving appropriate credit to each of the agencies involved. They also faulted him for referring to the investigation by its catchy moniker instead of identifying it as a Presidential Drug Task Force or an Organized Crime Drug Enforcement Task Force.

McMaster felt the criticism was unjustified. In a March 12, 1985, letter to Charles W. Blau, deputy associate attorney general, he sniped back at the DEA, mentioning that they had not supplied an appropriate amount of agents to the task force. He blamed the media for adopting the use of "Operation Jackpot" even though his press releases and remarks identified the investigation by its formal label and noted it was part of President Ronald Reagan's effort to curb drug trafficking. As to sharing credit, he pleaded, "I have talked myself blue in the face with the news media, asking, pleading, and jawboning, to convince them that they should report in their news stories that this effort is a joint one, a team effort, by several agencies."

Although many colleagues say McMaster was an adept politician eager for the spotlight, the U.S. attorney's claims to Blau were not untrue. Two months earlier, for example, when speaking in Columbia, South Carolina, to more than a hundred lawyers at a meeting of the Richland County Bar Association, McMaster praised the work of the nineteen agents working as part of Operation Jackpot and credited the agencies they represent.

"Where one area of expertise ends, another agency picks up, and it works out real well," said McMaster. "We think we're well on the way toward eliminating the major marijuana- and hashish-smuggling operations in South Carolina, and we're developing some cases on cocaine and heroin that we hope to report on soon."

As impressive as the number of convictions might have been, by 1985, Operation Jackpot had still failed to catch three alleged kingpins from the original indictments issued in May 1983: Barry "Flash" Foy, Lee Harvey, and Tom "Rolex" Rhoad. Additionally, Riley and Butler still were in Australia. Moreover, the investigation had suffered a setback in the fall of 1984, when Cam Currie, the assistant U.S. attorney who coordinated much of Operation Jackpot, became South Carolina's first female U.S. magistrate. At the time of her appointment, Assistant U.S. Attorney Bart Daniel described her as "the best lawyer I've ever seen or worked with."

"She's top flight," added Judge Falcon Hawkins. "I don't know [what] the U.S. attorney's office is going to do without her."

Currie would be most sorely missed for her expertise on civil law and the seizure of assets purchased with drug proceeds. It was through Currie's innovative legal maneuvers that Byers was jailed, and prevented from beginning a prison sentence, until he forfeited his hidden assets, including foreign bank accounts and sailboats. Of course since then, Byers dashed out of the Charleston County jail, hopped in an unmarked police car, and hightailed it to Knoxville, Tennessee, and on to destinations unknown.

As the weeks passed after Byers's escape, there was no sign of the fugitive. A month after the jailbreak, though, investigators caught a break, discovering that four $2,500 cashier's checks had been sent to the suspended jailer Albert W. Chubb from someone in Florida. The police immediately suspected it was a payoff from Byers. Soon, U.S. Marshal P. E. Morris was in Florida, requesting to look through photo logs and surveillance footage from each bank that issued a check. Morris noticed the same man purchasing each of the checks, but it definitely wasn't Byers.

The checks weren't the only clue associated with Florida. An informant told federal authorities that Byers's good friend and fellow Operation Jackpot fugitive Bob "Willie the Hog" Bauer was using a phone switch to place his calls, and the authorities were able to tap into the switch and determine that Bauer was calling an address near Fort Pierce, Florida, outside Port St. Lucie. Morris decided to stake out the house, parking a motor home down the street in the driveway of a residence owned by a retired Illinois police chief. He peered out the window, hoping to spy a familiar face, whether it be the man in the bank footage, Bauer, or Byers.

For two weeks Morris staked out the home, watching men come and go. To his annoyance, nearly every time men entered the house, they had their backs to Morris, making identification difficult. Rather than move the motor home to the other end of the street, Morris asked an attractive female deputy marshal from Miami to change into athletic shorts. When men were milling around the house, she jogged down the street. Predictably, they all pivoted their bodies to admire the running woman. As they turned to watch her pass, cameras inside the motor home snapped away.

After reviewing the photos, Morris identified Bauer and the man who purchased the cashier's checks. They began following Bauer, and soon identified the other man as Daniel Kenneth Riley, of no relation to Les Riley and his brother Roy. The marshals began following the men, but soon were forced to make arrests after their surveillance was compromised. They pulled Bauer over on a Florida highway and handcuffed him. Little did they know Bauer was on his way to a car show in Stuart, Florida, where he was due to meet Byers.

Bauer's arrest sent shockwaves through the already fractured smuggling community. Another confederate had fallen. Who knew who might be next? Foy soon got a phone call from Bauer's girlfriend, advising him to change his habits and address. The feds had found

Bauer's phonebook, she said, and your number is in it. It'd be best to move on.

Since being indicted eighteen months earlier, Foy had spent much of his time in New York, renting a Manhattan apartment. He'd gotten married to his longtime girlfriend, Jan Liafsha, and had two children, traveling through Europe, Canada, and the western United States with them. Foy would have preferred to stay abroad, away from investigators and on board his luxury sailboat, *Zakaniya,* but his wife complained of being sick on the sailboat, especially while pregnant. So they moved often, trying to stay ahead of David Forbes and other Jackpot investigators, knowing the agents were getting close, trying to trace their phone calls. Forbes had questioned Foy's in-laws on a few occasions, and one agent questioned his wife's elderly grandmother in Tennessee.

Foy had even been detained, briefly, when returning from Europe by way of Canada. After a jaunt to England, Paris, and Montreal with a blond woman he met on St. Barts, Foy had arranged for a Canadian cabbie to drive them to New York, picking out a remote border crossing for them to travel through. As they approached the American checkpoint, Foy sat in the back of the cab, the girl to one side and a six-pack of open beer to the other, and lots of cash in his luggage. The border guard was not amused by the alcohol, ordering Foy out of the car, but not before the fugitive was able to stuff cash into the cab's seat cushions.

Bringing him inside a Custom House, the border guards began checking Foy's identification and luggage. They combed through his clothes, asking why he didn't declare his Italian shirts. Aware of his rapidly changing fortunes and fearing the inevitable discovery of his fugitive status, Foy asked to use a bathroom, where he stashed some more money. While the guards were distracted, he bolted for the door and ran for miles. Foy tore through fields and swam down streams, trying to distance himself from unleashed bloodhounds and speeding state police cruisers, much like he did a decade or so earlier when he fled from the Columbia airport. He disguised his scent by hopping in cow pies. He inadvertently crossed back into Canada, realizing his misdirection when he spotted road signs bearing distances in kilometers. He trekked back into New York, staked out a country road from the woods, and eventually hitched a ride with a postman. Fabricating his story on the fly, Foy told the man he was a road laborer needing a ride to the hospital to meet his pregnant wife, who'd gone into labor. He inquired as to the kind stranger's name, promising him he'd name his newborn son after him.

The kingpin and mailman parted ways at a gas station, where Foy called a cab and made his way to Vermont for a flight back to New York City. Before reaching the airport, he shoplifted some clothes to replace his severely soiled duds. Meanwhile, the blond was left at the Canadian border, being interrogated about her fleet-footed companion. Upon arriving in New York, Foy called his friend and lawyer, Bob Moseley, though he wasn't too concerned about the lady's well-being.

"There's some money stashed in a Customs house," said Foy. "Can you go up and get it?"

Foy's half-serious request of Moseley betrayed the fact that for most of the fugitive smugglers, cash was becoming a scarce resource. In fact making money became a bigger concern for the men than getting caught, especially since all the kingpins wanted to maintain their luxurious standards of living. Apart from Byers, who made the U.S. Marshals Service's top fifteen most wanted list on account of having a rocket launcher aboard his sailboat *La Cautiva,* most of the other men were not high-priority targets. If they stayed out of South Carolina and Virginia, they figured, few people were desperate to find them, at least compared to violent criminals. The men felt comfortable traveling through the United States so long as they had good fake identification. They continued to live on the run using the names of dead men.

Since smuggling into South Carolina was out of the question, as were much of their familiar haunts on the East Coast owing to the disastrous hashish flotilla in 1981, the fugitive kingpins began scouting the West Coast for potential off-load sites. Foy began coordinating a deal with Harvey to bring untied Thai—lightly pressed marijuana— across the Pacific, and Foy recruited Rhoad to join him on a trip to Seattle so they could tour the nearby islands.

By this point, the thirty-seven-year-old Rhoad was not unfamiliar with the Pacific Ocean, having rented a cliff-top home in the ritzy San Diego suburb of La Jolla in March 1984. The house afforded breathtaking views of the ocean, though Rhoad confessed he more often watched television than the waves. Before Bauer was arrested, Rhoad told him he had developed an addiction to TV while living on the run.

In California Rhoad did not alter his flashy behavior. When he paid the first six months of rent for the home in La Jolla, he gave his landlord a shoebox full of $13,600. When he traveled, which was often, he paid travel agents in cash. When he bought a new $20,000 Jeep, he pulled a plastic bag full of cash out of the trunk of his classic Mercedes and brought it into a salesman's office. It was the registration of this Mercedes that would prove to be Rhoad's undoing. The Operation Jackpot agents ran searches for license plates and motor vehicle registrations relentlessly, always hopeful of finding new clues to a fugitive's whereabouts.

In 1985, nearly a year after Rhoad's move to La Jolla, U.S. Customs special agent Claude McDonald contacted colleagues in San Diego, asking them to look for the blue Mercedes. McDonald had tracked the car to a Cullen Lee Brown Jr., at an address in nearby Del Mar, California. The address turned out to be just a rented mailbox. Weeks later, agents learned that Brown was paying utilities at a home in La Jolla. On March 1, 1985, agents drove by the home, spying the Mercedes parked across the street. The next day, the agents returned and watched a short man exit the house and hop in a cab that headed for Lindbergh Field, the San Diego airport. Among his luggage was a bag of skis.

At the airport, agents watched the man check in for a flight to Montrose, Colorado, outside the ski resort of Telluride. They let him pass through security before approaching him and asking him for his identification. He produced a Florida driver's license in the name of Cullen Brown, with a distorted picture. As he was arrested, he insisted there was some mistake, that he didn't know a Tom Rhoad.

The ruse did not last long. The same evening, federal agents executed a search warrant on the La Jolla home, finding a closet full of assorted fake identifications, a book describing how to create "alternate" identification, as well as degrees from the University of South Carolina and its law school in the name of Thomas N. Rhoad III.

Beyond that, agent McDonald, Assistant U.S. Attorney Daniel, and cooperating witness and former Hilton Head lawyer Andy Pracht flew out to San Diego to make an identification of the suspect. When they walked in a room and found Rhoad, the suspect looked up, recognized Pracht, and realized he wasn't going to be released. After almost two years on the run, the diminutive and profane fugitive had been nabbed by Operation Jackpot.

"He broke into tears right then," says McDonald. "Just boo hoo."

If Rhoad had booked a flight two days earlier, he would have been safe in Colorado, skiing with none other than fellow fugitive Foy, who was waiting on him to deliver much-needed money. He could also have visited with Byers, who had rented a condo in the mountain town of Frisco, between Vail and Breckenridge. After his friends had been arrested in Florida, Byers thought it best to move on, purchasing a new AMC Eagle automobile and heading out West.

But Rhoad would likely have returned to San Diego. As long as the federal agents tracking him were patient, he would have eventually appeared in their sights. The inevitability of being caught was a difficult truth to swallow for nearly all the fugitive kingpins, and most believed they could live forever on the run, a step ahead of government investigators. If you didn't believe this, how could you get up each day, knowing that at least a decade in captivity could start at any minute when the police suddenly swarmed you and the handcuffs came out?

It was a frankly terrifying fate for the kingpins, one they refused to face. It meant exchanging landscapes of powdery ski slopes and waves crashing against cliffs for dusty recreation yards and concrete corridors of prison cells. It meant the color bleeding out of their rich lives. The chrome on their cars, the bronze of their skin, and the bright bottom paint on their sailboats would give way to the drab hues of prison life: beige walls, khaki uniforms, and gray bunks.

The gentlemen smugglers would not admit to such fears. Les Riley told authorities he moved to Australia not because of Operation Jackpot, but because life had begun moving too fast and his associations with drug smugglers began imperiling his family, estranging him from his wife and two children. Foy says he thought he'd never get caught, that his extravagant lifestyle was sustainable, that he could forever smuggle drugs into every side of the country to keep up with his expenses.

Keeping pace with these men could be taxing on lesser, rational mortals. Foy's wife says she drank excessively while on the run with her smuggler husband and their two young children.

"I lived in constant dread of the end, which I knew, quite well, was coming," says Liafsha. "[Barry] may say he didn't think it was coming to an end, but [Barry] is a liar. He was then, and I am sure he is now.

"Being an accomplished liar is a requirement for success in illegal activities," she added, parenthetically. "The most successful were the best and most audacious liars."

It's safe to reason, too, that without dread and by lying to oneself, a fugitive does himself more harm than good. A healthy fear of arrest benefits the fugitive, spurring him to change aliases more often, to keep a lower profile, to change vehicles and apartments frequently, to compromise his quality of life in exchange for a better chance of continued freedom. Without this fear, one doesn't worry about an informer blabbing to authorities or federal agents tracing phone calls made home or car registrations being tracked. But these things were happening, and each time another Operation Jackpot suspect was rounded up, the government learned more information about those who'd managed to stay on the run.

As Rhoad was being processed in San Diego and readied for a return to South Carolina, U.S. Marshal Morris hopped a flight from Miami to Denver, arriving in Colorado's capital dressed in thin pants and short sleeves. Weeks earlier he had learned about Byers's purchase of the new AMC Eagle and learned its vehicle identification number after visiting the Florida dealership from which Byers bought the car. He had his office make a national inquiry with motor vehicle departments, seeing if any state had a match. The answer was yes. A man in Frisco, Colorado, had recently registered the car, and Morris recognized the name as an alias previously used by Byers. Arriving in Colorado he quickly made his way to Frisco, joining other U.S. marshals in a hotel room, where they were watching Byers's rented condo through a telescope, though they didn't think he was home.

At the time, says Frisco Police Chief Ed Falconetti, Frisco's population was about fifteen hundred full-time residents, though it could swell to six thousand people during ski season. Many houses in the area were second homes or rental property, and the police kept busy with property crimes, whether theft, burglary, or the occasional armed robbery. Because Byers was thought to be interested in high-tech weaponry, including rocket launchers, the marshals and Frisco police force agreed he should be apprehended away from residents. The last thing they wanted, Falconetti says, was for Byers to hole up in his chalet, initiating a shootout.

On Saturday, March 16, 1985, the marshals spotted the AMC Eagle parked in front of the chalet. Nearby, too, was Byers's 1955 Gullwing Mercedes—an expensive, vintage automobile whose doors opened vertically, similar to a DeLorean or Lamborghini. Around four-thirty in the afternoon a man left the condo and hopped in the Eagle. Morris peered through the spotter scope and identified Byers, though he seemed to look a bit different. As Byers, age thirty-nine, drove away, the marshals and Frisco police officers scrambled to follow him in marked and unmarked police vehicles, intent on making an arrest.

Byers soon headed out of Frisco for the nearby town of Dillon, driving along a two-lane dam road that curled around the Dillon Reservoir. It was an isolated roadway, lined by pine and aspen. A quarter of a mile outside of Frisco, Byers suddenly turned around in the road, passing the first unmarked vehicle of marshals traveling behind him. The next police vehicle, however, pulled across the road, preventing Byers from passing. A Frisco police officer jumped out of the vehicle, a shotgun leveled at Byers's stopped car.

"Put your hands where I can see them or I'll blow your fucking head off," he screamed.

Byers did so and was handcuffed without putting up a fight. About the same time, other police knocked on his chalet door and arrested his girlfriend. When they searched the chalet hours later, they learned Byers had recently married the woman and that the couple had applied for passports under aliases. Even more surprising was Byers's appearance: A plastic surgeon had given him a facelift, removed a scar, and implanted hair plugs. He was barely recognizable.

When McMaster had gathered federal agents in 1982 to discuss the possibility of a financial investigation into South Carolina's drug smuggling networks, he was clear he wanted this potential investigation to be different, unique for its ability to snare the kingpins and financiers behind the illicit drug trade in the Palmetto State. He wanted trophies for the wall, entire drug smuggling operations toppled by cutting off the monster's head. He wanted Mr. Big, though he did not know there was an entire informal fraternity of Mr. Bigs in South Carolina, running up and down the East Coast, bombing loads in wherever they pleased. Obviously these men were adept at avoiding the law, but perhaps investigators and prosecutors underestimated how slippery the most talented gentlemen smugglers would remain even after their smuggling networks were exposed and dismantled. By remaining fugitives they prevented government investigators from fulfilling their ultimate mission: catching kingpins. Despite convicting almost a hundred men and a few women on smuggling-related charges, in three years the task force had few kingpin convictions to speak of, especially when it came to the men named in the original two Jackpot indictments.

The arrest of Rhoad and recapture of Byers finally turned the kingpin tide in the government's favor. The arrests proved the smuggling leaders, these almost mythical criminals able to evade detection despite the most brazen acts of criminality and consumption, were indeed fallible, susceptible to being captured through the betrayal of informers or their own sloppy, indiscreet living habits. The investigators were learning that if you pushed hard enough, one could break through the considerable smokescreen that surrounded these men. It was a law enforcement truth few people on the smuggling side of Operation Jackpot had recognized, enabling the drug runners' exalted reputations among fellow criminals to become self-perpetuating.

Skip Sanders, to whom many of the kingpins came calling when needing an isolated off-load spot on Edisto Island, writes:

the thing with byers and I suppose harvey [lee] was, their roles sort of went to their head. the same can be said for flash [barry foy] a little bit. i did hang out with him some, but not as an equal. he wanted to project that "front" you know. he once told me he got a cut for everything entering the carolina coast. and i thought to myself, "well, that's strange, i guess i won't tell him about the three loads that came in the past two months."

in actuality, no body ran shit. we all wanted to convey the illusion that we did. that's it. you want to do a boat load of weed? hop your ass on a sail boat, go off the coast of colombia [around Cartagena] with around 100k in cash, and you can instantly get loaded with ten thousand pounds of weed within a couple days. simple enough. but a few, like harvey, like flash, would portray this process as their own devise. and thereby instruct others where to go and sometimes reap as much as half of the load. and when a man suddenly assumes this much control over a process ultimately zero dependent upon him, he became protective as a "run something" tough guy. when actually, all he has of any value is the secret therein.

Two weeks after Byers was recaptured and less than a month after the arrest of Rhoad, another kingpin was removed from the dwindling list of Operation Jackpot fugitives. For weeks, Forbes had been prowling around New York State, looking for Foy, chasing leads in the Catskills and Manhattan. Many didn't pan out, and those that did were frustrating, bringing Forbes and fellow Jackpot investigator Chuck Pittard to places Foy had been some time earlier. He was still always a step ahead.

Toward the end of March 1985, they were back in New York City, interviewing a woman at her Manhattan apartment. She was a friend of Foy and holding onto some of his money and many fake identifications. She hadn't wanted to talk, but did so after Forbes gently suggested she could be arrested for aiding and abetting a fugitive. In the middle of the interview, the phone rang. To everyone's surprise, says Forbes, it was Foy on the line. He told the woman he was on a ski trip, but coming to New York with his family. They were in need of a place to stay, he said, so maybe she could find them a flat. He'd be arriving soon, just as soon as it stopped snowing. There was a blizzard outside.

The woman carried on the conversation while the agents scribbled questions on a notepad for her to ask. When she hung up, they were still unaware of Foy's exact location, but they started making inquiries with the National Weather Service as to where there was a blizzard. The answer, says Forbes, was "Telluride is catching hell."

After checking passenger lists of flights coming into New York from Colorado, they discovered reservations made in the name of a known Foy alias, all connecting through Denver. On March 28, 1985, undercover Customs agents in Denver identified Foy and his wife in the airport, but let him board his flight instead of making an arrest. Foy's wife says she knew something was amiss, having noticed strange men around them.

"Agents knew we were there, they sat next to me. I think they knew I knew, maybe not," writes Liafsha. "I told [Barry], advised him to leave the airport, but, as usual, he disregarded my advice."

After the flight left, the agents called New York, advising their colleagues that Foy was on his way, due to arrive just after nine o'clock that evening. Forbes headed to LaGuardia Airport, eager to make the arrest after nearly six months of work trying to locate the kingpin. Once the flight landed, he and other agents waited in the Jetway for Foy to emerge. Passenger after passenger streamed off the plane, but no one matching Foy's description. Forbes was flabbergasted. How could Foy have slipped through his fingers again, especially after the Customs agents in Colorado assured him he was on the plane? Desperate to solve the conundrum, Forbes rushed onto the plane with six other agents. They fanned down the two aisles of the large jet. It was empty, save for the flight crew and a family with young children in the back of the plane, gathering their things. The parents were striking, wearing three-quarter-length mink coats and leaving little doubt in the men's mind that Dad was Barry "Flash" Foy. The kingpin, who was wearing a gray three-piece suit under his coat, paid little attention to the plainclothes posse of federal agents heading his way, confusing them for the plane's cleaning crew.

"Barry Foy, you're under arrest," said a Customs agent, flashing his badge and confronting Foy in the left aisle. At the same time,

Forbes cut across the center row of seats and snapped handcuffs around Foy's wrists. As the metal clasps swung shut and clicked, Foy's fifteen-year career as a smuggler was over. He was three days short of his thirty-fourth birthday.

Unlike two years earlier, the summer months of 1985 would feature no spectacular show trials. The latest group of Operation Jackpot defendants were no mere hired hands with unfamiliar faces. It would be near impossible for Bob "The Boss" Byers, Barry "Flash" Foy, and Tom "Rolex" Rhoad, to shake their notoriety. The government could call dozens of witnesses able to point the men out in court and detail their innumerable transgressions. The kingpins had little chance of beating a conviction.

When Byers was returned to South Carolina to face charges related to his September 1984 escape from the Charleston County jail, U.S. marshals were careful not to allow him another chance to flee. He was kept locked in a five- by seven-foot cell twenty-four hours a day, and given limited use of a telephone. When he did call a relative or his lawyers, marshals dialed the phone number for him, handed him the receiver, and listened to his side of the conversation. Byers ultimately pleaded guilty to escape charges and was sentenced by Hawkins to eight years in prison, running consecutive to his original punishment. "The Boss" had thirty-three years in prison ahead of him. After pleading guilty, he kissed his pregnant wife and held her tight. He would not witness the birth of his daughter, nor her childhood.

In May 1985, Foy and Rhoad, bosom buddies and accused smuggling masterminds, were to be tried together. Foy gave notice that he might use a defense of insanity, while Rhoad planned to stick to a plea of not guilty. But three days before trial, the men reversed course and struck plea agreements with the government. Operation Jackpot may have been winding down, but the kingpins knew plenty of other drug traffickers around the country and world, and federal agents were eager for any information they might pry from Flash and Rolex. In exchange for their cooperation and pleading guilty to the kingpin statute, prosecutors would recommend a sentence of no more than

JASON RYAN

twenty years. Foy got just about all of that, handed a term of eighteen years in prison. During his sentencing hearing his lawyers disclosed that Foy had been previously diagnosed with psychotic tendencies and was a heavy user of cocaine and LSD, which contributed to his mental instability. Hawkins sympathized, but, in an escalation of his anti-drug rhetoric that squared him with the Reagan administration, stated his conviction that even at the height of the Cold War, drug smugglers like Foy were more dangerous to the United States than communists. In prison, Hawkins said, Foy could receive drug and psychological treatment.

A week earlier, Rhoad's defense counsel had been determined to do better for their client. They packed the courtroom with hometown supporters from Branchville and Bamberg, South Carolina. Those who could not make it had been asked to write letters, which were read in court, creating a glowing portrait at odds with Rhoad's conviction as a marijuana kingpin. The savings and loan president said she believed Rhoad wanted to make amends. The local superintendent said his behavior was always above reproach. The reverend's wife said Rhoad and his family loved the Lord, their church, their state, and their country. Rhoad's football coach recalled how the gutsy player, who suffered from asthma, was discharged from the hospital to play in the state championship game. He threw three touchdowns in the 35–7 rout.

At the same time, they confessed confusion at how the bright young man they knew in small-town South Carolina had lost his way so badly.

The government was effusive when describing Rhoad's cooperation, classifying him as one of the most helpful suspects they debriefed. Prosecutors described how he disclosed safety deposit box holdings across the country and wired money from his Bahamian bank accounts to a government account in Charleston. Letters from other police agencies around the country mentioned the unique information Rhoad disclosed to them about other suspects. On a scale of one to ten, said Forbes, Rhoad earned a ten in terms of his cooperation. One of Rhoad's lawyers, Robert B. Wallace, made a point of mentioning to Hawkins the harm that may come his way in prison for such actions.

"He will be ridiculed. He will suffer indecencies," said Wallace. "He will even suffer perhaps threats."

After the list of character witnesses was exhausted, another of Rhoad's lawyers, Sol Blatt Sr., began a lengthy impassioned address to the court. Blatt was a man of enormous stature in South Carolina, representing Barnwell County for nearly fifty-four years in the state's general assembly. For thirty-two of those years, he was speaker of the House. Blatt's influence was legendary, and he was a member of a small group of politicians known as the Barnwell Ring that occupied many of the leadership positions in South Carolina during the mid-twentieth century.

Now ninety years old and in poor health, Blatt, who came into the courtroom in a wheelchair, said this appearance was likely his last in a courtroom. With the same voice he used for countless stump speeches, courtroom arguments, and legislative oratory in his storied political and legal career, Blatt made a desperate plea on behalf of Rhoad as he leaned unsteadily against the defense table. He beseeched Hawkins to be merciful:

> *He's made his peace with his God. He believes God has forgiven him for his sins. And now I plead with your Honor to do that which God himself has done and give him a chance. Show him mercy. Some day we all must face our maker. Me soon. Because now, I have climbed down the mountainside into the valley from whence no traveler returns, and shortly, it can't be long, I must face my God, and I know if he does not show to me that mercy that I want and need so badly, that the penalty I will have to pay would be too extreme.*
>
> *Won't your honor do as much? Can your Honor do less than God himself would do? Isn't it only fair to a human being to say, well, you have sinned, you have repented, you have prayed, and you are saved? I will not throw a roadblock in your path.*

Blatt said he would have despaired should his own son, a federal judge in South Carolina alongside Hawkins, have become entangled in drug running. Finishing his speech, he charged Hawkins with the responsibility of Rhoad's salvation.

"My soul cries out to you to help him . . . Tom Rhoad is a fellow man of mine. He is a child of God. Won't you help that child of God as

God has helped him? God has forgiven him. You can do no less, your Honor. I plead with you to help this man in his hour of need, and I believe that God will bless you if you do."

For his part, Rhoad was contrite. He pledged to be an example of the destructive power of drugs and to use his legal knowledge to help fellow inmates straighten out their lives. He mentioned that his fiancée was in the courtroom, and that he longed to settle down with her. He said the last five months in jail provided him ample time to reflect on his past and to imagine his future. Choking back tears, Rhoad said he figured he could only look ahead:

> *When I get out, and I hope in the not too distant future, I would love to get into youth counseling, because I got a message for the youth of the country. I can tell them that if they use drugs, they are going to ruin their lives. If they get involved in selling drugs, they are going to go to jail . . . I am sorry for what I have done to society and sorry for what I have done to my family. Most of all, I am sorry for what I have done to myself. I have learned all the money in the world can't buy you happiness, and all the money in the world is not worth a dime compared to your freedom and your family.*

After hearing Rhoad's remarks, Hawkins called a recess for fifteen minutes. The judge, an acutely sensitive man when sentencing the most typical of defendants, was impressed by the considerable crowd in the courtroom and the comments made by Blatt, who was one of South Carolina's most venerable statesmen. But Hawkins was also a stickler for equal treatment, and he was careful to distance himself from political influence. For any difficulty he might have had in deciding an appropriate punishment, he was at least aided by the prosecutor's recommendation that the sentence not exceed twenty years in prison and the statutory requirement that a continuing criminal enterprise conviction not be less than ten years in prison.

When court reconvened, Hawkins spoke of the issues he grappled with in deciding punishment. That Rhoad was a lawyer bothered him, since he felt the criminal actions of all the lawyers convicted in Operation Jackpot tarnished his beloved profession. Regardless, he said, he would not punish Rhoad any more severely. When listening to Rhoad's remorse, he took it with a grain of salt, shrewdly observing that the kingpin's rehabilitation started the moment he was identified in San Diego. Before then, he was "living it up, doing everything he could from the fruits of his illegal activities."

Perhaps most frustrating to Hawkins was the fact that for every drug smuggling defendant he sentenced to years in prison—the number of which he had long lost count—the trafficking of illegal drugs had not lessened. In fact, despite Reagan's War on Drugs, there was even more of a drug problem in the United States. Hawkins mentioned listening to a radio report the day before, just before sentencing Byers to an additional eight years in prison:

The General Accounting Office, which reports to the Congress about the success of congressional committees among other things, report[ed] that the government's fight against smuggling drugs was lost. More coming in than ever came in with all these millions, maybe billions for all I know, of dollars that have been appropriated for that very purpose. So much cocaine in the country that the price is falling every day, meaning the supply is so great. Of course, if the price falls, then it makes it available to economic groups that could never have afforded it before.

Hawkins fretted that despite reading everything he could about drugs, hopeful of finding some solution, there seemed to be no stopping its use and import. He said they could all pray for the eradication of drugs, "but really I doubt if there's much hope for it. At least in my lifetime."

Still, the federal judge was not ready to throw in the towel. If drug smuggling was to be stopped in future generations, there must be deterrents. From the bench the best deterrent he could dispense was time behind bars. No matter how persuasive the speeches made in the courtroom, Hawkins believed he had an obligation to uphold the law that Rhoad and the associated gentlemen smugglers flagrantly flaunted. Justice required him to consider more than the recent emotional arguments:

They were eloquent pleas that the attorneys and others made for Mr. Rhoad, and I would have to be [an] awful cold-hearted, hard person not to have been affected by them, and I am affected by them. By the same token, I am also affected by the misery and the heartache that I see in our community and in our nation that comes about as a result of drug trafficking.

. . . I hope, Mr. Blatt, that [Mr. Rhoad] is conscientious and serious about working with misguided persons, because where he's going, there will be plenty of misguided people . . . a lot of misguided people who did not have the opportunities that were afforded Mr. Rhoad for education, stations in life.

Winding up his thoughts, Hawkins delivered the sentence. Rhoad would serve fifteen years in federal prison.

Just weeks before Byers, Foy, and Rhoad were sentenced, McMaster had resigned as U.S. attorney for the District of South Carolina, casting an eye toward his political future and asking not to be reappointed. In his four years as the state's top federal prosecutor, McMaster's most significant achievement was Operation Jackpot, resulting in the arrest and conviction of more than one hundred marijuana and hashish smugglers who had managed to avoid law enforcement for years. More important than these numbers was his belief that Operation Jackpot could be replicated in any part of the country, the task force serving as a model for effective drug enforcement. Before leaving office he sent a letter to each state representative, suggesting that a statewide drug task force be formed, along with a special grand jury.

McMaster's name was synonymous with the drug investigation, and indeed it was his efforts at the beginning of his appointment that created the task force and gave it the freedom to operate. If some employees bristled at his management, others credited him for letting them participate in the biggest and most interesting case of their careers. A few months after he left office, he described his role as an overseer and supporter, enabling competent staff to do the hard work:

I didn't do it. The agents did it, and the young deputy U.S. attorneys in my office were able to take their work and build good cases for court.

I'm just proud that I was able to help by putting the force of the U.S. attorney's office behind the effort, and I'm proud to have been a part of Operation Jackpot. If it had happened anywhere else, like maybe Washington or New York or California, Hollywood would come along and make a movie. It's that good a story, and it's true.

After leaving his U.S. attorney's position, McMaster said he would soon run for political office, but was mum on which one it might be. Privately he told friends he was interested in one day becoming president, but first might run for governor, lieutenant governor, or a congressional seat. The problem with these designs, noted South Carolina political columnist Lee Bandy, was that McMaster wasn't very well liked by fellow Republicans, with some members of his own party threatening to ambush him should he make a run, unless the thirty-six-year-old lawyer did "some serious fence-mending."

The biggest complaint about McMaster was that many of his actions as U.S. attorney were transparently political. He annoyed people from every camp. The smugglers, of course, despised him, accusing him of going overboard to punish them for nonviolent offenses. Defense attorneys were appalled at some of his pretrial comments, which seemed to violate a gag order imposed by Hawkins. In December 1983, Steven Bernholz, one of the North Carolina lawyers representing Les Riley while he was imprisoned in Australia, brought many of these comments to Hawkins's attention in a letter:

During the year or so that the "Jackpot" cases have been making countless headlines, we have observed with some mild chagrin the innumerable and widely reported pronouncements of the United States Attorney made in the context of formal press conferences, interviews, informal comments, and leaks. Even though I have not yet had the pleasure of meeting him, the handsome visage of Mr. McMaster has greeted me almost weekly in the newspapers I have read over morning tea. I already feel as if we are old friends. I admit that my vexation over this media campaign has, at times, become pronounced. On those several occasions, Mr. McMaster has clearly deviated from his own announced "policy" of not commenting "one way or another about the activities of Operation Jackpot," and then proceeded to make extrajudicial statements which appear to be calculated to and, in my opinion, do inflame the passions of the listener and reader.

Bandy, the political writer, commented that McMaster produced more news releases and press conferences than all his predecessors combined, and "no one can recall any other U.S. attorney being so public-relations conscious." Other critics pointed out that Operation Jackpot intercepted no drugs and rounded up smugglers who almost exclusively trafficked marijuana and hashish, not hard drugs like cocaine and heroin.

McMaster had critics within the government, too, and at least two veteran assistant U.S. attorneys in his office quit out of frustration with their boss. After McMaster finished his term, one of his staff members circulated a poem, which included this verse:

> *Oh, Henry—*
> *You leave behind a grateful public*
> *Who thinks you're greater than the Pope*
> *Because of Operation Crackpot,*
> *But, Henry, we're stuck with the DOPE.*

McMaster's successor, Vinton D. Lide, made numerous changes regarding the drug investigation task force when he took over. Most noticeably, the task force was no longer called Operation Jackpot, but the much more prosaic Presidential Drug Task Force for the District of South Carolina. Lide said the Jackpot moniker did not give proper credit to Reagan's drug enforcement initiatives. McMaster had argued that the catchy handle was crucial in helping create a success story the public could rally around. Another difference between the two men was their conduct during press conferences and the way they presented their charges against the smugglers to the public. Speaking of Riley and Butler, Lide said in 1985 that, "Of course, everyone is presumed innocent until proven guilty, and these charges are merely accusations right now."

Such a comment stands in stark contrast to one McMaster made two years earlier when discussing Les Riley and his brother Roy, neither of whom had been tried in court.

"They're criminals. They're both criminals," said McMaster. "Of course, they're not criminals until they're convicted, but they're still criminals."

If McMaster took his lumps from all sides, it was to be expected. He disturbed extensive smuggling networks, annoyed defense attorneys, and bucked bureaucrats and naysayers, delivering conviction after conviction. To mount Operation Jackpot, it probably required a bit of arrogance and entitlement, just as smuggling marijuana required those traits. McMaster was unapologetic about his performance:

If I could look back and point to anything I'm proud of, it's being part of Operation Jackpot. I think it is one of the singular most important achievements in law enforcement history, and the future investigation and prosecution of drug smugglers and drug dealers will profit from the financial approach we took in Operation Jackpot.

There is no doubt in my mind that Jackpot has changed the way these cases will be handled, and I sincerely believed it has crippled the drug smugglers' operations.

For nearly four years Lee "Smiley" Harvey had been a wanted man. Despite losing tons of hashish to the Atlantic Ocean and the police in 1981, he kept smuggling. Despite the arrests of Julian "Doc" Pernell, Barry "Ice Cream" Toombs, and dozens of others in Virginia in 1982, he kept smuggling. Despite Operation Jackpot and the arrest of his partner, Riley, in 1983, he kept smuggling. Toombs says Harvey moved beyond running drugs, that he was wrapped up with the mob, that the Lebanese were asking him to smuggle more than a billion dollars in gold and jewels outside their war-torn country to the Bahamas, the valuables concealed in slabs of hashish. It's hard to know if this is true.

Harvey outlasted almost every other kingpin he worked with, at least among the gentlemen smugglers. But not even Smiley could run forever, not if he kept visiting the same old haunts, as he was doing in Miami in 1985, with the DEA updating its files with every lead they received. When one vague tip came through to DEA agent Frank Hildebrandt from an anonymous caller on August 30, 1985, it was over for the kingpin. Hildebrandt entered the tip into the computer and, after chasing a few leads on his machine for a few days, determined he might be onto Harvey. Everyone but the CIA, it seemed, had a warrant out for the man.

Hildebrandt was a young agent at the time, with a sharp memory, and he recalled hearing about Virginia marijuana kingpins Harvey, Pernell, and Toombs from DEA agent Jim Mittica during a seminar at the federal law enforcement training center in Glynco, Georgia. So when the tip came through, he was interested, even though his supervisor and colleagues at the FBI dismissed it. Hildebrandt worked on it at night, though, determined to see if Harvey really was frequenting a condo on Key Biscayne, Florida, just across the bay from Miami. He introduced himself to a parking attendant, flashed his badge, and shared just enough information with the man to make him feel important. He asked the attendant to give him a call when Harvey came through. Meanwhile, Hildebrandt and other DEA agents staked out the condo complex and bars Harvey was known to frequent, looking for a sign of the kingpin. A week went by without any luck.

On September 9, 1985, Hildebrandt got the call—Harvey was in the condo. At ten o'clock that evening police and DEA agents filled the hallway outside Key Colony unit #1036. Police evacuated the condo across the hall, and one DEA agent was stationed on a ninth-floor balcony to thwart any attempts by Harvey to escape or destroy evidence. A DEA agent then picked up the phone and called to the residence. He identified himself and explained police and DEA agents had the condo surrounded. They were looking for Harvey, he said, and nobody needed to get hurt. Could Harvey, he asked, please step into the hall and surrender?

The door soon opened, and Harvey stepped out, along with his girlfriend and another man. Police rushed the kingpin and entered the condo, arresting Harvey without incident. Forty-five minutes later they received permission from Harvey's girlfriend to search the apartment, finding a fake driver's license that belonged to the fugitive, a boating manual for the vessel *Ragamuffin,* a cocaine free-basing pipe, and other papers. As Harvey was taken away, he asked his girlfriend to contact his family.

By two o'clock the next morning, Harvey was booked at the DEA's Miami office, fingerprinted, and photographed. For once he was without a smile. Instead the thirty-seven-year-old man with thick hair, a beard, a mustache, and glasses just looked tired. He said as much to the agents who arrested him, telling them he was glad it was all over. Harvey also told the agents that he knew a federal prosecutor had been gunning for him for years, that she wanted a piece of him.

A DEA agent rattled off the myriad charges against Harvey, including drug trafficking, possession of machine guns and silencers, tax evasion, operating a continuing criminal enterprise, racketeering, intimidation of a grand jury witness, and parole violations. Federal grand juries in at least three states had indicted him.

Harvey said nothing in response to the drug and kingpin charges. The weapons charge, however, was bogus, he told the agent. He had nothing to do with guns. Never had. Harvey, who was legendary for keeping his cool, soon became irritated. He considered the flood of allegations against him. It seemed preposterous.

"One man could not have done all this," he protested.

The government felt otherwise, and they convinced a federal judge in Alexandria, Virginia, of the same in a non-jury trial in January 1986, though the kingpin was acquitted of the gun charges. A month later U.S. District Judge Albert V. Bryan sentenced Harvey to forty years in prison.

After thirty months in Australian prisons, Riley and Butler learned their fates from the Australian High Court at Canberra on December 18, 1985, when a unanimous ruling decided the accused smugglers could be extradited under the kingpin statute and face a potential punishment of life imprisonment. Although Australia did not have a direct equivalent of the American kingpin statute, drug offenses listed in an extradition treaty were similar enough to warrant extradition on the charge, said the court, which dismissed some minor charges against Riley and Butler, including tax evasion and currency violations. The High Court's ruling was seen as an important one in the global war on drugs, as it claimed the American kingpin statute was an extraditable offense in more than forty nations in the former British Empire, including Australia, Canada, Great Britain, India, and New Zealand. American drug smugglers, it was hoped, could no longer find safe harbor in those countries.

In January 1986 Riley and Butler were returned to the United States to face charges from Operation Jackpot. The men prepared for trial, though it seemed a hopeless case given the overwhelming testimony against the men. As one of Riley's lawyers, Martin Bernholz, explains, "You can't argue to a jury that all eighty-seven people are lying."

By April the government dropped the continuing criminal enterprise against Butler, age fifty-four, on account of his age and limited role in smuggling ventures, a concession McMaster was unwilling to make when he was U.S. attorney. Butler struck a plea agreement with the government, as did Riley, who was not so fortunate to have the kingpin charge dropped. Although Riley agreed to plead guilty and disclose his assets, he refused to be debriefed about the involvement of his smuggling associates. On this point he was adamant, though his obstinacy confounded some of his former associates.

"We were all trying to make our time as short as possible," says one former smuggler, "and it seemed Les was trying to make it as long as possible."

On June 16, 1986, Riley stood before Hawkins in a Charleston courtroom. Behind him was a small crowd that included his wife, kids, parents, and ninety-year-old grandmother. Months earlier he celebrated his fortieth birthday in prison. Given that the *minimum* sentence for operating a continuing criminal enterprise was ten years, he'd spend his fiftieth birthday behind bars, possibly his sixtieth, and maybe all the other ones he had left, too. Among the 180 people charged in Operation Jackpot, a prosecutor said, there was no bigger boss than Riley. The government noted that he refused to name names, and alleged he was not forthcoming regarding his assets, doubting he spent all his money on legal fees, as he claimed. Alonzo B. Coleman Jr., one of Riley's lawyers, offered some explanation for Riley's refusal to talk about his coconspirators.

"That's probably about all he's got left in his view . . . the notion that even though a lot of the people had participated in ventures with him and whose names are on the records about what they have done, he leaves that to them to name their names," said Coleman. "He will tell the government everything he has done, but he feels like he cannot ever, ever say that he is going to name names of people that he has dealt with over the years."

Coleman also compared his client's life to the parable of the Prodigal Son. Riley did not leave home to seek a life of crime, he said, but rather fell into a smuggling career that, it was worth noting, was devoid of violence and involved a substance popular on college campuses across the country. He never committed a crime that he believed hurt someone.

When Riley spoke he was brief and contrite:

"I don't know if there are any words, your Honor, that I can say how sorry I am for what I have done. I just hope that you will show some mercy on me."

As was his habit, Hawkins then began to think aloud, explaining to those gathered in his court how he considered the matter at hand, and what would be appropriate punishment. He sympathized that marijuana was a popular substance across the country, and said that if Congress chose to decriminalize the drug, he'd have no strong opinions on that decision, though he reads plenty about the harmful effects of drugs, with many people stealing money and property to support their habits.

He sympathized, too, with the adventuresome aspects of Riley's crimes, and appreciated that smuggling marijuana was like "being a modern day pirate on the high seas" and "something that could get into a young fellow's blood." On the other hand, it was also just an easy way to make fast money.

Regarding Riley's extended extradition fight and his decision to not fully cooperate with the government, Hawkins found no fault, and even paid a bit of tribute to the defendant:

I don't quarrel with Mr. Riley about fighting extradition just as hard as he could. That's what the law is all about, and that's [why] I am here to uphold the law. I really don't quarrel with him about not ratting on his friends, if that's the right word, or squealing, because he had to weigh those things, and he has weighed them, and he's determined that he will stay on this side, even if it is a problem. It probably speaks well of Mr. Riley . . . When I first started practicing law, the lowest thing in the jail was a stool pigeon and informers, but times have changed. We have more educated criminals now, and he has chosen that path, and I am not going to hold that against him.

After this, Hawkins prepared to announce his judgment, advising Riley that he regretted punishing anyone, yet it was required of him, and he spent many hours pondering an appropriate penalty. With that he delivered Riley's sentence. For being a marijuana kingpin, Riley was to be committed to federal prison for a term of twenty-five years, with no chance of parole.

For the final time, Hawkins addressed the gentleman smuggler, who stayed polite to the end.

"Good luck to you, Mr. Riley"

"Thank you, sir."

Epilogue

Charleston, South Carolina
January 2011

Sometime in the mid-1980s, a mock newspaper article was written about Operation Jackpot, claiming the thirty-ninth trial in the investigation had started in Washington, D.C., with 427 government witnesses slated to testify. Trials had been shifted to the nation's capital, the article said, because buildings in Charleston, South Carolina had become too small. Yet even in Washington, officials were running out of space. The Capitol's rotunda could barely contain all thirty-two defendants and their attorneys. Discovery material was held in the Library of Congress, and witnesses were housed in the chambers of the Senate and House.

The mock article had no byline, but some say it was written by Dewey Greager, the DEA agent who was one of the five federal agents originally assigned to the Operation Jackpot task force and who went undercover to capture Bob "The Boss" Byers in Antigua in 1983. Greager died in 1997 and could not be asked about the parody, or his experiences in Operation Jackpot. Whoever wrote the article, however, communicated how overwhelming the investigation had become, especially with regard to the lengthy extradition battle concerning Les Riley and Wally Butler. To pay for the legal expenses associated with the case in Australia, the article said, the United States raised taxes by seventeen percent and Australia sold the states of "Queensland and Victoria to the Arabs." Riley, for his part, hired the former secretary general of the United Nations for additional defense counsel and vowed to "fight extradition to the end, or longer if necessary."

If the article was a bit silly—it mentioned a molecular-vision camera and an Inter-Solar Police Force (INTERSOL)—it was also fairly prophetic, correctly predicting that prosecutors in the case would use their experiences in Operation Jackpot as a springboard to more prominent positions, with Assistant U.S. Attorney Bart Daniel becoming the U.S. attorney for South Carolina in 1989, and his fellow prosecutor, Cam Littlejohn, becoming a respected defense attorney.

But for other prosecutors involved in the case, the article's predictions were inaccurate. Prosecutor Bob Jendron did not become chief justice of the U.S. Supreme court, but has remained an assistant U.S. attorney in South Carolina. Cam Currie is no longer a prosecutor, but now a federal judge in South Carolina. And Henry McMaster, despite the article's prediction, has not become vice president of the United States. At least not by the time this book was written.

McMaster, in fact, had a checkered political career after Operation Jackpot. Upon leaving the U.S. attorney's office, he hired a campaign staff and organized an election committee, yet for months did not designate which public office he would be running for. Many speculated McMaster would run for lieutenant governor. Although he had alienated some fellow Republicans, the former prosecutor had a strong reputation in the state, thanks to the success of Operation Jackpot. More than a hundred people had been convicted of smuggling-related crimes during his tenure as U.S. attorney and Crimestopper programs across the state had benefited from money seized in the investigation.

Eventually, McMaster announced he was challenging incumbent U.S. Senator Fritz Hollings in the 1986 elections. It was an ambitious goal to unseat the former Democratic governor who, for the last twenty years, had served in the Senate alongside South Carolina's other longstanding senator, Strom Thurmond. While campaigning, McMaster spoke often of the success of Operation Jackpot. During a televised debate, he challenged his opponent to take a drug test, allowing the senator to respond with his savage wit.

"I'll take a drug test," said Hollings, "if you'll take an IQ test."

McMaster lost the election.

In subsequent years McMaster served four terms as chairman of the South Carolina Republican Party. In 2002 he was elected South Carolina's attorney general, and won reelection four years later. In 2010, however, he lost a campaign for governor after placing third in the Republican primary.

Federal agents David Forbes and Claude McDonald are both retired, and Operation Jackpot was the case of their careers, though it wasn't without its stresses. McDonald suffered a heart attack in June 1986, the same month Les Riley and Wally Butler were sentenced to prison. After McDonald's open-heart surgery, he was surprised to receive a get-well card from Tom "Rolex" Rhoad, whom he had apprehended a year earlier.

Compared to the cops, fewer of the smugglers are alive. After being released from prison in 1998, Rhoad struggled with a cocaine habit. The fifty-eight-year-old died March 10, 2005, passing away in his sleep after previously suffering an aneurysm. Boat captain Willie Frank Steele, who trained as a triathlete after leaving prison, served less than six years behind bars. He crashed his motorcycle in Columbia, South Carolina, on July 26, 2007, and died at age fifty-six. Rhoad and Steele, like many of the smugglers, did not serve their full sentences, paroled early for good behavior.

Wally Butler served less than three years in prison and passed away on November 3, 2006, at the age of seventy-four. Lee Harvey died at the Mayo Clinic on April 7, 2001, from liver failure. At age fifty-two, Harvey was still a federal inmate. The Virginia prosecutor who put him behind bars, Karen Tandy, served as administrator of the DEA from July 2003 to November 2007.

Among the living is Skip Sanders, who followed his term in federal prison with a twelve-year stint in South Carolina prison for marijuana trafficking. He was released in 2009. Barry Toombs is a free man after three stints in prison. He still collects and deals antique lamps.

Alive, too, are Barry Foy and Les Riley. Foy served more than ten years in prison before his release in 1995. Riley was released in 1999 after nearly seventeen years in Australian and American prisons. He might have been released a bit earlier if not for a brief escape. In February 1992 Riley walked away from Federal Correctional Institution Tallahassee and went on the lam. He was arrested four months later in Sarasota, Florida, after attempting to obtain a passport in the name of Edwin Rogers Schooley, a five-year-old boy who had been squished to death by a circus elephant in Sarasota in 1950.

Without a doubt prison was difficult to endure for the marijuana kingpins. Foy describes going to prison as his life slowing down from one hundred miles per hour to five miles per hour. Bob Byers did just about as much time as Riley—nearly eighteen years—and emerged from prison a much different man, say friends, withdrawn and partial to yoga. It was Byers who wrote to Hawkins in November 1985, thanking him for his first contact visit with his wife and newborn child and asking for a reduction in his sentence. In this same letter, he expressed despair, ending the missive with a plea: "I am not the same man who stood before you on those other occasions. Time is the random wind that blows down the long corridor, slamming all the doors. Please help me!"

Foy's and Riley's lives since prison have lacked the glamour, riches, and excitement of their youth. They do not regret their careers as marijuana smugglers, save for getting caught and for spending so much time in prison, apart from their families and children. Many other smugglers feel the same way. Few are ashamed of their crimes, though some are reluctant to publicize their pasts today for fear of negative consequences from peers and professional colleagues.

If one thing has not dulled in the more than twenty-five years since Operation Jackpot, it is the smugglers' scorn for those they consider rats. When smuggler Tommy Liles mentioned Steele's fatal motorcycle accident to Riley, Riley asked if Steele's tire slipped on a piece of cheese. No, Liles replied, "His tail got caught in the spokes."

In a display of similar contempt, smuggler Ben Graham is fond of recounting "The Great Cheeze Incident." Once, says Graham, he and his brother Billy were dining at a McClellanville, South Carolina, restaurant after they had been paroled from federal prison. As they finished their meal, another former smuggler walked in—a man despised by the Grahams ever since he had cooperated with the government and testified against his friends. Before the brothers left, Ben poked his head into the kitchen and asked the cook to deliver a slice of cheese to the smuggler, compliments of the Grahams. When the suggestive side order was delivered, it infuriated the cooperating witness.

"That asshole called my parole officer and said I'd threatened him. The parole people called me in and said it had gone all the way to the Vice Presidential Task Force on Drugs in Washington and that I was up Shit Creek," says Graham, who worried for weeks that his parole might be revoked. "Much later, long after I was off parole, I found out that the people in the parole office thought it was as funny as I did, but they had to fuck with me."

Graham's story illustrates another truth, that the police who investigated the gentlemen smugglers look back fondly on that time of their careers, when they didn't have to fear catching a bullet during an investigation. Nowadays, they note, things are much different. Smuggling is less romantic and much more deadly. Trafficking by sailboat is a rarity, and the DEA estimates 80 percent of pot in the country is trucked across the border from Mexico. Because of fighting between Mexican drug gangs, there are shocking casualty counts south of the border, with many civilians, politicians, and police among the dead. In fact, more than twenty-five thousand Mexicans have died from drug violence since Mexico's President Felipe Calderon launched an offensive against drug gangs in December 2006.

That's not to say that there is a lack of ingenuity among today's smugglers. Illegal drugs are brought into this country through underground tunnels, by human mules that hide drug-filled condoms in their bodies, and by submarines made in South American jungles. Mexican gangs grow marijuana on public land in the United States, raising crops within national parks and forests. Americans also grow plenty of marijuana in the United States, whether indoors or outside, and some do so without risk of incarceration. Fifteen states have passed medical marijuana laws, decriminalizing patients' possession of small amounts of marijuana, and some of these states do not have criminal penalties for cultivation of small amounts of pot. Despite the loosening of marijuana laws for medical reasons, recreational pot use remains controversial from one coast to the other. In November 2010, Californians rejected a proposition to allow adults to legally possess up to an ounce of marijuana and grow pot for personal, non-medical use. In the gentlemen smugglers' home state of South Carolina, possession of up to an ounce of pot remains a misdemeanor, and cultivation of one hundred plants or less is a felony.

In August 2008 Ashley Brunson was sentenced in Charleston to thirty months in federal prison for his role in the smuggling rings targeted by Operation Jackpot. Because Judge David Norton credited him the fourteen months he had spent in jail while he awaited trial and sentencing, Brunson was instantly eligible for parole under old sentencing guidelines. He was released from custody in June 2009 and has returned to his home in coastal Mexico.

Brunson might not be the only one living abroad in paradise. Although Byers was said to have died in October 2004 in Punta Gorda, Florida, a day before his sixtieth birthday, his childhood friend and adult smuggling buddy Bob Roche isn't so quick to believe in his demise. Among those familiar with Operation Jackpot, it's a frequent source of speculation as to which kingpin might have buried some cash before their incarceration, or hid a sailboat, or maintained a Bahamian bank account that Uncle Sam never discovered. The smugglers made so much money, and kept it in so many places, it's hard to believe the government found it all.

Before Byers was imprisoned, says Roche, the kingpin kept money in the Cayman Islands and Minnesota, owned sailboats around the world, and had an attorney drive an RV packed with a million dollars into Canada, the cash destined for deposit into Canadian banks. Surely, Roche says, some of that money and a few of those sailboats could have escaped notice. After prison, Byers might easily have slipped off into the sunset, bound for the South Pacific to dust off his assets.

It's a nice thought, except for the fact that the state of Florida issued a death certificate in Byers's name.

Never mind that, says Roche.

"Has anyone seen his body?" he asks. "Check."

"If they haven't, go to Fiji."

Acknowledgments

This book started simply enough, a reporter digging through newspaper archives during his lunch hour, spurred on by his memory of a conversation eighteen months earlier in which he first learned of South Carolina's gentlemen smugglers. With each binder of news clippings I read, the story sprawled further and further, spanning decades, crossing oceans and continents, and involving an overwhelming array of daredevils, scofflaws, investigators, lawyers, and kingpins. It would not have been possible to tell this story without the cooperation of many of the men and women involved in Operation Jackpot, and I am grateful for them sharing very personal and sensitive information with me. I would like to thank all the people who granted me permission to quote them in this book, and consider it my good fortune to have made their acquaintance. Their amusing memories and varied perspectives made the book a pleasure to research, and I'd be remiss if I did not mention a few people who were especially helpful in my endeavor to tell the tale of South Carolina's gentlemen smugglers and Operation Jackpot.

Before researching this book, I never thought that I'd become familiar with some of the world's greatest marijuana kingpins, and my awareness of them came courtesy of Brooke Brunson, who shared a bit of her family history with me over lunch back in February 2005. I learned more about these men during an interview with former U.S. Attorney Henry McMaster and former Assistant U.S. Attorney John McIntosh in August 2006. McMaster and his staff in the South Carolina attorney general's office allowed me access to news clippings about Operation Jackpot and shared a number of photographs with me that appear in this book.

On the smuggling side, I enjoyed many memorable interviews. It's worth noting that boat captain Christy Campbell was the first smuggler to speak with me. Another native of Beaufort, South Carolina, Skip Sanders, proved an excellent pen pal and talented storyteller. It was always a good day when one of Sanders's letters appeared in my mailbox. John Jamison shared his stories and allowed me to reprint a portion of his poem "All Honey Isn't Sweet." The two South Carolina kingpins in the book who remain alive, Barry Foy and Les Riley, both made themselves available for many phone calls and visits. I am appreciative of their time and good-natured cooperation, and for allowing me to tell the story of their lives.

On the law enforcement side, retired federal agents David Forbes and Claude McDonald also received many of my phone calls and visits and provided me critical insights into their investigation and the evolution of Operation Jackpot. Former federal investigators Jim Mittica and Lance Lydon were equally as helpful about aspects of their drug investigation in Virginia, and retired DEA agent Frank Hildebrandt provided critical memories of the September 1985 arrest of Lee Harvey. Former Assistant U.S. Attorney Cameron Currie was helpful in arranging for the retrieval of court records related to Operation Jackpot. I would also like to thank Terry Sheahan and the U.S. marshals at the Charleston Federal Courthouse for their patience during my repeated visits.

Charleston's *Post and Courier* and Columbia's the *State* newspaper both allowed me to make copies of their large collections of news clippings about Operation Jackpot. In Charleston, Mark Berry was generous to me, as was author James Scott, who provided much counsel and encouragement about the publishing process. My friend Eric Hilmo answered every unusual military question I threw his way.

I owe many thanks to agent Jessica Papin at Dystel & Goderich Literary Management, who provided crucial enthusiasm for this story and thoughtful suggestions for its telling. She found a home for *Jackpot* at Lyons Press, where Keith Wallman provided even more energy and smart edits. I am indebted to both of them for helping me become an author.

My friends and family were reliable sources of love and support. They provided invaluable help during the writing of this book, particularly when my wife and I began a concurrent project of restoring a house. I am thankful for all the ways the Ryans and Garretts lessened our burdens. In particular, I'd like to recognize my brothers for being such marvelous companions through the years, as well as my parents, who have afforded me so many wonderful opportunities in life. They are exceptional, positive people who have always told me the sky is the limit. My grandparents, too, have always taken a keen interest in my pursuits and have been extremely supportive.

Lastly, I would like to thank the two Es in my life. My wife, Elizabeth, made many sacrifices during the three years I worked on this book, always keeping patience and encouragement in good supply. Eliot, our cat and my constant writing partner, offered his own, unique contributions to the manuscript each time he stepped across the keyboard.

Sources

In researching this story, speaking with dozens of devious men, and a handful of just as cunning women, one man warned me that I have been subjected to the biggest group of liars on this earth. A moment later, he passionately denied something that countless others told me was true. Was this man misinformed? Was he lying to protect someone? Were the others wrong? Who should I trust?

Because of lies, because of exaggerations, because of faulty and selective memories, because of ignorance, because rumors have been routinely passed on as fact, and because people on both sides of the law have agendas and grudges, a true account of Operation Jackpot and the marijuana and hashish smuggling that preceded it might seem impossible to obtain. After all, the federal task force in South Carolina, along with related drug investigations in other states, charged more than a hundred men with crimes defined by dishonesty, concealment, and underhandedness—including smuggling, money laundering, tax evasion, racketeering, and conspiracy.

Yet by conducting extensive interviews with the men and women involved in specific marijuana smuggling rings and Operation Jackpot, I believe all but the most insignificant distortions and discrepancies have been weeded out and any competing agendas offset. I have strived to make this book as true and accurate an account as possible, with great effort taken to print only what could be confirmed, unless otherwise noted.

No dialogue has been created. All conversations in the book are exactly as people recall them, or have been taken directly from trial and grand jury transcripts, news articles, police reports, letters, and other documents. Some people's comments have been printed without attribution, a condition they demanded in order to speak with me freely. It was a compromise I made as infrequently as possible. No names have been changed.

This book is not a comprehensive history of marijuana and hashish smuggling in the 1970s and 1980s. Indeed, it is not even a comprehensive history of all the loose smuggling networks targeted by Operation Jackpot. It is instead the story of a few talented smugglers and the law enforcement investigation that rounded them up. I regret that in the interest of telling a concise story, some fascinating people are only mentioned briefly, their adventures given short shrift. Surely these people's lives and illicit careers deserve their own books, too.

Formal Sources

Books and Articles

Bertram, Eva, et. al. *Drug War Politics: The Price of Denial.* Berkeley: University of California Press, Spring 1996.

Bottom, Bob. *Connections II: Crime rackets and networks of influence in Australia.* South Melbourne: The MacMillan Company of Australia, 1987.

Butler, Lindley S. *Pirates, Privateers, and Rebel Raiders of the Carolina Coast.* Chapel Hill and London: University of North Carolina Press, 2000.

Cochran, Hamilton. *Blockade Runners of the Confederacy.* Indianapolis and New York: The Bobbs-Merrill Company, Inc., 1958.

Daniel, E. Bart. "Operation Jackpot: The Investigation of Drug Assets." *Inside Drug Law,* December 1984, pp.1-3.

Flippo, Chet. "Misadventures in Paradise." *Rolling Stone,* October 4, 1979, pp. 36-40.

Gasque, Candace. "Interview with U.S. Attorney Henry Dargan McMaster." *The Carolana Magazine,* July 1985, pp.18-20, 32, 34-35, 39.

Gasque, Candace. "Part Two: Interview with Henry Dargan McMaster." *The Carolana Magazine,* August 1985, pp. 18-19, 27, 32-33.

Hobart-Hampden, C. Augustus. *Never Caught: Personal Adventures Connected with Twelve Successful in Blockade-Running During the American Civil War, 1863-1864.* London: Levey and Co., 1867.

Horner, Dave. *The Blockade-Runners: True Tales of Running the Yankee Blockade of the Confederate Coast.* New York: Dodd, Mead & Company, 1968.

Hughson, Shirley Carter. *The Carolina Pirates and Colonial Commerce, 1670-1740.* Baltimore: The Johns Hopkins Press, 1894.

Lamb, Chris. *I'll Be Sober in the Morning: Great Political Comebacks, Putdowns & Ripostes.* Charleston, SC: Frontline Press Ltd., 2007.

Mackey, Sandra. *Lebanon: Death of a Nation.* New York: Congdon & Weed, Inc., 1989.

McTeer, J.E. *High Sheriff of the Low Country.* Beaufort, SC: Beaufort Book Co., 1970.

"Operation Jackpot." *Alumni News* (The Citadel), Fall 1985, pp. 9-10.

Payne, Anthony, Paul Sutton, and Tony Thorndike. *Grenada: Revolution and Invasion.* New York: St. Martin's Press, 1984.

Perry, Robert J. *Dirty Money.* Lincoln, NE: iUniverse, Ins., 2006.

Taylor, Thomas E. *Running the Blockade: A Personal Narrative of Adventure, Risks, and Escapes During the American Civil War.* London: John Murray, Albemarle St., 1896.

Traboulsi, Fawwaz. *A History of Modern Lebanon.* London: Pluto Press, 2007.

Willoughby, Malcolm F. *Rum War at Sea.* Washington, D.C.: United States Government Printing Office, 1964.

Woodward, Bob. *Wired: The Short Life and Fast Times of John Belushi.* New York: Simon and Schuster, 1984.

Newspapers

Beaufort Gazette, Beaufort, South Carolina

Columbia Record, Columbia, South Carolina

Daily Sun, Lewiston, Maine

Evening Post, Charleston, South Carolina

Herald, Rock Hill, South Carolina

Herald-Journal, Spartanburg, South Carolina

Island Packet, Hilton Head Island, South Carolina

Miami Herald

New York Times

News and Courier, Charleston, South Carolina

Providence Sunday Journal

Southeastern Missourian, Cape Girardeau, Missouri

State, Columbia, South Carolina

Sun, Australia

Tallahassee Democrat, Tallahassee, Florida

Tico Times, San José, Costa Rica

Wall Street Journal

Washington Post

Notes

Prologue

viii "As it turned out": Dialogue in the prologue is taken from transcripts of a plea hearing in June 2008 and a sentencing hearing in August 2008 in *United States of America vs. Ashley Brunson*. These transcripts and court filings also provided details of Ashley Brunson's life abroad and of his 2007 arrest. The author attended the sentencing hearing as well.

xi "Barry, here he goes": interview with anonymous source.

Part I: The Gentlemen Smugglers
Chapter One

4 "Oh yeah, them boys": interview with Barry Foy, February 2008.

4 "We'd never do": interview with Les Riley, July 2010.

7 Riley had first visited: details of Riley's upbringing come from interviews with Les Riley in July 2010 and Roy Riley in May 2010.

9 "Y'all have any luck?": interview with Les Riley, July 2010.

10 "I got the key": interview with anonymous source.

10 "We thought he could": interview with anonymous source.

10 "He could tell his crew . . .": interview with Tommy Liles, June 2008.

11 "If you got one thousand pounds . . .": interview with Ken Smith, July 2010.

11 "We'll be right back": details of Barry Foy's youth were learned during interviews with Foy from 2008 to 2010.

11 "Started me down the road": interview with Barry Foy, February 2008.

12 "Some people are blessed": ibid.

12 "Right then . . . I knew": ibid.

13 "Halt, I'm going to shoot": ibid.

13 "Some name they gave me": ibid.

13 The favorable treatment: *Columbia Record* May 26, 1983.

14 "this case was postponed": ibid.

14 "We said, 'Well fuck'": interview with Barry Foy, February 2008.

14 "He's all happy": ibid.

14 By comparison, that same year; *Southeastern Missourian*, March 23, 1971.

15 "I hope to God": interview with Barry Foy, February 2008.

15 "You left me here, man": ibid.

16 "I was afraid": ibid.

16 "Stopped dead in the water": ibid.

17 "It looked so out": ibid.

17 In celebration, someone danced: e-mail from Jan Liafsha, May 2008.

17 "Sticks? . . . You gotta take": interview with anonymous source.

18 "I was upset with him": interview with Ken Smith, July 2010.

19 "You and your fucking lists": ibid.

19 "That's the time of year": interview with Les Riley, July 2010.

20 "Barry kept holding": interview with Ken Smith, July 2010.

20 "We basically relied": interview with Les Riley, July 2010.

21 "We smuggling reefer, motherfucker": interview with Tommy Liles, June 2008.

21 "Far out": interview with Les Riley, July 2010.

22 "We got a little bit more": interview with anonymous source.

22 "Oh shit. That's a fucking bale": interview with Barry Foy.

Chapter Two

24 "He walked in": interview with Buddy Ray "Fish Ray" Griffin Jr., July 2009.

25 "I was loving on her, man": interview with Barry Foy.

25 "We were young and simple in life": e-mail from Jan Liafsha, May 2008.

26 "When Jan got mad": interview with Bob Bauer, February 2010.

26 "What's so fucking funny": interview with Ken Smith, July 2010.

26 "an importer of tropical plants": interview with John Jamison, June 2008.

27 "If you guys are up to": interview with anonymous source.

28 During Foy's first trip: details of Foy and Byers' trip are from interviews with Barry Foy.

29 "That's their culture": interview with Mike Abell, February 2010.

29 "Fuck. Nooooo": interview with Bob Roche, February 2010.

30 "Where's Barry? Where's Barry, mon?": interview with anonymous source.

31 "People involved heavily": e-mail from Jim Mittica, July 2009.

32 "Our (purchase) costs": testimony of Julian Pernell in *United States of America v. Barry Joseph Foy, et al.*

32 "When Florida got warm": interview with Barry Foy, 2009.

34 "I had some in McClellanville": testimony of Julian Pernell in *United States of America v. Barry Joseph Foy, et al.*

35 "He was an alcoholic": transcript of interview of Bob Byers conducted by lawyer Gedney Howe.

35 After a 1962 arrest: Bob Byers's criminal record is listed in a federal pre-sentence investigation report.

36 "I had a pretty": interview of Bob Byers by lawyer Gedney Howe (date unknown).

37 In 1972, according to Byers's: affidavit by Mike Abell, April 1984.

37 Roche remembers even more debauchery: these memories of Bob Byers were gathered in separate interviews of Bob Roche, Mike Abell, and Bob Bauer, all in February 2010.

39 He was the "sweetest": interview with Liz Kennedy, February 2008.

39 "You've had enough": ibid.

39 "Barry . . . business is business": interview with anonymous source.

39 In response to complaints: Hughson, p. 22.

40 The appearance of Blackbeard: Butler, p. 31.

40 In 1718, Blackbeard blockaded Charleston: Butler, p. 37.

40 Rumrunners had a short heyday: Willoughby, p. 3.

40 In April 1861: Cochran, p. 13.

41 In 1862, for example: Cochran, p. 36.

41 The cotton bales: Hobart-Hampden, p. 27.

41 Meat, for example: details on the cargoes of blockade-runners can be found in Cochran, pp. 47–50.

42 "During the Confederate years": Cochran, p. 62.

42 "In Bermuda these men": Horner, p. 101.

43 "That was the best pussy": interview with Oliver Mayfield, July 2008.

43 "It must be borne": Hobart-Hampden, p. 2.

44 "Hunting, pig sticking": Taylor, p. 49.

44 "Pussy wasn't even fun": interview with Oliver Mayfield, July 2008.

45 "Needless to say": e-mail from Harold Stein, April 2008.

45 "There was always the undercurrent": interview with Lionel Lofton and Wells Dickson, June 2008.

45 The Customs Patrol office: interview with Mike Bell, May 2008.

46 "Most of the time": interview with Chuck Pittard, April 2008.

47 There they'd park along: descriptions of rumrunners' tactics are taken from Willoughby, p. 61.

47 "Beaufort County with its hundreds": McTeer, p. 5.

47 Billboards along coastal highway: interview with Mike Bell, May 2008.

48 Wary of being compromised: ibid.

48 Pernell and Toombs had met: testimony of Barry Toombs in *United States of America v. Barry Joseph Foy, et al.*

48 He was busted in 1972: testimony of Julian Pernell in *United States of America v. Barry Joseph Foy, et al.*

48 Toombs marveled at Pernell's ability: interview with Barry Toombs, May 2010.

49 "You get an adrenaline rush": ibid.

50 "All that was so unorganized": interview with Billy Graham, June 2008.

Chapter Three

51 They purchased a thirty-five-foot: interview with Les Riley, July 2010.

51 "no further north than Charleston": ibid.

52 "Developer Charles Fraser: www.seapines.com.

53 "Hilton Head had the Montessori schools": interview with Les Riley, July 2010.

53 "This was the biggest mistake": letter from Les Riley to Judge Falcon Hawkins (date unknown).

54 "Lee always had a smile": details of Lee Harvey's childhood were learned in an interview with Tom Harvey and Mike Harvey in May 2010.

55 All the girls at the University: interview with Cameron Currie, May 2007.

55 As Lee was finishing college: interview with Tom Harvey and Mike Harvey, May 2010.

55 "I'd wish to God": ibid.

55 "Things like that": ibid.

55 After graduating from the University: University of South Carolina, Office of Media Relations.

55 His graduate schooling would be interrupted: *Washington Post*, November 16, 1974.

56 "He was gone": interview with an anonymous source.

56 "He was a good guy": interview with Les Riley, July 2010.

56 "I've got people": ibid.

57 "He'll be right back": interview with Tom Harvey and Mike Harvey, May 2010.

57 "Oh my god": ibid.

58 "He was a charmer": interview with Barry Toombs, May 2010.

58 "No ambush was ever": details of this bust were gleaned from the appeals court opinion in *United States of America v. Donald George Maskeny, et al.*

59 "They're gonna give me": interview with anonymous source.

59 In 1978, eleven states: Bertram, p. 96.

60 "As for that tag": letter from Skip Sanders to author, March 25, 2008.

60 Among the men unshaken: biographical details for Christy Campbell were learned during an interview with Campbell in December 2007.

60 "bragging about how South Carolinians": affidavit prepared by Barry Toombs in support of the United States' request for extradition of Les Riley, May 1983.

60 Riley was happy: interview with Les Riley, July 2010.

61 "Christy was Lee's boy": interview with anonymous source.

61 In November 1978: details of the Coast Guard's seizure of the *Love Affair* are detailed in the testimony of U.S. Coast Guard Commander Thomas Braithewaite and Lieutenant Brian O'Keefe in hearings for *United States of America v. Robert Leslie Riley, et al.*

Chapter Four

62 "The first one": letter from Skip Sanders to author, March 7, 2008.

63 "see there. this is why": letter from Skip Sanders to author, June 8, 2009.

64 "How fast you going": interview with Barry Foy, July 2008.

64 For Bob "The Boss" Byers: interview with Bob Roche, February 2010.

65 "It's hard to tell": interview with Bob Bauer, February 2010.

65 Foy was going to make: interview with anonymous source.

65 In 1976, Foy was blamed: testimony of Barry Toombs in *United States of America v. Robert Leslie Riley, et al.*

65 They told him to "buzz off": testimony of Julian Pernell in *United States of America v. Barry Joseph Foy, et al.*

65 "Foy was burning his bridges": testimony of Barry Toombs in *United States of America v. Barry Joseph Foy, et al.*

65 Among Foy's new friends: Foy described his introduction to Tom Rhoad in an interview in February 2008.

66 His girlfriend lay bound: interview with Bob Bauer, February 2010.

66 He had also been spied: ibid.

66 Rhoad's buddies joked: interview with Kenny Thomas, June 2008.

67 When Rhoad had an apartment: interview with Barry Foy, April 2008.

67 Les Riley knew Rhoad: interview with Les Riley, July 2010.

67 "He had this massive Presidential": interview with John Jamison, June 2008.

67 "One night partying": letter from Skip Sanders to author, March 7, 2008.

68 "It ain't no fun": interview with Buddy "Fish Ray" Ray Griffin Jr., July 2009.

68 "Tom Rhoad—number eleven": interview with Bob Bauer, February 2010.

68 DDOA, or Drug Dealers of America: interview with John Jamison, June 2008.

68 Jamison recalls walking: ibid.

69 "Did your mom die": interview with Bob Bauer, February 2010.

70 "It is a crisis": Miller Center of Public Affairs, http://miller center.org/scripps/archive/speeches/detail/3402.

71 "Remember, every bale": interview with Bob Bauer, February 2010.

72 When he was honorably discharged: U.S. Army.

72 "Working hard doesn't mean": interview with Barry Toombs, May 2010.

73 As a rule, Les Riley: interview with Les Riley, July 2010.

73 One wonders . . . Nancy Reagan: www.hopajetworldwide.com/ hop.asp.

73 "Hey Willie, I've got a problem": interview with Bob Bauer, February 2010.

74 "If it fucks, flies": ibid.

74 "Ooh, don't throw us . . ." interview with anonymous source.

74 "It didn't take long": interview with Maura Mooney, December 2007.

75 "Sue asked me": ibid.

75 "St. Barts is a tiny": Flippo, 36.

76 "As I was coming in": letter from Freddy Fillingham to author, May 18, 2008.

77 Among the successful ventures: federal indictment of Barry Joseph Foy, et al., District of South Carolina (83-165).

77 Riley and Harvey were: federal indictment of Robert Leslie Riley, District of South Carolina, (83-166).

78 . . . using a sledgehammer: interview with Bob Bauer, February 2010.

79 Once, Butler and Riley constructed: interview with Les Riley, July 2010.

80 Property up and down: indictments of Foy and Riley.

Chapter Five

81 Cold seafood, booze, and Valium: descriptions of the *Second Life*'s voyage were obtained from interviews with Chris Campbell, Kenny O'Day, and anonymous sources, as well as the testimony of Campbell and O'Day in *United States of America v. Robert Leslie Riley, et al.*

81 "One happy ship of crazies": interview with anonymous source.

81 "It was no longer": interview with Christy Campbell, May 2008.

82 Among the world sailing community: www.volvooceanrace.com.

83 While the civil war: Traboulsi, p. 234 and Mackey, p. 229.

83 The obvious implication: interview with anonymous source.

84 In an odd but kind gesture: interview with Christy Campbell, May 2008.

86 "Who's got her": interview with anonymous source.

86 One slow-going day . . . the crew devised: ibid.

88 "One of three or four": www.volvooceanrace.com.

88 "You can't hit him": interview with Christy Campbell, May 2008.

88 "I had one bullet": ibid.

89 "He was a pretty nice": testimony of Christy Campbell in *United States of America v. Robert Leslie Riley, et al.*

89 "This has been two months": ibid.

89 Campbell's arrival and phone calls: descriptions of unloading the hashish and simultaneous boat chase were obtained from testimony of men present that night in *United States of America v. Robert Leslie Riley, et al.* and from interviews with some of these same men, including those noted below.

90 "He was going like a madman": interview with John Jamison, June 2008.

91 "That's when things:" testimony of Kenny O'Day in *United States of America v. Robert Leslie Riley, et al.*

91 "I'm going to go out": testimony of Walter Baxter in *United States of America v. Robert Leslie Riley, et al.*

92 "I don't like that": interview with John Jamison, June 2008.

92 "John, don't get crazy, don't get crazy": ibid.

93 "Pull it back": ibid.

93 "I thought you had two suspects": testimony of Tommy Simmons in *United States of America v. Robert Leslie Riley, et al.*

94 "He was incorrigible": interview with John Zwerling, February 2008.

Chapter Six

96 "You can get out": interview with anonymous source.

96 "We gotta pull over": interview with Barry Toombs, May 2010.

96 "You're caught up": ibid.

97 "That was when Frank met drugs": interview with Tommy Liles, June 2008.

97 "You know, some people say": interview with John Jamison, June 2008.

97 Harvey allegedly jeopardized ventures: Lee Harvey's excessive and dangerous drug use was mentioned by a multitude of smugglers who knew him well, including Les Riley, Barry Toombs, Bob Bauer, and others. While Lee Harvey's brothers Tom and Michael downplay the severity of his drug use, others say he nearly died a number of times from overdoses.

97 "But the little people": interview with Bob Bauer, February 2010.

98 "I was with Lee a lot": interview with Tom Harvey and Michael Harvey, May 2010.

98 ". . . let her possess you": from John Jamison's previously unpublished poem "All Honey Isn't Sweet."

99 Foy was fun: interview with Les Riley, July 2010.

99 "No wonder you can": ibid.

99 "Y'all are partners": ibid.

99 "Les had a big": interview with Barry Toombs, May 2010.

100 "Lee Harvey had problems paying": testimony of Frank Steele during *United States of America v. Robert Leslie Riley, et al.*

100 keep their wallet close: interview with Les Riley, July 2010.

100 "To me, that was a slap": interview with John Jamison, June 2008.

101 One smuggler labels Harvey: these descriptions of Harvey's alleged payment problems were from interviews with two separate anonymous sources.

101 "He picked me up": testimony of Steve Ravenel in *United States of America v. Robert Leslie Riley, et al.*

101 "This is what Les and Lee": interview with Bob Bauer, February 2010.

101 When men would come to Riley: interview with Les Riley, July 2010.

102 "Barry, one thing they teach": interview with Barry Toombs, May 2010.

102 "People were looking": interview with Les Riley, July 2010.

103 "Sometimes Lee Harvey": interview with Barry Toombs, May 2010.

104 Arriving on the island: IRS investigator David Forbes recalled his professional experience, early forays onto Hilton Head Island, and tips about Les Riley during interviews in November 2007.

104 "You need to look into Les Riley": ibid.

105 The year before . . . a DC-3 airplane: *Hilton Head Island Packet*, February 7, 1980.

105 One of Heyward's corporations: federal appeals court decision in *United States of America v. Heyward*.

106 "At one time": *Hilton Head Island Packet*, January 12, 1982.

106 "Something funny": interview with David Forbes, November 2007.

107 Here, too . . was the county courthouse: courthouse file in the South Carolina Room of the Beaufort County Library, Beaufort branch.

Chapter Seven

108 Barry "Ice Cream" Toombs claims Harvey: interview with Barry Toombs, May 2010.

108 More significantly, Harvey was alleged: *Providence Sunday Journal*, May 20, 1984.

109 The boat was controlled: Mark Hertzan's involvement in this massive smuggling run is described in Julian Pernell's testimony in *United States of America v. Robert Leslie Riley, et al.* Details of Hertzan's friendship with John Belushi are taken from Woodward, p. 151.

109 "You got this problem": *Wired*, p. 153.

109 The least amount of information: the route of the *Adeline C* is described in the *Providence Sunday Journal*, May 20, 1984.

110 In the weeks prior: the movements of the *Caroline C, Meermin,* and *Anonymous of Rorc* have been described in testimony by *Caroline C* captain Chris Campbell and *Anonymous of Rorc* captain Frank Steele during *United States of America v. Robert Leslie Riley, et al.*, as well

as interviews with Campbell in December 2007, with *Caroline C* sailor Dean Jacobs in February 2009, and with *Anonymous of Rorc* sailors Ken Brown and Ken Buckland in May 2008.

111 Now on the return voyage: letters from Kenny Gunn to his wife describing the crew's encounters with hurricanes were read by DEA agent Dewey Greager during federal grand jury testimony in September 1983 in Columbia, South Carolina.

112 As they docked the boat: Details of the docking of the *Caroline C* and some of the crew's subsequent arrest at the Savannah airport are detailed in police reports and testimony by a dockhand and assorted U.S. Customs officers during *United States of America v. Robert Leslie Riley, et al.*

113 "one of the best-built boats": interview with Ken Brown and Ken Buckland, May 2008.

113 "It didn't look": ibid.

113 Among other military awards: U.S. Army.

113 "My god, look at these magic mushrooms": interview with John Jamison, June 2008.

115 "Scared the shit out of me": interview with Ken Brown and Ken Buckland, May 2008.

116 "We were tacking back and forth": ibid.

117 "Well, it looks like": ibid.

118 A fellow smuggler and paramour: Madeline Wasserman, who also went by "Sarah," was convicted in New Jersey April 1983 for crimes related to the unsuccessful smuggling of hashish aboard the *Falcon*. Wasserman's and a coconspirator's convictions were reported in a United Press International article on April 21, 1983, entitled "Guilty verdicts in $36 million drug smuggling."

118 The crew on the *Meermin*: details of the *Meermin*'s arrival off New York, its rendezvous with other boats, and the aftermath of this smuggling episode were provided in interviews with Mike Abell in February 2010, Bob Bauer in February 2010, Ron Catanese in April 2008, Les Riley in July 2010, and with two anonymous sources. This section was also informed by the testimony of Abell and Wayne McDonald in *United States of America v. Robert Leslie Riley, et al.*

119 "Well, I'm going fishing": interview with anonymous source.

120 "the look": Skip Sanders describes his introduction to Bob Byers and his companions in a letter to the author, March 7, 2008.

120 "Just what is It": ibid.

120 "Ninety-something-year-old pillar": e-mail from Harold Stein to author, April 22, 2008.

120 "Not much of anything": letter from Skip Sanders to author, March 7, 2008.

121 Four vans were parked there: details of the vans come from police reports and interviews with Dave McDonald in June 2008, Chuck Pittard in April 2008, and Bob Roche in February 2010.

121 "If you own the plantation": letter from Skip Sanders to author, June 3, 2008.

121 "radars and all that": July 29, 2008.

122 "Island blacks have the uncanny": ibid.

123 The kindest adjective . . . was *ratty*: all quotes and dialogue attributed to Louis Jefferson came from an interview with Jefferson in July 2008.

124 "Louis don't mess around": all quotes and dialogue attributed to Mike Bell came from an interview with Bell in May 2008.

126 Byers ordered someone: details of the smuggler's activities at West Bank Plantation were learned from police reports, letters from Skip Sanders to the author, interviews with Mike Abell in February 2010, Bob Roche in February 2010, and testimony or police debriefings of Ray Zeman, Dennis York, and Mike Martin.

126 "hop on the speedboat": letter from Skip Sanders to author, June 3, 2008.

127 "There was no way": interview with Ken Brown and Ken Buckland, May 2008.

127 "How many men": Louis Jefferson described the preferred boarding procedure in an interview in July 2008.

128 "There was about six or seven": grand jury testimony of Dennis York in Columbia, South Carolina, April 1982.

129 "We can't do this": interview with Clark Settles, May 2008.

130 Officers joked Huggins: ibid.

130 Patterson found a handgun: interview with Dean Patterson, May 2008.

130 "Where were you all": letter from Skip Sanders to author, June 3, 2008.

131 "Skipper, I tell ya": ibid.

131 After ten days of sailing: details of the voyage of the hash-laden scallop boat were learned through the testimony of Julian Pernell in the second trial of *United States of America v. Robert Leslie Riley, et al.*

132 Hertzan, the owner: Woodward, p. 283, and *New York Times*, February 4, 1982.

Part II: Operation Jackpot
Chapter Eight

134 Although Carter lost South Carolina: The American Presidency Project, www.presidency.ucsb.edu.

134 "Now, I've come to Columbia": Ronald Reagan Presidential Library, online speech archives, remarks delivered July 24, 1986.

135 "The drug problem": *Rock Hill Herald*, January 27, 1981.

136 "tall, personable" "bright and hard-working": editorial from the *State* printed in the *Herald-Journal*, February 12, 1981.

136 Lydon pledged to help: *Columbia State*, February 23, 1981.

136 "Jack for money": interview with Holly Gatling, May 2008.

136 "stretched his long, well-jogged": *Columbia State*, February 17, 1981.

136 "Mrs. McMaster was very pleased": interview with Holly Gatling, May 2008.

137 "If you break the law": *Columbia State*, June 6, 1981.

137 "Some people don't think": Gasque, p. 18.

138 "fail to see the forest": *Columbia State*, June 6, 1981.

138 "Some people may think": ibid.

138 Riley, in fact, had known: interview with Les Riley, September 2010.

138 The same year McMaster: Wellesley's meetings with McMaster were described in an interview with Tim Wellesley in February 2010.

139 Authorities in California: details of the investigation of Araujo were learned through Robert J. Perry's *Dirty Money*.

140 Araujo pleaded guilty: *Lewiston (ME) Daily Sun*, September 24, 1981.

140 McMaster latched onto the idea: *Columbia State* October 6, 1985.

141 "You have to have": interview with Tim Wellesley, February 2010.

141 At the meeting: the initial meeting of what would become Operation Jackpot was described by David Forbes in the fall of 2007 and Claude McDonald in March 2008.

143 "We had nothing": interview with Claude McDonald, August 2007.

143 He had come to Charleston: Claude McDonald's biographical information was learned in an interview with McDonald in March 2008.

146 As Forbes and McDonald discovered: beyond interviews with David Forbes and Claude McDonald, information about the beginnings of Operation Jackpot can be found in Margaret O'Shea's series on Operation Jackpot in *Columbia State* in October 1985.

146 "He's living high on the hog": interview with David Forbes, November 2007.

147 "We threw out": *Charleston News and Courier/Charleston Evening Post*, January 29, 1984.

147 In the locker: *Columbia State*, October 6, 1985.

147 "Before we left his house": interview with David Forbes, November 2007.

148 "I had a tiger": ibid.

149 "I can't believe": interview with Mike Lemnah, January 2008.

149 "Mark was kind of ": ibid.

149 "It sounds simple": ibid.

149 "You'd get a call": interview with Wells Dickson and Lionel Lofton, June 2008.

150 "Gee, this is a big house": testimony of Jimmy MacNeal, *United States of America v. Barry Joseph Foy, et al.*

150 "He knew, but he wouldn't": interview with David Forbes, August 2007.

151 "The pressure is frankly": letter from Wally Butler to David Forbes, undated.

151 "We all had different skills": *Columbia State*, October 6, 1985.

151 "as the shot heard": interview with Bart Daniel, March 2007.

152 "I wish it could be written": Daniel, p. 1.

153 "the whole concept": interview with Mike Lemnah, January 2008.

153: Two weeks after taking: a list of seized assets is detailed in *Charleston Evening Post*, October 14, 1982 and December 21, 1982.

153 "Operation Jack Pot": *Charleston Evening Post*, December 15, 1982.

153 "The U.S. Government is snatching": *Miami Herald*, March 19, 1984.

Chapter Nine

154 "It was the hardest kind": *Washington Post*, April 17, 1983.

155 "She wasn't afraid": interview with Lance Lydon, May 2010.

155 "It was cowboys and Indians": ibid.

156 "dressed to the nines": interview with Lance Lydon, May 2010.

156 Outside the grand jury room: *Washington Post*, October 29, 1981.

156 A judge jailed O'Day: ibid.

157 "We really had to work": interview with Lance Lydon, May 2010.

157 One valuable asset: *Washington Post*, November 17, 1981.

158 Despite the recalcitrant witnesses: *Washington Post*, July 1982.

158 "At some point": interview with Lance Lydon, May 2010.

158 "The government also subpoenaed:" *Washington Post*, May 6, 1982.

158 "fishing expedition . . . impede the grand jury": *Washington Post*, October 29, 1981.

159 "those were not pleasant days": interview with Bill Moffitt, February 2008.

159 "Karen was one of the most": e-mail from Jim Mittica to the author, May 11, 2009.

159 "Her main goal in life": interview with anonymous source.

159 The professor's answer: Costa Rica: interview with Barry Toombs, May 2010.

159 American fugitives, in particular: *San Jose (Costa Rica) Tico Times*, August 20, 1982.

160 "until all this blows over": *San Jose (Costa Rica) Tico Times*, August 13, 1982.

160 "their assets for their asses": the phone call between Julian Pernell and Karen Tandy was described in interviews with Barry Toombs and Lance Lydon, both in May 2010, as well as *San Jose (Costa Rica) Tico Times*, August 13, 1982.

161 "I remember going out": e-mail from Jim Mittica to the author, May 11, 2009.

161 "They had plans to kidnap us": second trial of *United States of America v. Robert Leslie Riley*.

162 "The best thing": interview with Barry Toombs, May 2010.

162 "When I left the country": e-mail from Jim Mittica to author, May 16, 2009.

162 "Let us not forget": Ronald Reagan Presidential Library, online speech archives, remarks delivered September 14, 1986.

163 "scorched earth policy": remarks given by Associate Attorney General Stephen S. Trott, according to Bertram, p. 113.

163 "We're rejecting the helpless attitude": Bertram, p. 112.

163 "It is high time": Bertram, p. 113.

164 "Public Enemy Number 1": Bertram, p. 106.

164 "a growing menace to the general welfare": Bertram, p. 105.

164 This recommendation was supported: Bertram, p. 95.

164 "I don't give a hoot": Bertram, p. 94.

164 "penalties against possession of a drug": Bertram, p. 97.

164 Despite asking for more: Bertram, p. 110.

165 "He didn't know diddly-squat": descriptions of Lofton's and Dickson's differences and dissatisfaction with Henry McMaster come from an interview with Lionel Lofton and Wells Dickson in June 2008.

166 "In my opinion": correspondence between McMaster and the White House is contained in the Ronald Reagan Presidential Library.

167 "Here he is again": this internal White House correspondence is among the Henry McMaster–Ronald Reagan correspondence in the Ronald Reagan Presidential Library.

167 "Of course, we had been filing": Gasque, August 1985, p. 19.

167 "If it wasn't for Henry": interview with Mike Lemnah, January 2008.

167 "The supervisor here": interview with David Forbes, November 2007.

168 "Strom wouldn't put up with that": interview with Tim Wellesley, February 2010.

169 "It will not happen": interview with Bart Daniel, March 2007.

169 By voluntarily giving up: *Columbia Record*, August 22, 1983.

169 "That's the most money": *Columbia State*, April 21, 1984.

170 "He was so pissed": interview with Mike Lemnah, January 2008.

170 "[It was] a lot of work": ibid.

170 "touchy-feely": interview with Clark Settles, May 2008.

171 "We got your ass": interview with David Forbes, November 2007.

171 One of their favorite tactics: interview with anonymous source.

171 "Look, Wells, we just gotta": interview with Lionel Lofton and Wells Dickson, June 2008.

172 It didn't help when: letter from Ben Graham to author, May 25, 2008.

173 "I was a little disappointed": interview with Kenny O'Day, May 2010.

173 "When you've got them": interview with David Forbes, August 2007.

Chapter Ten

174 "who overlooked a lot": interview with Les Riley, July 2010.

174 "I saw that there": letter from Les Riley to Judge Falcon Hawkins, unknown date.

175 "Surely, we reasoned, no one": ibid.

175 "I want to talk to you": details of Les Riley's arrest in Australia are gathered from reports by the Australian Federal Police and interviews with Les Riley, July 2010.

176 "Are you from South Carolina": Australian Federal Police reports.

177 "I'm worried about my wife": ibid.

177 "Federal Police, step out": ibid.

177 "How did you find me": ibid.

178 "We just got scared": ibid.

179 "America's 'Most Wanted Man'": *Australia Sun*, May 6, 1983.

179 In the last ten years: federal indictment of Barry Joseph Foy, et al., District of South Carolina, (83-165), and federal indictment of Robert Leslie Riley, District of South Carolina, (83-166).

180 "most of it got through": *Charleston Evening Post*, May 24, 1983.

181 "The defendants included": ibid.

181 "the message I continually got": letter from Skip Sanders to author, April 16, 2008.

183 One smuggler recalls spreading rotting: interview with anonymous source.

183 "The government has a funny way": testimony of Julian Pernell in second trial of *United States of America v. Robert Leslie Riley, et al.*

184 Hawkins had joined the military: biographical information for Judge Falcon Hawkins was learned from an oral interview of Hawkins by Herbert Hartsook for the South Carolina Bar Foundation, January 2000, and *Columbia State*, July 22, 2005.

185 "crazy about it": oral interview of Hawkins by Hartsook, January 2000.

185 "He was one of the smartest": *Columbia State*, July 22, 2005.

185 "I don't say this": oral interview of Hawkins by Hartsook, January 2000.

185 "[Hollings] kind of believed": ibid.

186 "I don't get upset": ibid.

186 "Usually, if it was a bad": interview with Patty Kasell and Fritz Hollings, July 2008.

187 "There's really nothing much": *Charleston News and Courier*, October 6, 1982.

Chapter Eleven

189 "I call this the case": *Columbia State*, August 1, 1983.

190 "These aren't the little": *Columbia State*, August 10, 1983.

190 "They don't have ten thousand": transcript of *United States of America v. Barry Joseph Foy, et al.*

190 "Your Honor, I again note": ibid.

191 Surely, the prosecutors figured: *Columbia State*, August 2, 1983.

191 "there weren't any nuns": *Columbia State*, August 10, 1983.

191 Some witnesses had been offered money: such offers to witnesses, and actual payoffs, were revealed to the author by more than one smuggler regarding a number of Operation Jackpot–related trials and grand juries.

192 "There was a captain": testimony of Steve Ravenel in *United States of America v. Barry Joseph Foy, et al.*

193 "Threw it away": testimony of Julian Morse Jr. in *United States of America v. Barry Joseph Foy, et al.*

193 "there must be some witnesses": transcript of *United States of America v. Barry Joseph Foy, et al.*

193 "I don't know": ibid.

194 Despite her familiarity: the shirt-switching incident was described in an interview with Mike McEachern, April 2008.

194 "I can't stand this": testimony of Maura Mooney in *United States of America v. Barry Joseph Foy, et al.*

194 "You got a lot": transcript of *United States of America v. Barry Joseph Foy, et al.*

194 "How do they pay you": ibid.

194 "Hey Don": testimony of Maura Mooney in *United States of America v. Barry Joseph Foy, et al.*

194 "Judge . . . she went up": transcript of *United States of America v. Barry Joseph Foy, et al.*

195 "What do you want": ibid.

195 "This Operation Jackpot": ibid.

196 "It was just a mess": interview with Cam Littlejohn, June 2007.

196 "As far as the Operation Jackpot": *Columbia State*, August 12, 1983.

197 "a gentleman identifying himself": testimony of Brian O'Keefe during a pretrial hearing for *United States of America v. Robert Leslie Riley, et al.*

198 "hardly ever do we get": transcript of a pretrial hearing for *United States of America v. Robert Leslie Riley, et al.*

198 "I wish the court": ibid.

198 "Why's that?" ibid.

198 "I never forget a man": testimony of Rachel Fischer during a pretrial hearing for *United States of America v. Robert Leslie Riley, et al.*

199 "Guys, Christy Campbell just turned": interview with Tom Harvey and Mike Harvey, May 2010.

199 "I could wring": ibid.

199 "join the party": letter from Skip Sanders to author, April 16, 2008.

200 "notoriously anti-establishment": e-mail from Jim Mittica, July 13, 2009.

200 "They rarely had the merits": e-mail from Jim Mittica, August 15, 2009.

201 "hardball": interview with Cam Currie, February 2008.

202 "The crossing over": transcript of *United States of America v. Robert Leslie Riley, et al.*

202 "We are not talking": ibid.

202 "Someone said to me": ibid.

203 "Down there it was": interview with John Zwerling, February 2008.

203 For Moffitt, there was uneasiness: interview with Bill Moffitt, February 2008.

204 "fix the jury": transcript of *United States of America v. Robert Leslie Riley, et al.*

204 "He sent me lots": ibid.

204 "I'm not going to have": ibid.

205 "prove their virtue": ibid.

205 "He asked me": ibid.

205 "Things aren't working too well": ibid.

206 "What they are bargaining with": ibid.

206 "So you got": ibid.

206 "most reluctant government witness": *Columbia State*, November 8, 1983.

206 "It's been instilled": testimony of Kenny O'Day in *United States of America v. Robert Leslie Riley, et al.*

206 "Oh yes . . . I'm an old girl": transcript of *United States of America v. Robert Leslie Riley, et al.*

207 "that's supposed to be good": Life cereal commercial, as seen on YouTube in 2010.

207 "No matter how reprehensible": transcript of *United States of America v. Robert Leslie Riley, et al.*

207 "Please understand that": ibid.

208 "When you have a case": ibid.

208 "I don't know where": ibid.

208 "I have never": ibid.

209 "He told us": ibid.

210 "There's been a change": ibid.

Chapter Twelve

211 Willie Frank Steele sat: details of Steele's call to investigators and the information he divulged about the sailboat *La Cautiva* come principally from interviews with David Forbes in the fall of 2007.

211 "That's her": ibid.

212 "handed (the feds) Bob Byers": interview with an anonymous source.

212 "You don't talk about snitching": interview with Ken Smith, July 2010.

212 "Dude, did you tell": ibid.

214 "On the small island": Ronald Reagan Presidential Library, online speech archives, remarks delivered March 23, 1983.

214 "There was quite a civil": Bob Byers's account of fighting in Grenada comes from a transcript of an interview of Byers conducted by lawyer Gedney Howe sometime after Byers's arrest in November 1983.

215 On October 25, six days: Payne, p. 158.

216 "When the invasion was over": interview of Bob Byers by Gedney Howe.

216 In exchange for soft drinks: Byers's trade for a rocket launcher was described in interviews with Byers's friend Bob Roche in February 2010 and U.S. Marshal P. E. Morris in April 2008. The weapon was also referenced by U.S. Marshals Director Stanley Morris in an Associated Press article in *Columbia State* on February 9, 1984.

217 "just bowled us over": *Columbia State*, November 28, 1983.

217 "a message to all the millionaire": *Columbia State*, November 18, 1983.

218 "I'm looking at her now": Forbes and Greager's trip to Antigua was described by Forbes in interviews in the fall of 2007.

220 "Ain't no doubt that's him": ibid.

220 "Bob, it just ain't": ibid.

221 "go-fer": testimony of Wayne McDonald in second trial of *United States of America v. Robert Leslie Riley, et al.*

221 "He was bottom": *Charleston News and Courier*, December 8, 1983.

221 "I'm very close": *Columbia State*, July 31, 1983.

222 "in the dope business": *Charleston Evening Post*, December 14, 1983.

222 "If that eagle": ibid.

222 "We're confident": *Charleston News and Courier*, December 16, 1983.

223 "My son gave it": interview with Mike Lemnah, January 2008.

223 "finest collection of Tiffany glass": *New York Times*, March 11, 1984.

223 "the most fanciful and fragile": ibid.

224 "I think we've done": *Washington Post*, March 26, 1984.

224 "When a sale": *New York Times*, March 25, 1984.

224 "Fantastic . . . It was a risk": *Washington Post*, March 26, 1984.

224 "finest stock": transcript of sentencing hearing for Roy Riley, March 9, 1984.

225 "I don't think": transcript of sentencing hearing for Mike Harvey, February 22, 1984.

226 "I would like to say": transcript of sentencing hearing for Christy Campbell, unknown date.

226 "he determined, rather than divulge": transcript of sentencing hearing for Roy Riley, March 9, 1984.

227 "We have no sympathy": *Charleston News and Courier,* March 9, 1984.

227 That luxury sailboat: according to an anonymous government source, the sailboat *La Cautiva* was sailed near Cuba, allowing the CIA to eavesdrop on the country through electronic equipment aboard the boat. The CIA responded to an inquiry from the author regarding *La Cautiva* by saying the agency "can neither confirm nor deny the existence or nonexistence of records responsive to your request."

227 "We think [Byers]": letter from Henry McMaster to D. Lowell Johnson, May 18, 1984, contained in the National Archives.

228 "Our problem is": letter from Henry McMaster to William French Smith, April 16, 1984, contained in the National Archives.

228 "We think it is important": ibid.

228 Through memos among senior staff: an Office of the Attorney General memo from Rob Steinberg to Lowell Jensen, April 27, 1984, can be found in the National Archives.

229 "After several hours": letter from Bart Daniel to Henry McMaster, May 14, 1984, contained in the National Archives.

229 "he's probably going to tell": interview with David Forbes, November 2007.

230 In five years: *Charleston Evening Post*, June 4, 1984.

230 "One of the few:" *Wall Street Journal*, August 12, 1985.

230 This ring, the government alleged: *Charleston News and Courier*, September 22, 1984.

231 "Amend's trial began in October:" *Wall Street Journal*, August 12, 1985.

231 "the premier law enforcement association": *Columbia State*, October 25, 1984.

231 "Drug smugglers are like": *Charleston News and Courier*, January 29, 1984.

232 *Time* magazine wrote: Bertram, p. 113.

232 When describing the ceasefire: *Charleston Evening Post*, August 24, 1984.

233 "amazing," "of the one hundred": ibid.

233 "Even if you discounted": *Charleston Evening Post*, August 30, 1984.

234 "I feel like the side": Byers's jail scribblings and cards are contained in an FBI file.

234 "Don't say anything": *Charleston News and Courier*, date omitted from news clipping.

235 "I got a call at night": interview with Claude McDonald, March 2008.

236 "I never heard": ibid.

236 "the involvement of the Federal": letter from U.S. Senator Fritz Hollings to FBI Director William H. Webster, October 11, 1984, contained in an FBI file.

236 McMaster couldn't believe it: *Charleston News and Courier*, October 11, 1984.

236 "Are you out of ": interview with Claude McDonald, March 2008.

237 "I'll be leaving": *Columbia State*, December 12, 1984.

237 "[But] there's any number": *Charleston News and Courier*, September 27, 1984.

237 "armed and dangerous": *Columbia State*, February 9, 1985.

Chapter Thirteen

238 Bernholz compared it to chum: interview with Martin Bernholz, March 2010.

238 Prisoners were often put: Les Riley described his time in Australian prison during an interview in July 2010.

239 "nightmare," "I have witnessed": letter from Les Riley to Judge Falcon Hawkins, unknown date.

239 During the short commute: details of the treatment of Les Riley and Wally Butler were learned from interviews with Riley in July 2010, a report by the Australian Federal Police, and a letter from the Commonwealth Ombudsman to Riley's Australian attorney after Riley lodged a complaint regarding his treatment.

239 "They treated Les": interview with Martin Bernholz, March 2010.

240 "lost," "I get to the point": *Beaufort (SC) Gazette*, October 11, 1983.

241 "I have talked myself": Henry McMaster's March 12, 1985 letter to Charles W. Blau can be found in the National Archives.

242 "Where one area of expertise": *Columbia State*, January 24, 1985.

242 "She's top flight": *Charleston News and Courier*, September 29, 1984.

243 Soon, U.S. Marshal: P. E. Morris's pursuit of Bob Byers was described in an interview with Morris in April 2008.

244 Since being indicted: Barry Foy described his time as a fugitive in interviews from 2008 to 2010.

244 Forbes had questioned: e-mail from Jan Liafsha, June 2008.

245 "There's some money stashed": interview with Barry Foy, August 2009.

246 When he paid: details of Tom Rhoad's life in California and his arrest were learned from the testimony of federal agent Simon during a pretrial hearing for Rhoad.

247 "He broke into tears": interview with Claude McDonald, March 2008.

248 "I lived in constant dread": e-mail from Jan Liafsha, June 2008.

248 Arriving in Colorado: details of Byers's arrest were learned from interviews with P. E. Morris in April 2008 and Ed Falconetti in July 2008.

249 "Put your hands": interview with anonymous source.

249 Even more surprising: interviews with Bart Daniel in March 2007and Bob Roche in February 2010.

251 "the thing with Byers": letter from Skip Sanders to the author, April 16, 2008.

251 Two weeks after Byers: details of Foy's arrest come from interviews with David Forbes in the fall of 2007 and Barry Foy from 2008 to 2010.

252 "Telluride is catching hell": interview with David Forbes, November 2007.

252 "Agents knew we were there": e-mail from Jan Liafsha, June 2008.

252 "Barry Foy, you're under arrest": interview with David Forbes, November 2007.

254 "He will be ridiculed": transcript of sentencing hearing for Tom Rhoad, July 19, 1985.

255 "He's made his peace": ibid.

256 Choking back tears": *Charleston News and Courier*, July 20, 1985.

256 "When I get out": transcript of sentencing hearing for Tom Rhoad, July 19, 1985.

257 "living it up": ibid.

257 "The General Accounting Office": ibid.

259 "I didn't do it": *Columbia State*, October 6, 1985.

259 Privately, he told friends: *Columbia State*, January 13, 1985.

259 "some serious fence-mending: ibid.

259 "During the year or so": letter from Steven Bernholz to Judge Falcon Hawkins, December 15, 1983.

260 "no one can recall": *Columbia State*, January 13, 1985.

260 Oh Henry—You leave behind: *Columbia State*, October 6, 1985.

261 "Of course, everyone is presumed": *Columbia State*, December 19, 1985.

261 "They're criminals. They're both criminals": *Columbia State*, July 31, 1983.

261 "If I could look back": *Columbia State*, October 6, 1985.

261 Toombs says Harvey moved beyond: interview with Barry Toombs, May 2010.

262 When one vague tip: details of Lee Harvey's arrest were learned in an interview with Frank Hildebrandt in July 2009 and an arrest report released by the DEA.

263 "One man could not": DEA investigation report, December 31, 1985.

264 "The High Court's ruling: *Charleston News and Courier*, December 19, 1985.

264 "You can't argue": interview with Martin Bernholz, March 2010.

264 "We were all trying": interview with anonymous source.

265 "That's probably about all": transcript of Les Riley's sentencing hearing, June 16, 1986.

265 "I don't know": ibid.

265 "being a modern day pirate": ibid.

266 "I don't quarrel": ibid.

266 "Good luck to you": ibid.

266 "Thank you, sir": ibid.

Epilogue

268 "I'll take a drug test": Lamb, p. 179.

269 He was arrested four months: *Tallahassee Democrat*, July 3, 1992.

270 "I am not the same": letter from Bob Byers to Judge Falcon Hawkins, November 12, 1985.

270 "His tail got caught": interview with Tommy Liles, June 2008.

270 "The Great Cheeze Incident": letter from Ben Graham to the author, May 2008.

270 "That asshole called": ibid.

271 the DEA estimates 80 percent: DEA public affairs office.

271 In fact, more than twenty-five thousand Mexicans: *Washington Post*, August 2, 2010.

271 In the gentlemen smugglers' home state: norml.org

272 "Has anyone seen his body": interview with Bob Roche, February 2010.

Index

About the Author

Jason Ryan is a South Carolina journalist and former staff reporter for the *State* newspaper. He was born in Connecticut and is a graaduate of Georgetown University. He lives with his wife in Charleston. *Jackpot* is his first book.